Tippecanoe and Trinkets Too

Tippecanoe and Trinkets Too

The Material Culture of American Presidential Campaigns

1828–1984

Roger A. Fischer

University of Illinois Press
Urbana and Chicago

This book is printed on acid-free paper.

Library of Congress Cataloging-in-Publication Data

Fischer, Roger A., 1939–
 Tippecanoe and trinkets too.

 Bibliography: p.
 Includes index.
 1. Presidents—United States—Election—History.
2. United States—Politics and government.
3. Campaign paraphernalia—United States—History.
4. Material culture—United States. 5. Political
collectibles—United States. I. Title
E176.1.F53   1988   324.973   86–30924
ISBN 0–252–00960–6

Contents

Preface

This volume was motivated by a desire to assist two disparate groups: the curators, antiquarians, and collectors who gather and preserve the physical relics of past American presidential campaigns and the academic historians who create the scholarly interpretations of those quadrennial contests. The first group contains many dedicated and gifted individuals endowed with almost encyclopedic knowledge of campaign artifacts, but who often appear to be at best only dimly aware of the historical context, the political circumstances that ordained the production, design and thematic characteristics, distribution, and functional roles of the objects they treasure. I hope that this volume will prove useful to them in developing this broader understanding of the role played by material culture in American presidential campaigns. Political historians, on the other hand, have traditionally limited their scholarly inquiries to the recorded verbiage of this or that election or sequence of elections, confining their quests for enlightenment to such documentary sources of evidence as party platforms and position papers, public and private statements by the candidates, newspaper editorials, the letters and speeches of party luminaries, and the like. Despite the success attained by archaeologists in reconstructing whole civilizations through their physical remains, American political historians have with few exceptions either ignored presidential campaign material culture altogether or utilized it only as pictorial window dressing. To them, this volume is a plea to abandon this self-imposed tunnel vision and to begin to reflect in their research and its fruits the true multifaceted complexity that has characterized these efforts to capture the White House.

One facet of presidential electioneering for more than a century and a half has been the use of material objects to attract votes. From the medalets, thread boxes, and bandannas promoting Andrew Jackson or John Quincy Adams in 1828 through the buttons, bumper stickers, and other items featuring Ronald Reagan or Walter Mondale in 1984, every presidential race has inspired and utilized material objects for partisan purposes. Tens of thousands of artifact varieties have been produced for use as badges, regalia, mass visual devices, or personal keep-sakes. Marvelously eclectic, the genre encompasses objects as small as a bobby pin and as large as a highway billboard or a boulevard banner twenty feet high and three times as long, as mundane as a thimble or matchbook and as exotic as a walking-stick crafted from the petrified reproductive organ of a bull, as tasteful as a cut crystal 1860 Abraham Lincoln bowl, and as monumentally tasteless as a 1956 stamp predicting that Dwight Eisenhower's re-election would trigger his death from a fatal heart attack.

These objects would be worthy of serious scholarly attention even if they were merely campaign ephemera or trivia (as they are so commonly characterized, even by material culturists), for as Ivor Noel Hume has properly reminded us, "we do the past a disservice if we fail to make use of any and every scrap of evidence that it has left us." I believe, however, that to dismiss such artifacts as trivial or ephemeral in political importance is to fail to truly comprehend the dynamics of campaigning for public office in the United States, especially during the long stretch from the dawn of the politics of popular entertainment in the days of Jackson and the elder Harrison to the birth of the electronic age after World War I. In a period of limited literacy, few amusements, and very little idle time, it is difficult to believe that large numbers of Americans made their choices by poring over newspaper editorials or party platforms. In 1840, the Whigs found themselves too busy staging parades, teach-ins on the glories of the log cabin, rolling large balls from town to town, and other such activities to even bother to fashion a platform. With the advent of politics as spectator entertainment, banners, floats, badges, and other campaign artifacts became the very sum and substance of the political process. Throughout the remainder of the nineteenth century and into the twentieth, such ritual activities as the lavish "Wide-Awake" torchlight parades that promoted Lincoln as "the rail-splitter of the West," the many participatory rites of the intensely waged Victorian campaigns, and the free silver and sound money demonstrations of 1896 continued to provide colorful and exuberant forums for objects as partisan devices, flamboyant exhibits of thematics and symbolism witnessed by millions of Americans not given to reading party platforms and the like. Even in the modern age of television and freeways, the material dimension remains something more than ephemeral or trivial to the process of choosing our national leaders. To ignore it is to present a rather skewed perspective of the American political tradition.

In defining the scope of this volume, I have made several rather arbitrary judgments on which items to include and which to omit. Because the study is limited to the role played by material culture in campaigns for the presidency, I have essentially ignored the vast quantities of artifacts inspired by presidential victory celebrations, inaugurations, pilgrimages, and deaths, as well as the host of postcampaign items reflecting upon winners in office or losers in exile. Although there has developed no precise definition of the term *material culture* (a pretentious phrase born of convenience and the desire for academic respectability) and no clear consensus about its proper limits, I have followed accepted tradition in excluding types of campaign items (biographies, flyers, song sheets, cartoons, broadsides) that were essentially literary or artistic in nature. In doing so, I have not tried to impose my own distorted views on which types of campaign material merit serious scrutiny by political historians, because the popular literature, music, and art created for presidential campaigns unquestionably deserve more attention than they have received from the scholarly community. For reasons of space, I have excluded from this study the tremendous volume of objects created for campaigns for Congress, state and local offices, and for the adoption of such ideological imperatives as prohibition and women's suffrage (except in instances where these movements were mirrored in the artifacts produced for presidential campaigns). I have done so with reluctance, because many of these items exhibit qualities of thematic and functional creativity frequently absent in presidential campaign objects.

In researching and writing this volume I have been the recipient of many considerations and kindnesses. I have had the good fortune to serve on the faculty of an institution that is uncommonly supportive of scholarly research and publication; I thank the University of Minnesota for research travel stipends during the summers of 1979 and 1980 and for a leave during the fall quarter of 1981. I am grateful to Robert Franz, acting Dean of UMD's College of Liberal Arts, for many kindnesses and much support. For their wise counsel and encouragement in pursuing a topic that many other acquaintances regard as frivolous, I am indebted to my colleagues Craig Grau and Fred Schroeder and to Smithsonian Institution associate curator Edith Mayo and National Park Service regional archaeologist David Orr. I thank the University of Hartford for making a home for the J. Doyle DeWitt Collection of Political Americana and for making many of its items available for photographs. My debt to my colleague Ronald Marchese and to University of Minnesota, Duluth, photographer Kenneth Moran for their outstanding photographic contributions to this volume is considerable. The American Political Items Collectors generously allowed the use of many photographs from its archives, as did the Smithsonian Institution. Appreciation is extended to both worthy organizations, as it is to the Kent State University Press for its permission to repeat nearly verbatim several passages from my article "The Republican Presidential Campaigns of 1856 and 1860," which appeared in *Civil War History* (1981).

The many friends I have acquired through the common bond of collecting political Americana who have contributed to this effort directly or indirectly in a multitude of ways are too numerous to list, but for their ideas, photographs, campaign objects, auction catalogs, and encouragement

I would like to extend particular thanks to Robert Hultkrantz, Joseph M. Jacobs, Michael Kelly, James Kotche, Erroll Leslie, H. Joseph Levine, Robert Lowe, John Pfeifer, Robert Platt, Morton Rose, Robert Rouse, Morris Shenk, John Vargo, and Joe Wasserman.

I owe an extra measure of gratitude to a few very special individuals. Michigan State University political scientist Charles Press read this manuscript and provided much encouragement and many cogent suggestions for improvement, as did Louis A. Warren Lincoln Library and Museum director Mark E. Neely, Jr., whose support and expertise made him a vital resource from the beginning of this project. Robert Fratkin, my long-time collaborator on the APIC *Keynoter*, contributed his boundless generosity, energy, and enthusiasm in more ways than I can enumerate, as well as his extraordinary knowledge of twentieth-century campaign material. A close friend and valued collaborator, Edmund B. Sullivan, unselfishly supplied me with many photographs taken for this volume and others from his outstanding volume *Collecting Political Americana*, the hospitality of the J. Doyle DeWitt Collection, his personal collection, and his home, and the benefit of an unparalleled wealth of information on nineteenth-century political items. Finally, to my lovely wife Susan and to our sons Brian, David, and Timothy, I owe a very special debt for their loyalty, consideration, and support during a period in which the normal stresses of modern family life were compounded considerably by my "publish or perish" workaholia.

1

Genesis

The practice of using material objects to win votes for American political candidates owes its origin in large part to a monumental temper tantrum. In the presidential contest of 1824, Andrew Jackson led his three rivals—John Qunicy Adams, William H. Crawford, and Henry Clay—in popular and electoral votes, but was denied the presidency when Clay threw his support to Adams in the House of Representatives. Adams then appointed Clay secretary of state, traditionally the stepping-stone to the White House. Believing that they had been victimized by a "corrupt bargain," Jackson and his lieutenants reacted with carefully orchestrated rage, did what they could to sabotage the Adams presidency, and prepared for revenge in 1828. The result was a generation of raucous, vitriolic political warfare that essentially created the modern American system of campaigning for public office. One key characteristic of this new political style was the introduction of manufactured and handmade objects of all sorts—visual items to capture the attention of the voters, and an amazing array of trinkets and geegaws to win or keep their affection. During the two campaigns in which Jackson exacted revenge, upon Adams in 1828 and then Clay in 1832, such items as snuff and thread boxes, metal tokens and garment buttons, cloth ribbons and bandannas, glass flasks and cup plates, and ceramic pitchers and plates became the first material objects used to convey partisan propaganda to the electorate.

Although voters in many areas exhibited their political loyalties at public meetings and the polls long before this by wearing bits of colored ribbon on their coats or twigs, bucktails, or cockades on their hats, our first several presidential contests were waged without mass-produced campaign items to sway public opinion. While the early struggles between Republicans and Federalists were often characterized by extreme partisanship,[1] overt grassroots campaigns for national office had not yet become a component of our political process. One major reason for this was that through 1812, a majority of presidential electors was chosen not by the voters but by state legislatures. This arrangement continued in nine states in 1816 and 1820 and six in 1824, before our modern practice of choosing electors by popular vote became nearly universal in 1828.[2]

A second compelling reason for the absence of grass-roots presidential campaigns was that prevailing political decorum mandated that candidates play what British scholar M. J. Heale has aptly described as the role of the "mute tribune." Our political culture during the early national period looked upon constitutional republics as fragile creations, more likely than not to fall prey to mob anarchy or tyrannical despotism. The presidency, even with the restraints imposed by the Founding Fathers, was viewed widely as a source of potential mischief, and the appearance of unseemly lust for the office was likely to doom the chances of any man to win it. Accordingly, candidates commonly paid homage to the maxim of South Carolina congressman William Lowndes that "the Presidency is not an office to be either solicited or declined," issued nothing but lofty expressions that the sovereign will of the people would be served, and stayed in seclusion unless prevented from doing so by the burdens of office. In 1796, for example, John Adams raised a barn and tended his crops on his farm in Quincy, while Thomas Jefferson supervised the renovation of Monticello. Deviations, most notably the exertions of Aaron Burr in 1800 and De Witt Clinton in 1812, served only to reinforce prevailing etiquette.[3] Correspondingly, supporters were expected to confine their efforts to decorous displays of appreciation for the republican ideals and tested statesmanship of their favorite. Not until 1828 would an evolving electoral system and angry polarization make possible the brash effrontery of a popular campaign for the presidency.

As a result, the relatively small number of known objects featuring our first five presidents had little to do directly with their campaigns for the office. Most were created to celebrate inaugurations, others for memorial or general patriotic or commemorative purposes. Although these objects were not campaign items, they could be considered their direct ancestors, creating artifact types and design motifs later adapted to partisan purposes during political campaigns.

American presidential material culture began with the presidency itself, when George Washington was inaugurated as our first chief executive in 1789, and nearly fifty known varieties of garment buttons were fashioned from brass, copper, silvered copper, silver, and pewter to commemorate the event (fig. 1).[4] All were simple devices consisting of metal discs (often coin or token planchets) with attached shanks, except for one variety with two oval discs joined to create a cuff link. Most of these buttons bore the legend "Long Live the President," with others inscribed with such sentiments as "Unity Prosperity & Independence," "The Majesty of the People," "March the Fourth 1789 Memorable Era," "Remember March Fourth, 1789," and

"E Pluribus Unum." Favorite design features were various renditions of the initials "GW," chains of thirteen oval links encircling the initials of the states, and eagles with shields on their breasts and arrows and olive branches in their talons, almost always surmounted with sunbursts to symbolize the birth of a new form of government.

Washington apparently wore a set of these eagle-sunburst buttons when he took the oath of office in New York on April 30. Secretary of War-designate Henry Knox commissioned one William Rollinson to execute the set, which arrived at Mount Vernon on March 30, prompting Washington to write delightedly to Knox that the buttons "really do credit to the manufactures of this Country" and ask for an additional six to trim the brown broadcloth suit he planned to wear "in the manner I wish it to be."[5] His request was apparently fulfilled, for Senator William Maclay of Pennsylvania attended the inaugural and recorded in his diary that the new president had been clad "in deep brown, with metal buttons, with an eagle on them."[6] Many of the other eagle-sunburst varieties were probably copies of the Rollinson design, struck after the inauguration for sale throughout the new republic to citizens eager for mementos of the event.

Washington's accession to the presidency also inspired the creation of a red and white cotton bandanna and at least two Liverpool transfer tankards. The bandanna featured an oval inauguration scene surrounded by oval-framed portraits of Washington, John Adams, Thomas Jefferson, William Penn, Benjamin Franklin, and Christopher Columbus, and allegorical representations of Commerce and Agriculture.[7] The tankards (fig. 2) both featured military busts of Washington flanked by figures of Justice and Liberty, the toasts "My Favorite Son" and "Long Live the President of the United States," and this marvelous curse:

> Deafness to the Ear that will patiently hear
> & Dumbness to the Tongue that will utter
> A Calumny against the immortal Washington.

These mugs, made possible by a process developed in England a generation before whereby designs were printed on paper from steel or copper plates and then fired onto inexpensive white earthenware, were typical of many ceramic objects exported to the United States by various Liverpool and Staffordshire potteries featuring important individuals and events from the Revolution until after the War of 1812.[8]

Washington's second inauguration in 1793 seems to have inspired only a pair of brass tokens featuring obverse military busts and reverse designs consisting of rays emanating from an eye past fifteen stars to the legend "Success to the United States." A few of the other objects honoring Washington—tapestries, christening cups, brooches, plates, snuff boxes, Battersea curtain tie-backs, a host of bandannas, and Liverpool transfer pitchers, tankards, and mugs—might have been created as tributes to his

Figs. 1 and 2. Among the memorabilia produced to commemorate George Washington's 1789 inauguration were these clothing buttons struck in brass and silvered copper and this Liverpool transfer tankard laying a curse upon detractors of Columbia's "Favorite Son." (Edmund B. Sullivan)

Fig. 3. Hand-painted 1801 linen banner exulting "T. Jefferson President of the United States of America, John Adams no More." (Smithsonian Institution)

presidency, although almost all appear to be memorial or commemorative objects manufactured after his death in 1799 to pay homage to the man who would remain for generations our most enduring national icon.[9]

Subsequent presidents also inspired objects, although on a much diminished scale. Among the items produced to celebrate Adams's inauguration as our second president were two Liverpool transfer pitchers, a leather bridle rosette inscribed "John Adams M. 4. 1797," a copper clothing button, and two types of shanked buttons, one of them featuring a bewigged "Jo[n] Adams ESC" in colonial attire. Jefferson's presidency inspired such memorabilia as an 1801 inaugural medalet executed by German-born John M. Reich of Philadelphia, a magnificent hand-painted linen portrait banner (fig. 3) also made in 1801, a silvered copper shank button, two Liverpool transfer mugs, and at least three Liverpool transfer pitchers, two of them inaugural in nature and the other (featuring Jefferson as a cow pulled in opposite directions by John Bull and Napoleon) satirizing his difficulties with Great Britain and France during his second term.[10]

An 1807 letter from Senator Samuel Latham Mitchill to his wife in New York, acquired by the University of Michigan Library, makes clear that material objects were not totally divorced from campaign politics before the 1820s. In need of new razors, he visited a Washington establishment and discovered British imports engraved to suit American partisan leanings. According to Mitchill:

> Orders are sent from this place to Sheffield, the great manufactory of hard ware in England, for Razors to be manufactured to suit the two prevailing parties in the U. S. and they came forth with appropriate Words elegantly burnished on one side of their Blades. For the Republicans, these instruments are adorned with the Words 'a true Jeffersonian,' and for the Federalists with 'a true Washingtonian,' and more recently to favour the pretensions of the Secretary of State to the Presidential Chair, Razors are sold here in great Numbers with the Words 'a true Madisonian' superbly legible on the steel.

A stalwart Republican, Mitchill purchased both a Jeffersonian and a Madisonian model and commented to his wife, "It is in this way that the Printing of Callico Curtains, the figuring of Staffordshire Crockery, and the casting of Gypsum Medallions have all been instrumental in procuring renown for certain persons."[11] His observation proved to be prophetic; in less than a generation, fabrics, ceramics, medallions, and other types of objects would be exploited commonly to "procure renown" for candidates for the presidency. Unfortunately, no surviving specimens of these Sheffield razors are known to exist. Quite possibly, the "a true Madisonian" variety represents the earliest American campaign artifact.

Madison's 1809 inauguration was commemorated by a Liverpool transfer pitcher (fig. 4), and his 1813 inaugural by a large medal designed by Moritz Furst. The presidency of James Monroe inspired a small token struck in brass and copper varieties and a clothing button of the genre known popularly as "backname" buttons, with a plain gilt obverse and "Monroe" and the manufacturer's quality mark "Extra Strong" inscribed on its reverse. Monroe was also featured on several varieties of the small christening cups or maxim mugs so much in vogue as gifts for children at that time, but whether they were produced to honor his presidency or issued as parts of sets cannot be determined, for very similar cups featuring Washington and the elder Adams have also survived.[12]

These early inaugural and commemorative items were the true ancestors of later presidential campaign items. Small brass and copper tokens similar in manufacture and design to the ones struck to honor Washington's 1793 inaugural would become the most ubiquitous of all nineteenth-century campaign trinkets, rivaled in variety and quantity only by ribbons and by gilt metal garment buttons much like those made to commemorate his 1789 inauguration. Washington's portrayal in uniform on the 1789 tankards and 1793 token obverses would be duplicated to enormous political advantage by such subsequent soldier-statesmen as Jackson, William Henry Harrison,

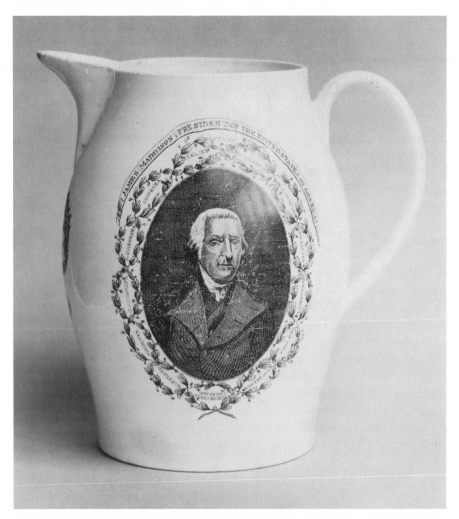

Fig. 4. Liverpool transfer pitcher commemorating James Madison's 1809 inauguration; on reverse is Republican version of "Hail Columbia, Happy Land" celebrating
victory of Thomas Jefferson in "Revolution of 1800." (Smithsonian Institution)

and Zachary Taylor. Colorful cloth bandannas similar to the one honoring
the accession of Washington would be printed for supporters of Jackson and
Adams in 1828 and would later develop into a common byproduct of presidential campaigns. Liverpool transferware and maxim mugs would not
survive into the era of campaign material culture, but the almost insatiable
middle-class American appetite for such bric-a-brac would be fed by a new
generation of political ceramics, ranging in cost and quality from the exquisite lusterware pitchers and plates to the more mundane "Columbian Star"
Staffordshire pottery of John Ridgway. Papier-mache snuff boxes similar to
one made as a Washington memorial souvenir would bear the likenesses of

such presidential candidates as Jackson, Clay, Harrison, Taylor, and Martin Van Buren.

These early inaugural and commemorative items were prophetic in another sense as well. Although (with the possible exception of Senator Mitchill's "a true Madisonian" Sheffield razor) they were not created or used for campaign purposes, a number of them demonstrate a growing tendency to use physical objects as vehicles for extremely partisan sentiments. The unknown artist who painted the words "T. Jefferson President of the United States of America/John Adams no More" onto an 1801 banner (fig. 3) left little doubt of his intention to denigrate the defeated Federalist as well as to pay tribute to his conqueror. A Liverpool transfer pitcher celebrating Jefferson's victory carried this militantly partisan adaptation of the popular patriotic air "Hail Columbia":

> Hail Columbia happy Land
> Hail ye patriotic band
> Who late oppos'd oppressive laws
> And now stand firm in freedom's cause
> Rejoice for now the storm is gone
> Columbia owns her chosen son
> The rights of man shall be our boast
> And jefferson our favorite toast
> Republicans behold your chief
> He comes to give your fears relief
> Now arm'd in virtue firm and true
> Looks for support to Heaven and you.

The market for anti-Federalist verse apparently remained fairly lucrative, for a Liverpool pitcher produced to commemorate James Madison's 1809 inauguration featured the same transfer. Madison's 1813 inaugural medal, struck at a time when Federalist New England was stridently protesting our involvement in the War of 1812, bore on its reverse the message "Protection Against Invasion Is Due from Every Society to the Parts Composing It." From such items to ones created overtly for campaign purposes was but a very short step.

Precisely when that step was first taken, when objects began to be designed, made, and utilized for the express purpose of influencing a mass electorate, is unclear. That the bitterly contested 1828 rematch between Adams and Jackson engendered a variety of objects clearly produced and used to win votes is apparent, but many authorities on American political material culture have argued that the tradition was already well established by 1828. A specialist on clothing buttons has postulated that the Monroe backname button was created as a campaign item, either for 1816 or 1820.[13] This would seem quite improbable, for Monroe was virtually unopposed in 1816, when the half-hearted Federalist campaign of Rufus King was waged in only a few states, and unopposed altogether in 1820. Moreover, a small button with its message on its back side, tight up against the fabric, would surely have made a rather ineffective propaganda mechanism.

Other authorities have attributed various Jackson items to his 1824 presidential bid. A brown ceramic crock (fig. 5) made in New Haven, Connecticut, which bore the legend "25,000 Majority/GNL Jackson" beneath a clipper ship, has been classified by Smithsonian personnel as an 1824 campaign object, although its text makes its genesis as a post-1824 protest item much more likely.[14] Similar arguments have been advanced on behalf of several objects featuring Jackson as the "Hero of New Orleans," including lusterware pitchers, ceramic plates, six small brass tokens struck in Waterbury, Connecticut, and some papier-mache snuff boxes bearing youthful portraits.[15] It appears quite improbable that such items were created expressly for the 1824 Jackson presidential campaign, because 1824 was a contest (one of the last of its type) simply not characterized by the extensive activity at the grass-roots level likely to engender partisan trinkets or bric-a-brac. Moreover, breakthroughs in political material culture generally occur simultaneously among the various candidates, but no Adams or Clay campaign items can be attributed to 1824, and no items of any sort promoting William H. Crawford have ever been reported. Apparently no direct evidence exists to settle this question, because documentation is lacking, type parallels are inconclusive, and the Hero of New Orleans theme common to these objects was central to the Tennessean's identity as a national icon from his 1815 victory over Lord Pakenham's forces until long after his death thirty years later.

As a symbol of national glory whose three presidential campaigns did much to establish the cult of personality in national politics, Jackson inspired an impressive variety of material memorabilia. Included were more than two dozen different metal tokens or medalets, many holed to wear as little badges or lapel ornaments, and a dozen or more gilt metal garment buttons, eight of these of the backname variety. Textile items featuring Jackson included beautiful silk bandannas (fig.6), several designs of cotton yard goods or "chintzes" (fig.7), and a few silk ribbons. A dozen or more styles of flasks and a tumbler featuring a cameo likeness imbedded in the base were among the glass mementos. Ceramic objects decorated by his image included dinner plates (fig. 8) and ornate and expensive copper luster pitchers (fig.9) imported from Britain and France. Other Jackson items included several different types of papier-mache snuff boxes (fig. 10), a rather gaudy tortoise-shell comb (fig. 11), and at least four varieties of cardboard, gilt paper, and velvet thread boxes (figs. 12, 13) imported from France and displaying political maxims on the velvet pincushion outer lids and paper portraits attached to the inner lids. [16]

It is clear from newspaper accounts and historical scholarship, as well as from the rarity of most mass-produced Jackson items and the complete absence of comments about them and advertisements for them in the news-

Fig. 5. This New Haven, Connecticut "25,000 Majority GNL Jackson" earthenware crock has inspired a lively controversy over its date of manufacture. (Smithsonian Institution)

Figs. 6 and 7. Silk bandanna recalling heroics of "Major General Andrew Jackson" at New Orleans and cotton chintz exploiting same theme with legend "Magnanimous in Peace, Victorious in War." (Edmund B. Sullivan)

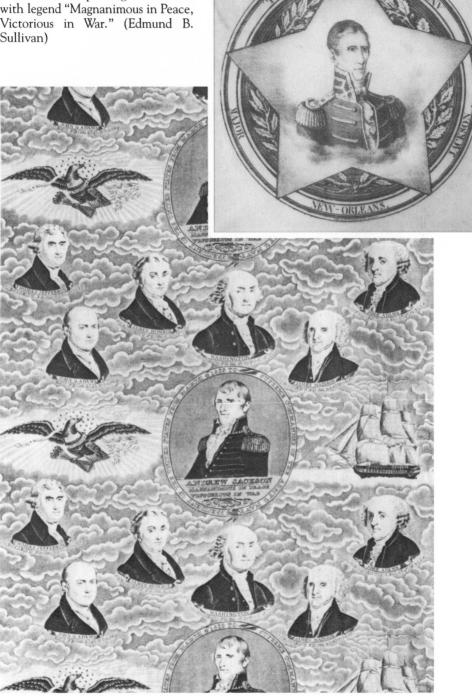

Figs. 8 and 9. Imported copper luster plate and pitcher featuring same transfer design of "General Jackson, the Hero of New Orleans." (Smithsonian Institution)

Figs. 10 and 11. Papier-mache snuff box with youthful likeness of "General Andrew Jackson" in parade regalia and tortoise-shell comb featuring Jackson flanked by Lafayette and Washington and legend "New Orleans." (Fig. 10, Edmund B. Sullivan; Fig. 11, Smithsonian Institution)

Figs. 12 and 13. 1828 French velvet thread box, closed to reveal "Jackson Triumphant" pincushion design and opened to display portrait. (Smithsonian Institution)

papers of the day,[17] that the physical objects that played a meaningful role in Jackson's campaigns (1828 in particular) came not from the factories or kilns of England and France or the foundries or textile mills of New England, but from the American hardwood forests. Jackson had won the nickname Old Hickory, a major political asset in reinforcing his reputation for natural strength, on a march from Natchez to Nashville in 1813, when he surrendered his horse to an ailing soldier, fashioned a hickory walking-stick, and made the journey on foot.[18] During the 1828 campaign his supporters (organized into Hickory Clubs) marked such occasions as the anniversary of his victory over the British at New Orleans and Independence Day by gathering in public squares and fields to plant hickory saplings or raise hickory poles. One enterprising New Jersey Jacksonian running low on firewood reportedly secured "several cords of hickory, a good long pole to raise for the Hero, and a pleasant laugh at his friends" by asking each fellow Democrat in his community to donate a hickory pole for July 4![19] More common as badges than ribbons or medalets were hickory sprigs. Among the manufactured items echoing this theme were an "Old Hickory Forever" velvet thread box and an 1832 Pennsylvania silk ribbon featuring the verse "Freemen, Cheer the Hickory Tree; In Storms Its Boughs Have Sheltered Thee."

A large majority of Jackson objects presented him as the Hero of New Orleans, either by stating so directly or simply by portraying him in military attire, usually accompanied by legends utilizing his rank. Tokens featuring military busts of "Gen[l] Andrew Jackson" proclaimed him "Hero of New Orleans," as did plates and lusterware pitchers. Medalets with military bust obverses featured such sentiments on the reverses as "We Commemo[at] the Glorious Victories of our Hero in War & in Peace" and "The Gallant & Successful Defender of New Orleans." Two bore stylized scenes of battle, as did several patterns of cotton yard goods. Another chintz variety, every known type of Jackson flask, several snuff boxes, a garment button, the thread boxes, and both silk bandannas featured military busts, often accompanied by such legends as "Major General Andrew Jackson New-Orleans" or "G[NL] Andrew Jackson." A small oval cuff-link button bore the words "General Jackson" surrounding a shield, while "New Orleans" read a tortoise-shell comb.

Because Jackson's battlefield exploits transformed him almost overnight into a national celebrity nearly a decade before he first vied for the presidency, some of these Hero of New Orleans items—most likely the lusterware pitchers and plates, tortoise-shell comb, snuff boxes with young portraits, battle-scene chintzes, and possibly a few tokens—were perhaps made and marketed before 1824, not for political purposes but simply to exploit for profit the popularity of a new cult hero. Lafayette's 1824–25 grand tour inspired a copious array of similar memorabilia, and the nostalgic outpouring of affection for him was much less intense than was the adulation showered upon the Tennessean who had "conquered the conquerors of Napoleon" and avenged the torching of Washington.

Enough of these objects can be attributed to his 1828 and 1832 campaigns and the inaugural celebrations that followed, however, to document the enduring importance of the Hero of New Orleans theme to Jackson's political success. In 1828, a pair of medalets saluted "General Jackson" as "The Gallant & Successful Defender of New Orleans & Candidate for the Presidency of the United States of America 1828," and the thread boxes portrayed him in military regalia, one of them also admonishing on the pincushion lid "Don't Forget New Orleans." Among the goods produced for his exuberant 1829 inauguration were a trio of tokens reiterating the "Gallant & Successful Defender" theme, and two proclaiming him "Hero of New Orleans," plus a cotton fabric pattern featuring a military bust and the motto "Magnanimous in Peace, Victorious in War." The war hero theme appears to have been represented on 1832 campaign items only by a white metal token with an equestrian portrayal of Jackson and by the military bust flasks, but his 1833 inauguration inspired two medalets bearing the "Gallant & Successful Defender" slogan, and three that read "We Commemo[at] the Glorious Victories of our Hero in War & in Peace."

These campaign trinkets do little to challenge the rather harsh judgement of historian Edward Pessen that the Democratic party was born as "a heterogeneous catchall whose great national leader had taken pains to avoid committing himself on the important issues."[20] If Jackson's 1828 vendetta against Adams was identified in the public mind with positions on salient questions of national policy, the souvenirs and badges it inspired do not reflect it. Apart from a thread box that read "Jackson and no Corruption," a rather blunt reminder of the 1825 "corrupt bargain" between Adams and Clay, no known 1828 Jackson objects transcended Hero of New Orleans or Old Hickory thematics.

This lack of issue-oriented items may have been expected in 1828, a singularly venomous contest waged primarily with character assassination by both sides (Jackson was accused of multiple murders and of having lived in sin with his beloved Rachel, the arch-puritan Adams of having procured young American virgins for the Russian tsar), but Jackson's re-election over Clay in a much more ideological contest in 1832 inspired only two known issue-related campaign items. A token struck in New York attacked both the Bank of the United States and the defiance of federal sovereignty over the states by South Carolina's "nullifiers" with a reverse that read "The Bank Must Perish/the Union Must and Shall Be Preserved." A silk ribbon (fig. 14) from Philadelphia urged, "Jackson, Sutherland, Democracy, and no Bank/Equal Rights to all Legal Voters." This item may well represent the first known "coattail" campaign object of a material nature, linking the popularity of Jackson with that of Pennsylvania Congressman Joel Barlow

Sutherland. Its legend remains something of a mystery, because Sutherland was an avid supporter of the bank (headquartered in his district) who subsequently fell prey to a Democratic party purge over the issue. No known Jackson campaign items from either 1828 or 1832 made reference to the tariff or federal funding for internal improvement projects, topics on which his political fortunes rode to a great extent upon his ability to be "all things to all men."

The few campaign items inspired by John Quincy Adams's unsuccessful 1828 re-election effort developed neither an ideological focus nor a popular image with which the voters could identify. A redware tile (fig. 15) apparently cast in a hand-carved wooden bread mold now in the Smithsonian collection, the only known issue-oriented Adams campaign object, featured a standing portrait and the legend " "Peece [sic] Liberty/Home Industry." A mirror in a ringed pewter casing held a rather stoic likeness of Adams on the reverse. The only known Adams flask featured a bust on one side with an eagle on the other. French thread boxes (fig. 16) imported for sale to Adams partisans carried such maxims as "Victory for Adams," "Adams and Liberty," "Be Firm for Adams," and "Adams Forever." Cotton bandannas and white metal tokens tried to exploit Adams's incumbency with the legend "His Excellency John Quincy Adams."[21] Faced with a well-orchestrated, often vicious effort by Jacksonians to portray him as an effete aristocrat given to "kingly pomp and splendour" and "royal extravagances,"[22] Adams was not especially well served by "Adams Forever" thread boxes or "His Excellency" tokens and bandannas. The material remains of his 1828 campaign do much to explain why he was defeated so decisively, particularly in the rough-hewn constituencies west of the Appalachians.

Some of the campaign items inspired by Henry Clay's attempt to unseat Jackson in 1832 were both more thematic and more imaginative in symbolism. Two trinkets paid homage to Clay's American System agenda for national economic development, a small gilt copper clothing button proclaiming the Kentuckian "The Champion of Internal Improvs" and a rather large white metal token identifying him as "The Champion of Republicanism and the American System." Two white metal tokens executed by Charles C. Wright of New York sought to depict Clay as a statesman-like alternative to the rustic Jackson by portraying him in the classic togaed bust motif (fig. 17), like a modern Pericles or Cincinnatus, with reverses featuring lists of several of his major legislative and diplomatic achievements to further accentuate this theme. Three varieties of gilt brass clothing buttons also bore togaed Clay busts. His 1832 campaign also inspired portrait snuff boxes, a backname button, two styles of glass cup plates (fig. 18) made by the Boston and Sandwich Glass Company (for holding cups after hot coffee or tea had been poured into saucers to cool and drink), and probably three or four varieties of flasks.[23] Supporters of the "Sage of Ash-

Figs. 14 and 15. Two of the more unusual campaign items ever produced, an 1832 Jackson–Joel Barlow Sutherland campaign ribbon curiously linking Sutherland to Jackson's vendetta against the Bank of the United States and an 1828 John Quincy Adams redware tile apparently made from a hand-carved wooden bread mold. (Fig. 15, Smithsonian Institution)

land" unable to purchase such "store-bought" items displayed their political loyalty with ash poles similar to the hickory poles exhibited by Jackson stalwarts.

The use of material objects as partisan weapons in political campaigns thus began in earnest during the 1828 and 1832 presidential races, although its permanence as a basic facet of American elective politics was by no means assured. The practice, in fact, appears to have been abandoned almost altogether during Martin Van Buren's victory over three Whig adversaries in 1836. Unable to come up with a single candidate capable of

Fig. 16. 1828 French velvet thread box open to display Adams's likeness. (Smithsonian Institution)

challenging Jackson's heir apparent nationally, the new Whig coalition
resorted to the ploy of fielding such regional nominees as Daniel Webster,
William Henry Harrison, and Hugh Lawson White in hopes of creating an
electoral deadlock. The result was a rather dull campaign that appears to
have inspired little grass-roots activity or popular enthusiasm, two ingre-
dients necessary for a copious harvest of trinkets. A large red, white, and
blue silk banner hung from a tavern to celebrate a campaign appearance in
Tappen, New York, and a white metal token proclaiming him "Our Next
President" are the only known Van Buren campaign objects that can be

Figs. 17 and 18. 1832 Henry Clay campaign medalet featuring Kentuckian clad in classical Roman toga to emphasize his stature as a national statesman and glass cup plate pressed by the Boston and Sandwich Glass Company. (Kenneth J. Moran)

linked with relative safety to his 1836 race, although two or three other tokens, a copper luster pitcher, one or two snuff boxes, and a few styles of ribbons might possibly have seen use in 1836. The only Harrison item possibly used in 1836 is a token patterned after the congressional medal given him for his heroics at the Battle of Thames, the lone Webster 1836 possibility is a snuff box, and no White campaign items of any sort have ever been reported.[24] In 1836, the politics of trinketry gave every sign of being a dying phenomenon in presidential campaigns.

The Whigs proved much more prolific, however, inspiring political items for other purposes. Garment buttons, tokens, and ribbons produced to celebrate their creation, promote local Whig candidates, and protest Jackson and Van Buren monetary policies were largely responsible for keeping alive the tradition of political material culture between 1832 and 1840. The Whigs wasted no time. Their genesis as a formal organization of Jackson's adversaries in 1834 inspired the creation of at least thirteen varieties of brass garment buttons, some silk ribbons, and seventeen different types of brass or copper tokens.[25] Nearly all of the clothing buttons featured the Whig symbol, a liberty cap upon a pole. This device, so prominent in the iconography of the American Revolution, represented an obvious attempt to build upon their exploitation of the name of the old antiroyalist faction to combat what they believed to be the monarchical policies of the Democrat they branded "King Andrew." To make the analogy ever more apparent, the buttons read "Whigs of 76 & 34" or "True Whigs of 76 & 34," a few adding "For the Constitution" or "E Pluribus Unum" for good measure. This theme was symbolized on the ribbons (figs. 19, 20) with the portrait of Washington, whom the Whigs labored mightily throughout their brief existence to depict as the spiritual founding father of Whiggery.

Some of the tokens were created by Thomas Lovett of New York for local distribution. Three celebrated Whig victories in the April 1834, municipal elections. Two bore liberty cap obverses reading "The Glorious Whig Victories of 1834" and clipper ship reverses admonishing "Fellow Citizens, Save your Constitution," and the third featured a clipper ship obverse exulting "For the Constitution, Hurra!" and a reverse inscribed "Flourish Commerce, Flourish Industry/Whigs of N. York Victorious les Trois Jours April 8. 9. & 10. 1834." A token touted Whig gubernatorial hopeful Gulian C. Verplanck as "A Faithful Friend to our Country," while eventual party nominee William Henry Seward received the same accolade on a trio of tokens and "The Glory and Pride of our Nation" on another. These gubernatorial tokens were the first known trinkets produced solely for candidates for lesser offices than the presidency.

Other 1834 Whig tokens included some outstanding satiric pieces (fig. 21) prompted by Jackson's removal of the federal deposits from the Bank of the United States. These tokens essentially depicted King Andrew as an irresponsible tyrant and pretentious ass whose monetary policies endangered

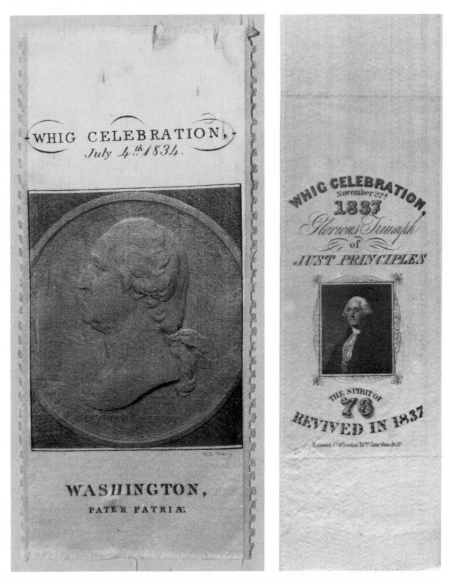

Figs. 19 and 20. Silk ribbon badges from Whig celebrations in Boston in 1834 and New York in 1837, both featuring George Washington as the ultimate symbol of a party that portrayed itself as heir to the Spirit of '76. (Kenneth J. Moran)

the economy and the Constitution alike. Three featured jackasses branded "LL.D.," a reference to an honorary degree conferred by Harvard upon the allegedly illiterate Tennessean,[26] a theme echoed by an 1834 copper cent counterstruck "The Hero of New Orleans/Rex and Jackass." Two tokens portrayed Jackson exiting from a vault with a sword in one hand and money bags in the other and were captioned "I Take the Responsibility" (a legend inspired by his assurance to his Cabinet in September 1833, that he was "very willing to let the public know that I take the whole responsibility" for removing the deposits). Others bore obverse Jackson busts with the legend "My Experiement, My Currency, My Glory" and reverses with running hogs labeled "My Third Heat" and Congressman Samuel Beardsley's unfortunate exhortation "Perish Credit, Perish Commerce."[27] Satiric shinplaster notes were also printed depicting Jackson as an ass carrying saddlebags marked "Deposits" down the road to ruin. These tokens and notes were created primarily as protest items rather than partisan trinkets, but they were used widely in 1834 for campaign purposes until public opinion turned decisively against the bank, and Whigs abandoned the issue.

After almost altogether ignoring material culture as a means of denying Van Buren the presidency in 1836, the Whigs appear to have rediscovered the art once they were again in their comfortable reactive role as a not-so-loyal opposition. Silk ribbons commemorating a November 22, 1837, "Whig Celebration (fig. 20), apparently an effort to generate excitement for the forthcoming off-year elections, proclaimed the "Glorious Triumph of Just Principles" accompanied by a double reminder of their alleged philosophical birthright, a portrait of George Washington and the legend "The Spirit of 76 Revived in 1837."

When Van Buren reacted to the Panic of 1837 by proposing his "independent subtreasury" system as an alternative to reviving the Bank of the United States, one result was a deluge of satiric Whig protest items similar to the ones motivated by Jackson's bank vendetta in 1834. According to Thomas Hart Benton, the Missouri senator whose hatred for paper money was so intense that he was known as "Old Bullion" and silver and gold coins were popularly referred to as "Benton mint-drops," banknotes were printed featuring "caricatures and grotesque pictures and devices, and reproachful sentences . . . and exhibited every where to excite contempt," many of which were mailed to Benton and other hard-money disciples "plentifully sprinkled over with taunting expressions." Also distributed were "pieces in imitation of gold and silver coins . . . intended to act on the thoughtless and ignorant through appeals to their eyes and passions."[28]

To test Old Bullion's notoriously fragile sense of humor even further, two of these "derisory manufactures" made him the butt of their satire, copper tokens featuring reverses reading "Bentonian Currency/Mint Drop" and "Benton Experiment/Mint Drop," the latter also bearing a hideous female head labeled "Loco Foco" on its obverse. Other tokens (fig. 22) depicted a turtle lugging a strongbox labeled "Sub-Treasury" surrounded by the inscription "Executive Experiment/1837 Fiscal Agent." Reverses (fig. 23) featured a jackass encircled by the legend "I Follow in the Steps of My Illustrious Predecessor." Several varieties of tokens were struck by the Scovill Manufacturing Company of Waterbury, Connecticut, to promote Daniel Webster's 1840 presidential aspirations. Most likely circulated in the Northeast during 1838 and 1839, they featured on one side the clipper ship "Constitution" sailing proudly inside the legend "Webster Credit Currency 1841," and on the other side the vessel "Experiement" foundering upon the rocks in turbulent seas, surrounded by the legend "Van Buren Metallic Currency 1837."[29]

Largely ignored by historians and curators alike, these satiric off-year pieces protesting Jackson's war on the bank and Van Buren's subtreasury proposal, coupled with a virtual absence of 1836 Whig presidential campaign items, speak volumes on the basic nature of early Whiggery. Created primarily to mold anti-Jacksonians into a stronger reactive force, the Whig coalition during the 1830s was held together less by consensus on major issues or even by a common bond of opportunism than it was by a shared hatred for "King Andrew," his expansion of executive prerogatives, and his heir Van Buren. It functioned enthusiastically in a purely negative capacity as a not-so-loyal opposition to the Democrats, but proved singularly incapable of pursuing power on its own behalf. The trinkets the Whig coalition engendered during this period demonstrate a much greater talent for denigrating the character and policies of opposition presidents than for promoting the virtues of Whig candidates and causes. Probably more than any other political artifacts produced during this era, these "derisory manufactures" reflect the raucous partisanship of our modern political system in the years of its infancy.

In general, the campaign items created during the period from the 1825 "corrupt bargain" through the 1830s demonstrate both a huge potential for political material culture and some rather substantial early limitations. A rather diverse variety of object types was introduced, including some soon doomed to extinction as partisan weapons (chintzes, cup plates, lusterware, thread boxes) along with the tokens, ribbons, clothing buttons, and bandannas destined to develop into staples of political trinketry in the years ahead. This generation of campaign items clearly established the viability of physical objects as conduits of partisan propaganda to a mass electorate, but it represented only a tentative first step in that direction. With the exceptions of some pieces depicting Jackson as the Hero of New Orleans and a togaed Clay as a latter-day Cincinnatus, these items appear to have been created by men oblivious to the virtually unlimited potential for political symbolism in designs, shaped, textures, and coloration. The possibility of using objects to exploit issues was made manifest by several off-year Whig tokens and notes, but remained almost untouched by presidential campaign items. Most pre-1840 political trinkets were relatively expensive, thus useless for winning the hearts of working-class Americans. Most limiting of all, these items were primarily personal in nature, intended exclusively for the gratification of the recipient, rather than designed to advertise the merits of candidates or causes to presumably uncommitted bystanders. A quantum advance in the art of political trinketry, however, lay just ahead.

Figs. 21, 22, and 23. Among the many varieties of Whig tokens satirizing the fiscal policies of Andrew Jackson and his heir Martin Van Buren were these 1834 examples above and 1837 medalets below. (Kenneth J. Moran)

NOTES

1. A splendid example of this acrimony was the dying plea of Daniel Webster's staunchly Federalist father Ebenezer, who was stricken in a New Hampshire village recently carried by Thomas Jefferson and begged, "Carry me back home! I don't want to die in a Republican town." See Richard N. Current, *Daniel Webster and the Rise of National Conservatism* (Boston, 1955), 5.

2. M. J. Heale, *The Presidential Quest: Candidates and Images in American Political Culture, 1789–1852* (London, 1982), 20–21, 33–34.

3. For an excellent analysis of the "mute tribune" ideal and covert efforts to circumvent it during pre-Jacksonian elections, see Heale, *The Presidential Quest*, 1–22.

4. Edmund B. Sullivan, *American Political Badges and Medalets, 1789–1892* (Lawrence, Mass., 1981), 1–7; Alphaeus H. Albert, *Record of American Uniform and Historical Buttons with Supplement* (Hightstown, N. J., 1973), 387–97.

5. George Washington to Henry Knox, April 10, 1789, in *The Writings of George Washington* 30, ed. John C. Fitzpatrick (Washington, 1929), 280.

6. Edgar S. Maclay, ed., *Journal of William Maclay: United States Senator from Pennsylvania* (New York, 1890), 9.

7. Herbert R. Collins, *Threads of History: Americana Recorded on Cloth, 1775 to the Present* (Washington, 1979),52.

8. See Marian Klamkin, *American Patriotic and Political China* (New York, 1973), 12–17; G. Bernard Hughes, *English and Scottish Earthenware, 1660–1860* (London, 1961), 123–31; and Robert H. Macauley, *Liverpool Transfer Designs on Anglo-American Pottery* (New York, 1942). For a thorough and superbly illustrated survey of similar objects commemorating British individuals and events, see John May and Jennifer May, *Commemorative Pottery, 1780–1900.* (London, 1972). The Washington inaugural tankard not pictured in this volume is illustrated in Klamkin, *Patriotic and Political China*, 62, and in Theodore L. Hake, *Political Buttons: Book III, 1789–1916* (York, Pa., 1978), 15.

9. For the 1793 inaugural tokens, see Sullivan, *Political Badges and Medalets*, 9. A general representation of Washington memorial and commemorative objects produced during the early nineteenth century may be found in Collins, *Threads of History*, 53–60; Klamkin, *Patriotic and Political China*, 60–69; and Hake, *Political Buttons, III*, 14–15. Washington continued to serve as a favorite subject for the producers of plates, flasks, ribbons, statuary, and other memorabilia, especially during such events as Lafayette's 1824–25 return visit to the United States, the centennial of Washington's birth in 1832, and the national centennial in 1876.

10. Sullivan, *Political Badges and Medalets*, 11–12, 15; Collins, *Threads of History*, 60; Klamkin, *Patriotic and Political China*, 70–74; Hake, *Political Buttons, III*, 15–16.

11. Quoted in *The Quarto* (newsletter of Clements Library Associates of the University of Michigan), no. 136 (March 1983): 4.

12. Klamkin, *Patriotic and Political China*, 76–78; Sullivan, *Political Badges and Medalets*, 17; Albert, *Uniform and Historical Buttons*, 420. For a brief but informative description of "backname buttons," see Alphaeus H. Albert, "Backname Buttons," *The APIC Keynoter* (journal of the American Political Items Collectors) 80 (Summer 1980): 21. "Maxim mugs" were apparently so named because many varieties featured the "Poor Richard" sayings of Benjamin Franklin.

13. Albert, "Backname Buttons," 21.

14. Although Jackson's 1824 popular majority over Adams was nearly forty-five thousand votes, not the twenty-five thousand indicated on the crock, the reference was probably to the 1824 popular vote, because Jackson's 1828 and 1832 majorities were approximately one hundred fifty thousand. This was not a reference to Connecticut alone, which Old Hickory never carried. Because the reference to 1824 was ex post facto, the crock was probably made after the "corrupt bargain" in 1825.

15. Assertions that Jackson's 1824 campaign inspired items apparently began with J. Doyle DeWitt, A Century of Campaign Buttons, 1789–1889 (Hartford, 1959), 10–12, which attributes several small brass tokens struck in Waterbury, Connecticut, to 1824. This claim was reiterated in Hake, Political Buttons, III, 20, 243; Edmund B. Sullivan, Collecting Political Americana (New York, 1980), 72; Sullivan, Political Badges and Medalets (essentially a revised and expanded edition of the DeWitt volume), 19–21 and Heale, The Presidential Quest, 50. In Collecting Political Americana, 88, 151, Sullivan has advanced the premise that plates and snuff boxes bearing youthful portraits of Jackson (figs. 8 and 10) were produced in 1824 or even earlier. A more likely candidate as an 1824 campaign item, in my opinion, would be the tortoise-shell comb (fig. 11) featuring small busts of Washington and Lafayette, because Lafayette's return to the United States in 1824 created a vogue for the Frenchman as an American patriotic icon.

16. For a general representation of Jackson material, see Roger A. Fischer and Edmund B. Sullivan, American Political Ribbons and Ribbon Badges, 1825–1981 (Lincoln, Mass., 1985), 20–26; Sullivan, Political Badges and Medalets, 19–28, 31–33, 42; Albert, Uniform and Historical Buttons, 420–22; Collins, Threads of History, 68, 77–78; Klamkin, Patriotic and Political China, 97–101; Hake, Political Buttons, III, 19–20; Sullivan, Collecting Political Americana, 72, 88, 102–3, 132–33, 151, 170–71; Bessie M. Lindsey, American Historical Glass, rev. ed. (Rutland, Vt., 1967), 278–79; Helen McKearin and Kenneth M. Wilson, American Bottles and Flasks and Their Ancestry (New York, 1978), 475–78; Donald L. Ackerman, "Snuff Boxes," The APPA Standard (journal of the Association for the Preservation of Political Americana) 4 (Summer 1977): 14–16; and Ackerman, "Thread Boxes," APPA Standard 4 (Autumn 1977): 12.

17. A thorough search of the leading Jackson and Adams newspapers in 1828 yielded only an ad for Masonic mourning ribbons for DeWitt Clinton at $1.50 per dozen in the April 8, 1828 National Intelligencer.

18. See John William Ward, Andrew Jackson: Symbol for an Age (New York, 1955), 54–57.

19. Belvidere (N. J.) Apollo, quoted in National Intelligencer, Aug. 23, 1828.

20. Edward Pessen, Jacksonian America: Society, Personality, and Politics rev. ed. (Homewood, Ill., 1978), 200.

21. Klamkin, Patriotic and Political China, 98; Sullivan, Political Badges and Medalets, 29–30; Hake, Political Buttons, III, 18; Collins, Threads of History, 76; McKearin and Wilson, Bottles and Flasks, 475–76; and Ackerman, "Thread Boxes," 12.

22. A key tenet of the 1828 Jackson campaign was its contrasting the manly simplicity of Old Hickory with "the kingly pomp that is displayed by the present incumbent," accusing Adams (incorrectly) of such "royal extravagances" as purchasing an imported billiard table for the East Room with public funds. See Robert V.

Remini, *The Election of Andrew Jackson* (Philadelphia, 1963), 102–4; and Pessen, *Jacksonian America*, 166–67.

23. See Sullivan, *Political Badges and Medalets*, 33–35; Albert, *Uniform and Historical Buttons*, 432–34; Ruth Webb Lee and James H. Rose, *American Glass Cup Plates* (Northborough, Mass., 1948), 40–41, 307, 312; and Sullivan, *Collecting Political Americana*, 103–5, 151.

24. Sullivan, *Political Badges and Medalets*, 45–48; Collins, *Threads of History*, 86; and Sullivan, *Collecting Political Americana*, 88, 151.

25. Albert, *Uniform and Historical Buttons*, 422–24; Sullivan, *Political Badges and Medalets*, 37–43; and Fischer and Sullivan, *Political Ribbons and Ribbon Badges*, 27.

26. For an excellent account of this incident, the Whig reaction to it, and its political ramifications, see Ward, *Andrew Jackson*, 83–88.

27. For background on the incidents that inspired these satiric tokens, see Robert V. Remini, *Andrew Jackson and the Bank War* (New York, 1967), 142–47; and Arthur M. Schlesinger, Jr., *The Age of Jackson* (Boston, 1945), 108.

28. Thomas Hart Benton, *Thirty Years' View* (New York, 1856), vol. 2, 26.

29. Sullivan, *Political Badges and Medalets*, 49–52.

2

Down to the People
1840–54

In 1840, the politics of popular amusement truly came of age, as the Whigs went "down to the people" (in the telling phrase of editor Richard S. Elliott) to elect William Henry Harrison our ninth president with a campaign that stands as a landmark in the carnivalization of American elective politics. Its victim, Van Buren, denounced it as "a political Saturnalia" and its unwitting role-model Jackson as "Logg cabin hard cider and coon humbugery," and Whig elder-statesman John Quincy Adams saw it as a sign of "a revolution in the habits and manners of the people," but the canvass was perhaps characterized best in one of its own chants as the "great commotion." In lieu of a platform (which only encouraged lying, party leaders explained solemnly) or other discourse on the major public questions of the day, the Whigs gave the voters a candidate so mute on the issues he acquired the nickname "General Mum," homilies on the innate nobility of log cabins, such slogans as "Tippecanoe and Tyler too," lurid propaganda contrasting their homespun "Ohio Ploughman" with the "grovelling demagogue" Van Buren and his "eastern officeholder pimps," and new forms of political theater that involved hundreds of thousands of Americans in a participatory role for the first time. Banal and colorful, enthusiastic and profoundly irrelevant, the Harrison campaign was an effort worthy of the talents of P. T. Barnum or Cecil B. deMille.

In its participatory dimensions alone, the great commotion transformed the art of campaigning for public office in the United States.[1] Rallies were not new, strictly speaking, but the celebrations two and three days long that drew estimated crowds of one hundred thousand to Baltimore in May, Nashville in August, and Dayton in September (the same weekend some sixty thousand congregated at Bunker Hill), and "fifteen acres of men" to the Tippecanoe battlefield in Indiana in May were unlike anything yet

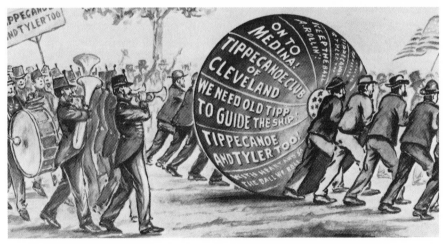

Figs. 24 and 25. Captured in these contemporary prints of 1840 "Tippecanoe and Tyler Too" campaign revelry are a mobile log cabin, used as a float during the parade and a dispensary of hard cider afterward, and a slogan ball rolled to promote the Whig cause from Cleveland to Lexington. (Smithsonian Institution)

experienced in American politics. Stump speeches had been standard campaign fare for years, but not two-day talkathons by platoons of orators (including for the first time a nominee himself) to crowds as large as the forty thousand estimated in Nashville. Campaign songs were not unknown before 1840, but Harrison was the first man literally "sung into the Presidency," as Philip Hone put it, with such tunes as "The Hard Cider Quick Step" and the "Log Cabin or Tippecanoe Waltz" created to enliven Whig rallies. Men had most likely marched for candidates before, but the political parade that came to be a hallowed American tradition for generations—with its bands, floats, banners, and the like—was born in 1840. Twenty-five

Fig. 26. Among the many silk ribbon badges worn at the gigantic Harrison "New England Convention" at Bunker Hill in September 1840, were these varieties sported by delegations from as near as Newton and Lynn and as far as Georgia.

thousand men were said to have formed the procession in Baltimore and thirty thousand in Nashville, while a parade in Cincinnati in October resulted in a line of march three miles long. Even villages held scaled-down versions of such extravaganzas (fig. 24). Another 1840 innovation not destined for such immortality was the rolling of huge buckskin-covered balls (fig. 25) decorated with partisan doggerel, either in parades or from town to town, often over considerable distances.[2]

All of this activity created an extraordinary environment for material culture. The rallies and parades begat posters, silk ribbon badges (fig. 26), floats, and cloth banners of every sort—large cotton ones for streets and platforms and smaller marching banners (fig. 27) for parades, including some truly outstanding examples of American folk art hand-painted in oil onto silk, satin, or cotton. To a March 1840, Harrison rally in Hartford, Connecticut, delegations from surrounding towns brought banners that read "Meridan—Strike for Our Country," "North Haven—Know, Man of

Fig. 27. Featuring a magnificent eagle motif on one side and a plea for high wages and log cabins on the other (facing page), this hand-printed cotton sailcloth banner led an 1840 Independence Day Whig parade through the streets of Stoneham, Massachusetts. (Smithsonian Institution)

Kinderhook, the People Will Meet You at the Polls," "New Haven, the 'Gibralter of Whiggery'—Her Troops Prefer Tippecanoe Venison to 'Stubble' Fed Beef," and "Old Milford, They Call Her 'Sleepy Hollow'—She's Wide Awake for Harrison and Reform." An Erie, Pennsylvania, Whig rally in September featured a banner that rhymed, "With Tip and Tyler, We'll Burst Van's Biler." At a Rockford, Illinois, rally on October 7, 1840, banners included "Beloit Is True for Tippecanoe," "Whigs of Byron—For Our Country We Rally," "Pacatonic—No Tonic for Van Buren," and a beautiful scarlet satin variety from Galena that featured a log-cabin design above the legend "Public Justice Is Certain—Nov. 1840."[3] Along with the buckskin balls,

FOR

HARRISON & TYLER,

And no reduction of the prices of labour.

THE LOG CABIN,

The house our fathers lived in.

STONEHAM,
JULY 4, 1840.

these were our first political visuals, the remote ancestors of our modern billboards, bumper stickers, and lawn signs.

At the same time, this great commotion was transforming the unlikely Harrison into something of an instant folk icon worthy of adorning an amazing array of mass-produced trinkets and bric-a-brac that domestic and foreign firms were quick to market, and Whig enthusiasts equally quick to buy. Before it ran its course, the "Tippecanoe and Tyler Too" campaign inspired a harvest of souvenir items seldom if ever surpassed in quantity and variety in nearly two centuries of American politics.[4] Included were examples of virtually every type of item used politically in the United States before 1840—thread boxes, papier-mache snuff boxes, flasks, cotton chintzes, at least twenty varieties of silk kerchiefs or bandannas, almost as many different Sandwich glass cup plates, more than five dozen known types of clothing buttons, an equal number of medalets and tokens, nearly two

Fig. 28. Often sold inexpensively in complete sets, John Ridgway's "Columbian Star" Staffordshire china sold briskly in the United States for more than a generation after the 1840 campaign. (Edmund B. Sullivan)

hundred styles of silk ribbons, and an eclectic array of ceramic mementos that ranged from exquisite and expensive copper luster pitchers to Ridgway's "Columbian Star" Staffordshire pottery priced at seven cents per plate. Produced in several colors in two basic patterns (fig. 28), Ridgway's china services and tea sets represented something of a breakthrough in American political ceramics, the first items created essentially for everyday use rather than primarily decorative purposes.

In addition to the visual devices made for parades and rallies, other 1840 innovations in our political material culture included lacquered wooden hairbrushes, ceramic caneheads, brass belt buckles, pewter spoons, lithographic prints, stationery, song sheets, and almanacs. Imaginative entrepreneurs even exploited the enthusiasm to market such consumables as "Tippecanoe Tobacco" and "Log Cabin Bitters" and such toiletries as "Tippecanoe Shaving Soap or Log-Cabin Emollient" and "Tippecanoe Extract," the latter promoted as "a compound of the finest essences, and a most delicate perfume for handkerchiefs, gloves and the hair, leaving a rich and durable fragrance."[5]

Most of these objects faithfully mirrored the Whig strategy of presenting Harrison to the public in the twin roles of military hero and symbol of the rustic virtues of log-cabin America, the precise formula used so successfully by the Democrats in their marketing of Andrew Jackson. The war hero image had worked surprisingly well for Harrison in 1836,[6] when he had carried seven states as a regional Whig candidate, and was a theme exploited even more enthusiastically by his forces in 1840. He appeared in military bust motif (almost always identified as "Maj. Gen. W. H. Harrison") on more than fifty types of medalets (fig. 29), many silk ribbons, bandannas, a thread box, garment buttons, flag banners, sulphide brooches (fig. 30), ceramic plates, glass cup plates, lithograph prints, and snuff boxes. Several ribbons, tokens, and flag banners saluted him as "Hero of Tippecanoe," plates bore the motto "Hero of the Thames," a log-cabin cup plate read "Fort Meigs," and a number of ribbons identified him as the "Hero of Tippecanoe, Thames and Fort Meigs." Bandannas reminded recipients that Harrison had commanded the Northwestern Army during the War of 1812, cotton yard goods featured cannons, and medalets read "The Hero & Statesman" and "Honor Where Honor's Due."

More creative in design were prints, snuff boxes, ribbons, and medalets featuring stylized scenes of Harrison in combat at Tippecanoe or Thames, and ribbons, medalets, clothing buttons, and a magnificent silk bandanna (fig. 31) portraying him in the classic equestrian manner, with sabre ready and atop his spirited charger. More grandiose in assessing Harrison's contribution as a warrior were flag banners that a contingent of women from McHenry County, Illinois waved during a Rockford rally that saluted him as the "Ohio Farmer, the Defender of Our Homes and Children, the Friend of the West, and the Foe of the Savage."[7] A ribbon proclaimed "Washington the Father of his Country, Harrison a Chip of the Old Block," and others (fig. 32) pictured Harrison with Washington and Lafayette over the legend "First in War—First in Peace—First in the Hearts of Their Countrymen." If such pieces were consistent with Whig efforts to portray their leading men as heirs to the traditions of 1776 and the Founding Fathers, completely incongruous with their attempts to present Harrison as a rustic "farmer of Ohio" who had left "the plough to save his country" were other styles of ribbons (fig. 32) depicting "Old Tip" as an American Napoleon Bonaparte, down to the Corsican's hairstyle and renowned hand-in-jacket pose.

Even more ubiquitous on 1840 Harrison objects than such symbols of his martial glory, especially on items designed once the main focus of the Whig campaign developed, were representations of what Jackson so aptly described as "Logg cabin hard cider and coon humbugery." The genesis of the log cabin and cider barrel as the ultimate Harrison campaign symbols was apparently a sarcastic suggestion in the Van Burenite Baltimore *Republican* in December 1839, that a barrel of hard cider and a modest pension might induce the elderly Harrison to "sit out the remainder of his days in his log cabin by the side of a 'sea coal' fire, and study moral philosophy." After the gibe had been given a wider circulation than it probably deserved in other

Figs. 29, 30, and 31. Typical of 1840 Whig efforts to exploit William Henry Harrison's image as a war hero were this military bust medalet and sulphide lapel pin and equestrian silk bandanna. (Figs. 29, 30, Edmund B. Sullivan)

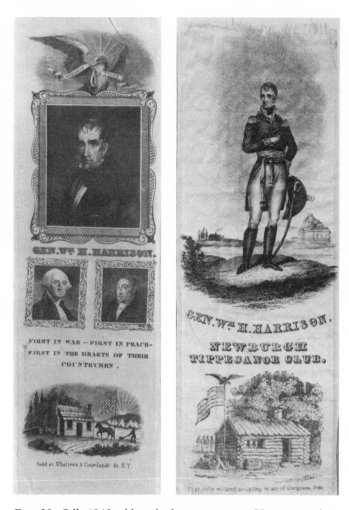

Fig. 32. Silk 1840 ribbon badges presenting Harrison as heir to Washington and Lafayette and as Americanized version of Napoleon Bonaparte.

Democratic newspapers, Whig editors began interpreting it as a slur by "Eastern officeholders' pimps" against the great American yeomanry and began promoting Harrison as the "Log-Cabin Candidate."[8] Within weeks, what had begun as a mundane effort to put a Whig in the White House had been cleverly transformed into a holy crusade, as the Albany *Evening Journal* waxed eloquent on behalf of "virtues that dwell in obscurity—of the hopes of the humble—of the privations of the poor—of toil and danger—of perseverance and patient endurance—of hospitality and charity and frugality."[9] Soon the aristocratic New Yorker Philip Hone was donning buckskins to eulogize log cabins, and Daniel Webster was shedding public tears over the "edifying lessons" they provided.

Figs. 33 and 34. Among the many 1840 Harrison campaign items displaying the log-cabin symbol were these medalets and ribbon badges (facing page).

Hone's buckskin and Webster's tears were by no means the only elements of absurdity in log cabins and cider barrels as symbols for a man who lived in a palatial home and enjoyed imported wines and a party more renowned for its sympathies for tariff protection and national banks than for "the privations of the poor," but in American political imagery absurdity has rarely been a barrier to effectiveness. Log cabins and cider barrels were also splendid symbols for exploitation through the aborning medium of material culture, beginning with some illuminated transparencies featuring log cabins, raccoon skins, and cider barrels designed in January 1840 by a pair of Pennsylvania Whigs, banker Thomas Elder and editor Richard S. Elliott.[10] Soon log-cabin headquarters were springing up throughout the land, invariably equipped with at least one barrel of hard cider to be dispensed freely at all but the most decorous of Whig gatherings. Cabins were not only used as campaign headquarters, but they were also put on wheels to use as parade floats. A large one carried eighty of Abraham Lincoln's Sangamon County cohorts in a Springfield, Illinois, celebration. Smaller log-cabin floats (fig. 24) were often built to use as post-parade dispensaries of cider and other drinks to marchers thirsty from carrying cabin banners and transparencies.

In Albany, silversmith John T. Crew began making and marketing little silver log-cabin breast pins so distinctive that even the opposition *Daily Argus* described them as "handsomely designed and executed in the best manner."[11] Log cabins adorned most Harrison ribbon badges (fig. 34), ban-

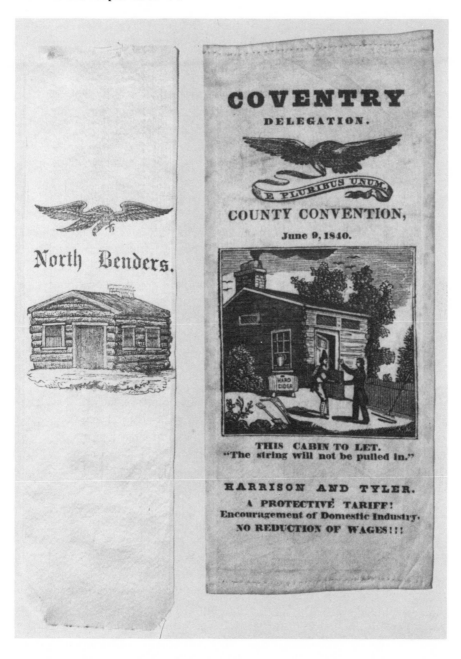

dannas, patterns of yard goods, medalets (fig. 33), gilt clothing buttons, jewelry devices, and glass cup plates (fig. 35), plus stationery, pewter spoons, brass belt buckles, and glass tumblers (fig. 36). They were featured on most ceramic plates and pitchers as well, although in a few cases transfers designed by British artists unfamiliar with American folk architecture portrayed two-story English log cottages (fig. 37) instead. Cabin scenes graced most song sheets, many with such cabin-related titles as "The Log Cabin Song" and "Log Cabin or Tippecanoe Waltz." Medalets paid tribute to "The Log Cabin of North Bend" and its occupant, "The Log Cabin Candidate." "Log Cabin Bitters" came bottled in little glass figural cabins. Two styles of silk bandannas, perhaps the only Harrison log-cabin campaign items to concede that Old Tip did not actually live in such a humble dwelling, turned this into a virtue by exhibiting an impressive mansion behind a cabin, explaining, "the back ground is a representation of the Farm House which the old General has been able of late years to construct by many hard knocks and industry."

A standard feature on these cabins was the latchstring, invariably let out as a symbol of rustic hospitality. The inspiration for this was most likely Harrison's farewell remarks to his troops, when he had promised them, "If you ever come to Vincennes, you will always find a plate and a knife and fork at my table, and I assure you that you will never find my door shut and the string of the latch pulled in." Designers of even the tiniest brass button included the dangling latchstring. Silk ribbons (fig. 34) depicted Harrison welcoming a visitor to his log cabin above the legend "The String Will Not Be Pulled In."

Cider barrels were nearly as ubiquitous on Harrison campaign items as were log cabins. Wooden barrels inscribed "Harrison Cider/Boston O. K." were attached to poles and carried as parade standards. Harrison walking sticks were made and marketed with figural barrel-shaped ceramic caneheads (fig. 41) inscribed "Hard Cider" on one end and "Tippecanoe" on the other. "Hard Cider" barrels formed border designs on silk bandannas. A banner proclaimed, "Van Buren Is Running: Hard Cider Is Coming," and a ribbon carried the gibe "Hard Cider—Not so Hard as Van Burenism." Cider barrels appeared as accent pieces in cabin scenes on cup plates, tumblers, ribbons, clothing buttons, sulphides, and nearly every known campaign medalet. An understandable exception was a Harrison log-cabin token handmade by a man whose views on strong drink may be deduced from the legend "Drink no Spirit/Say Thy Prayers/Read the Bible/Avoid Bad Company."

Some of the more creative and thematically ambitious of all Harrison campaign objects were those portraying him as a simple backwoods farmer, in fundamental contrast to the Whig presentation of Van Buren as a venal, sleek aristocrat. A variety of items including banners, pitchers, ribbons, and bandannas that pictured Old Tip welcoming a disabled veteran to his log cabin (fig. 38) identified Harrison variously as "The Ohio Farmer," "The Farmer of North Bend," and "The Ohio Ploughman." He was portrayed with team and plow on several hand-painted banners, including a silk variety declaring Lyme, New Hampshire "The Soil Where Locofocoism Can't Flourish" and a cotton banner used in southern Ohio to promote him

Figs. 35 and 36. Glass Harrison campaign items featuring log cabins included this cup plate and unusual hand-etched tumbler. (Fig. 36, Smithsonian Institution)

Fig. 37. A transfer design featuring a two-story English log cottage, not an American log cabin, graces this imported 1840 Harrison campaign pitcher, the handiwork of a British artisan unfamiliar with American vernacular architecture. (Smithsonian Institution)

as "The People's Friend." Medalets presented him as "The People's Choice" and "Candidate of the People," and several varieties of ribbons identified him as "The Poor Man's Friend." A log-cabin banner from North Carolina read "Republican Simplicity/Locofoco Arrogance." The rather deliberate effort to depict Harrison as a modern Cincinnatus led to several items. Flag banners featuring "The Hero of Tippecanoe" with shovel in hand in front of his log cabin noted, "As long as the leaders of Rome were taken from the plough, to the plough were they willing to return." A token was inscribed "He Leaves the Plough to Save His Country," and a ribbon read "A Frequent Change of Rulers, Is the Soul of Republicanism"—certainly one of

Fig. 38. 1840 campaign bandanna depicting Harrison as "The Ohio Farmer" welcoming a disabled comrade-in-arms to his humble log cabin. (Smithsonian Institution)

the more piously phrased pleas to "throw the rascals out" in American political history.

Whig efforts to portray themselves as the champions of a persecuted peasantry occasionally reached truly ridiculous proportions. In eastern Pennsylvania, Harrisonites promoting such "proletarian" causes as a protective tariff and restoration of a national bank wore ribbons that read "Arise! ye hard-handed inmates of our country's Log Cabins, and put to rout a corrupt and venal administration."

Despite the Van Buren legacy of three years of hard times following the "Panic of '37," 1840 Whig campaign objects were remarkably mute on national economic priorities and other important public questions. Many items bore the slogan "Harrison and Reform," but none provided any clues as to what exactly this meant. A few ribbons echoed traditional Whig efforts to portray the party as guardian of the legacy of limited government under law bequeathed by the Founding Fathers with such legends as "The Constitution Inviolate, the Laws Supreme," "We Hold the Constitution & Laws SACRED," and "Harrison, Tyler and Constitutional Liberty." Ribbons reflecting the essentially anti-party image of Whiggery included one that read "Government by the People—not a Party" and a Frederick County, Virginia, variety with the motto "We Strike for Retrenchment and Reform." Among the very few mass-produced Harrison campaign items to feature economic themes were Pennsylvania silk ribbon badges bearing such rhetoric as "The Currency of Washington Is All We Want" and "A Protective Tariff! Encouragement of Domestic Industry. No Reduction of Wages!!!"

Other issue-related 1840 Harrison campaign objects were invariably banners handmade by local enthusiasts. Some such examples of 1840 political folk art read "Tip, Tyler and the Tariff," "Harrison the Poor Man's Friend— We Want Work," and (fig. 27) "Harrison & Tyler and no reduction in the prices of labour." An especially pointed commentary on labor economics was displayed on a banner made for the Cincinnati demonstration in October: "Matty's policy, 12½ cts. a day and French soup—OUR policy, 2 Dolls. a day and Roast Beef." A Vermilion County, Illinois, contingent at the Tippecanoe celebration exhibited even more creativity in depicting the legacy of Van Buren fiscal policies. To a battered gig festooned with signs that read "A Picture of the Times" they hitched an unfortunate horse that "looked as if he had been mortgaged to the buzzards, but had by some accident delayed Death's grasp"[12] to create one of the more memorable living visuals ever used in an American political campaign. Such colorful examples of grass-roots enthusiasm were exceptions, however, to a general tendency among Whigs in 1840 to use material objects to exalt Indian-killing, log cabins, and hard cider, while ignoring altogether salient issues.

With the rallies, processions, songfests, cabin-raisings, ball-rollings, and other participatory rites that comprised the Harrison campaign, the politics of popular entertainment truly came of age in the United States. Material culture simultaneously evolved into one of its basic components as a result of the vast array of "Tippecanoe and Tyler too" banners, floats, badges, trinkets, and assorted keepsake items inspired by the great commotion. Yet in 1840 and for many elections to come, both this new style of campaigning and its material dimension were virtually monopolized by the Whigs. In 1840, for example, a "Shall the Banks or the People Rule?" Roxbury, Massachusetts, headquarters banner is the only large Van Buren visual device cited in contemporary newspapers and subsequent historical accounts, and the major private and museum collections also indicate an absence of such items promoting Van Buren. A half-hearted effort was made in Ohio to rekindle the old spirit of the Jackson campaigns by erecting hickory poles to mark the anniversary of the Battle of New Orleans, but Whig critics were quick to point out that the 1840 Democratic nominee was Van Buren, who had not fought at New Orleans, and to suggest that poles made of slippery elm might be more appropriate.[13]

This same disparity in material culture between the two parties in 1840 extended to personal campaign items as well, for the major collections and reference volumes include only a few Van Buren sulphides, clothing buttons, and snuff boxes, a copper luster pitcher, a dozen or more ribbon badges, and at most a dozen types of medalets.[14] Moreover, every known variety of 1840 Van Buren campaign items except for a few of the medalets appears for sale or auction only rarely, a good indication that they were produced and marketed in very small quantities. It had not yet become the general practice in 1840 for a producer of campaign material to market matching items for each major party nominee, but in the few instances where this was done, the Harrison piece is seen much more commonly than its Van Buren mate.

Predictably, these few Van Buren campaign items tended to be much more issue-oriented and much less given to exaltation of symbolism or hero-worship than were the Harrison objects. A few ribbons and medalets featured such puffery as tributes to Van Buren as "New York's Favourite Son" and "The Firm and Fearless Advocate of Democracy" and to him and running-mate Richard M. Johnson as "Enlightened Heroes of Patriotic Liberty." A pair of ribbons (fig. 39) with the legends "No White Slavery" and "We Pledge Ourselves to a Firm and Uncompromising Opposition to all Alien and Sedition Gag Law and Black Cockade Candidates, Although Disguised by the Name of Whig" provided the only echoes on campaign items of a rather desperate effort by the Democratic press to portray Harrison as a covert Federalist and advocate of the practice of sentencing poor white convicts to slave labor.[15] Much more typical, however, were the Van Buren ribbons and medalets that emphasized such Democratic fiscal initiatives as the subtreasury. More than half of all known varieties of 1840 Van

Fig. 39. The most salacious 1840 Van Buren campaign items, these silk ribbons implied that opponent William Henry Harrison was a latter-day Federalist who favored making slave laborers of white convicts unable to pay their fines.

Buren ribbons made mention of the independent treasury, and another featured the terse motto "No Bank Monopoly." Among the medalets were varieties (fig. 40) with such inscriptions as "A Uniform & Sound Currency—the Sub Treasury" and "The People's Money—Safe Bind, Safe Find," the latter surrounding a representation of a safe inscribed "OK."[16]

Precisely why such a great disparity in campaign trinkets and visuals existed in 1840 remains something of a mystery. A potential market surely existed for Van Buren material, for he attracted nearly 47 percent of the popular vote and carried or lost narrowly such states as Pennsylvania, New York, New Jersey, New Hampshire, and Illinois, where political material culture had become well established as a feature in campaigns. Although the Van Burenites did not go in for massive rallies and theatrical extravaganzas, accounts of their meetings and other activities indicated no lack of spirit or interest among the Democratic faithful. The idea that Whigs were usually much wealthier than Democrats and could thus afford more easily the mementos not given out to members of political clubs or at rallies has been laid to rest by a generation of historical scholarship. Whig voters were slightly more prevalent in urban areas, where campaign materials were more readily available, but demographics do little to explain the disparity.

Such factors as incumbency and the diverse backgrounds of the two candidates cannot be dismissed so lightly. A recent study of the political culture of the era argues persuasively that the Whigs and Democrats developed very different styles of campaigning, primarily because they were quite dissimilar in nature and tended to choose altogether different types of candidates. Essentially an "anti-party party" throughout its brief existence and never faced with the burden of running an incumbent president for re-election, the Whig party tended to award its nominations to nonpolitical men of great popular renown, primarily war heroes long on image and short on experience in public affairs. The Democrats, however, tended to choose their candidates on the basis of service to the party and the Jacksonian tradition, less-glamorous figures but (however obscure most of them may have been) more widely known as political entities. By this line of reasoning, Whig candidacies were naturally suited to the new politics of popular entertainment—and its material component—and Democratic candidacies were not.[17]

Incumbency and candidate backgrounds admittedly played a key role in the disparity in material culture evidenced in 1840. The Democrats, running a sitting president well known to most Americans exclusively in a political context, simply could not have exploited successfully the sort of fanciful, essentially escapist personality politics that the Whigs were utilizing on behalf of a dark-horse warrior of bygone battles. In 1828, when their nominee had been another agrarian warrior and the opponent a beleaguered incumbent, a career diplomat, and the son of a president, the tables had been turned. From John Quincy Adams through Jimmy Carter, incumbency has nearly always negated image politics totally divorced from reality—even for such candidates as Carter whose initial campaigns had been largely triumphs of image over substance. Too, image campaigns have rarely been successful for nominees like Van Buren (or Stephen Douglas or Hubert Humphrey) whose identities have been so exclusively political. Nevertheless, this thesis cannot explain fully why the Whigs exploited so successfully the politics of material culture in 1840 and the Democrats made virtually no effort to follow suit. Nor can it completely account for the total dominance of Whigs over Democrats in this facet of campaigning after 1840, for never again would a Whig do battle against a Democratic incumbent, on at least two occasions (Cass in 1848 and Pierce in 1852) the Democrats ran men whose obscurity surpassed Harrison's, and in 1844 the Whigs exploited material culture creatively and enthusiastically on behalf of that ultimate professional politician (and civilian), Henry Clay.

To explain more fully why material culture became the nearly exclusive province of the Whigs in 1840 and afterward, to these elements of party difference identified by scholars must be added generous measures of accident and emotion. It is likely that the Democrats entered 1840 contemptuous of the "derisory manufactures" used to lampoon their economic dogma in 1834 and 1837 and rather cool toward campaigning gimmicks of any sort after three comfortable consecutive victories in presidential elections. Then, springing from the altogether improbable source of snob wit in a Van Buren newspaper, the presidential canvass evolved almost overnight into a profoundly irrelevant referendum on log cabins and hard cider, to the mutual amazement of delighted Whigs and incredulous Democrats. Recognizing a blessing of great proportions in the sentiment that attended unveilings of log-cabin transparencies, Whig leaders quickly and easily overcame their misgivings over the dark underside of grass-roots democracy and embarked with enthusiastic opportunism upon a new, unrestrained avenue of political expression that was tailor-made for material objects of all sorts. Caught totally by surprise by this sudden mania for nostalgic symbols, the bright and rational men who headed the Democratic effort (their doubts over Van Buren's bromide that "the sober second thought of the people is always right" perhaps blunted a little by their string of popular successes) gambled upon their common sense and political instincts that this "barrels and balls" madness could not possibly carry the day.

To Van Buren from the Hermitage came Jackson's appraisal of Whig campaign tactics as so much "Logg cabin hard cider and coon humbugery,"[18] and this tone of derision permeated Democratic newspaper accounts of Whig activities throughout the summer and autumn. In a commentary on "Log Cabin Breast Pins, Hard Cider Canes, and Tippecanoe Perfume for the Hair," the Albany *Argus* literally dripped with sarcasm over the unlikely prospect of a "restless Western settler" clearing his land "decorated with a log cabin breast pin, his hair redolent with Tippecanoe extract and glossy as a soap-lock, one hand holding an axe-helve and the other resting on a hard cider rattan [fig. 41] . . . the size of a man's little finger, mounted with a miniature ivory cider barrel" that sold for $2.00.[19] Such commentaries do not convey the impression of a dispirited campaign whistling past the graveyard. If anything, such light satire and accounts of Van Buren rallies seemed to make a conscious effort to play up the contrast between the businesslike decorum of Democratic gatherings (staged without banners and the like) and the revelries staged by the Ciderites.

After the voters had rendered their verdict, Democratic incredulity turned to bitterness. In his autobiography, Van Buren sourly attributed his defeat to the "debaucheries of a political Saturnalia, in which reason and

Fig. 40. Medallic tributes to the "independent subtreasury," Van Buren's substitute for the Bank of the United States.

Fig. 41. This 1840 Harrison campaign cane, complete with ceramic cider barrel canehead inscribed "Tippecanoe" on one end and "Hard Cider" on the other, was one of several Whig souvenir items satirized by the Democratic press. (Smithsonian Institution)

justice had been derided," and in 1844 the Democratic party wrote into its platform condemnations of "factitious symbols" and "displays and appeals insulting to the judgment and subversive to the intellect of the people."[20] Such statements suggest that to other factors accounting for the disparity between Democrats and Whigs in the realm of campaign material culture after 1840 must be added a quite natural Democratic aversion to blatant hypocrisy. In any event, in 1844 and subsequent campaigns the Democrats departed very little from their vow of abstinence from "displays and appeals" promoting "factitious symbols." This was especially telling in 1844, when

Fig. 42. Among the many types of lapel devices marketed as political badges were these 1844 Polk and Clay varieties, consisting of paper portraits under glass encased in pewter frames.

the effectiveness of "barrels and balls" theatrics was fresh in their minds, the career politician Henry Clay the opposition candidate, and their own "Young Hickory," James K. Polk, a nominee sufficiently Jacksonian and personally obscure to make symbolic appeals on mass visuals and personal trinkets quite tempting. Yet newspaper accounts of Polk campaign activities made virtually no mention of transparencies, banners, or floats, and the reference works and major collections contain only a few styles of Polk parade flags and one truly exceptional silk banner six feet long, with hand-painted busts of Polk and George M. Dallas and the motto "Just and Equal Protection to All."[21]

The Polk campaign did inspire a much larger assortment of lapel devices and personal keepsake items than the 1840 Van Buren effort, but only a small fraction of the array available to Clay supporters. Moreover, many Polk–Dallas badges and mementos have Clay–Theodore Frelinghuysen mates, a reliable indication that they were created not for specific Democratic campaign functions, but rather for general retail distribution by vendors and storekeepers. The lesson that political enthusiasm made for brisk business had been learned in 1840, and by 1844 producers were ready with myriad styles of ribbons, medalets, and glass and ceramic bric-a-brac, plus a number of innovations. Among the items offered commercially to political partisans for the first time in 1844 were looped "shell" lapel ornaments stamped from thin brass sheets, pewter-rimmed lapel devices (fig. 42) containing Polk's and Clay's paper portraits under glass, and multicolored lithograph prints of the candidates and their running-mates (figs. 43, 44) produced by such popular printmakers as Nathaniel Currier of New York and Kellogg and Hanmer of Hartford. Sold for a dime or fifteen cents apiece, these gaudy prints lithographed in mass quantities and then colored individually by platoons of watercolorists (usually immigrant women) did much to familiarize millions of Americans with the likenesses of their leaders before the advent of photography and mass-circulation newspapers and magazines. In 1844 and increasingly thereafter, a growing commercialization worked to diminish the direct role of campaign organizations in designing and producing material culture.

In addition to these prints and lapel devices, snuff boxes and cigar cases featuring Polk's likeness, a gilt clothing button, a few varieties of medalets, and more than two dozen styles of silk ribbons were produced for Democratic loyalists in 1844.[22] Understandably, nearly half of these items sought to exploit the Texas question, because annexation was the issue responsible for Polk's dark-horse nomination and provided his best chances for a victory over Clay, especially among the militantly expansionist voters of the South and West. Prints, parade flags, ribbons, and shell lapel pins featured star motifs to symbolize the Lone Star Republic, as did a "Polk, Dallas, Texas" medalet. A ribbon (fig. 45) featured a large star inscribed "Texas," the pledge "Alone but not Deserted," and the advice of Andrew Jackson, "Let Polk, Dallas & Texas Be the Watchword & Countersign and Victory Is Certain." Two ribbons, one urging "Tariff, Texas, and Oregon" and the other "Oregon, Texas, and Democracy" tried to broaden the appeal of expansion for free-staters. Another Polk ribbon made land greed appear almost saintly with the legend "Extension of the Area of Freedom/Restoration of Our Ancient Boundary," as did a medalet imploring "Enlarge the Boundaries of Freedom."

Other Polk campaign items sought in several ways to portray Polk as a loyal son of the Democratic tradition of Jefferson and Jackson. This lineage was made manifest on a ribbon (fig. 45) printed by R. M. Gaw of Philadelphia that bore the names of Jackson and Van Buren on a pedestal under a bust of Jefferson. The legacy of Jackson was symbolized on a medalet by a hickory pole and on a Pennsylvania ribbon by a hickory tree and the couplet "Freemen, Cheer the Hickory Tree, in Storms Its Boughs Have Sheltered Thee." Traditional Democratic campaign appeals to working-class voters through egalitarian sentiments included the aforementioned "Just and Equal Protection to All" silk banner, an "Equal Laws and Equal Rights!" ribbon, an "Equal Protection to All Classes" medalet, and a shell badge presenting Polk as the "Friend of Equal Rights." Echoes of Jackson's vendetta against the Bank of the United States included such ribbon rhetoric as "No Bank," "Texas and no Bank," and "No United States Bank/No National Debt, if Possible." The only evidence on any of these items of an effort to exploit personality politics on Polk's behalf were ribbons, prints, and a medalet proclaiming him "The Young Hickory," as much a salute to the venerable Jackson as to his fellow Tennessean.

Fig. 43. This multicolored lithograph print, featuring Polk and running-mate
George M. Dallas, was the first of many "Grand National Banner" varieties marketed by Nathaniel Currier and then by Currier and Ives. (Smithsonian Institution)

Fig. 44. Featuring Clay, Theodore Frelinghuysen, and a scene suggesting the industrial, maritime, and agricultural prosperity that a Clay presidency would bring, this colorful and imaginative print was produced by the Hartford, Connecticut, firm of Kellogg and Hanmer. (Smithsonian Institution)

Fig. 45. These imaginative and well-executed silk ribbons designed by K. P. Water of New York and R. M. Gaw of Philadelphia provide excellent examples of the exploitation of Polk as a champion of Texas annexation and as heir to the Democratic tradition of Jefferson and Jackson.

Much more numerous and collectively much more imaginative in thematic expression were the items inspired by Clay's third and last formal bid for the White House. Clay's 1844 campaign engendered an array of visual devices, badges, and memorabilia nearly equal in volume, variety, and creativity to the material culture of Harrison's 1840 great commotion. Such gala events as the May 2 procession in Baltimore to celebrate Clay's nomination and the massive September 29 "Dayton Barbecue" begat an enormous number of hand-painted or mass-produced banners, several styles of parade flags, and many transparencies and floats. Ball-rollings were once again in vogue. More than one hundred known varieties of silk ribbons made their appearance, as did nearly four dozen types of metal tokens, many styles of clothing buttons, brass shell badges and sundry lapel devices, and Sandwich glass cup plates, plus some beautiful hand-painted ceramic cup plates (fig. 46), prints, song sheets, flasks, cigar cases, snuff boxes, and unusual figural ceramic caneheads and clay pipes.[23]

Motivated by their enormous success with the politics of personality and rustic populism four years before, the Whigs made something of an effort to follow suit in 1844 by portraying Clay as another "good ol' boy," man of the soil, and symbol of the American Dream. Tokens and ribbons proclaimed him "The Mill Boy of the Slashes," the nickname invented by Clay himself to foster the illusion that he had risen from humble origins. Tokens and ribbons, often with pastoral scenes of a farmer plowing a field (fig. 47), identified him as "The Farmer of Ashland" or "The Ashland Farmer." Other items promoted Clay as "Old Kentucky," "Harry of the West," or simply "Harry." One token presented him as "The Man of the People/The Star of the West." But still another Clay nickname, "the Old Coon," provided the primary mechanism for bringing the Kentuckian's image "down to the people." Raccoons in cages were often exhibited at Clay rallies and parades. Tokens carried raccoon motifs and the slogan "The Same Old Coon," as did several varieties of cotton parade flags (figs. 48, 49). Ribbons bore caricatures of coons rolling balls or committing sundry acts of violence upon Democratic roosters while taunting them, "Why Don't You Crow?"

On the whole, however, 1844 Whig material culture represented a sharp departure from the "Logg cabin hard cider and coon humbugery" of the Harrison campaign, primarily because the Whig standard-bearer was Henry Clay—for four decades the ultimate Washington insider, architect of two great national compromises, the American System, and the Whig party itself, and twice before a presidential contender. Moreover, his unusually consistent beliefs in a protective tariff, a national bank, and federal funding of internal improvement projects had formed the very basis of national dialogue over federal economic policy for more than a generation. With Clay as their candidate, the Whigs lacked the luxury of waging a purely escapist campaign, choosing instead to accentuate Clay's stature and posi-

Fig. 46. This small ceramic Henry Clay plate was apparently pressed from a die created for a nearly identical Sandwich glass cup plate, then trimmed and hand-painted. Unlike the glass cup plates, which were used functionally as receptacles for dripping cups, this exquisite piece was probably created purely for decorative purposes. (Kenneth J. Moran)

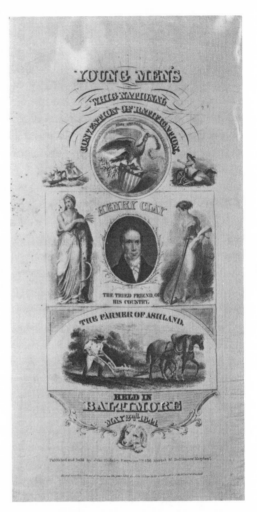

Fig. 47. This elaborate silk Clay ribbon, with its plowing motif and "The Farmer of Ashland" slogan, is representative of 1844 Whig efforts to portray the urbane planter and career politician as a humble man of the soil, à la William Henry Harrison.

tions on the issues. Cigar cases (fig. 50) and ribbons (fig. 51) proclaimed him "The American Statesman." Many tokens and garment buttons reiterated the 1832 concept of portraying Clay clad in a toga like a modern Pericles or Cincinnatus. Others bore such patriotic maxims as "United We Stand/Divided We Fall" and "Liberty and Union/Now and Forever/One and Inseparable" or long lists of the major milestones in his public career. Ribbons depicted Clay in patrician pose with the legend "The People's Welfare My Reward" or a John Greenleaf Whittier poem exulting "The shrine of old idolatries before his kindling light grows dim."

Even greater emphasis was placed upon Clay's remedies for the nation's economic ills. A ribbon proclaimed him "Champion of the American System." A parade flag urged "A National Currency, Revenue, and Protection." A banner used in a parade in Abingdon, Virginia, read almost like a party platform, insisting "Uniform Bank Currency/Revenue on Imports/Protection of American Industry/Distribution of the Proceeds of the Public Lands Among the States/One Presidential Term/Reduction of Executive Power." A Clay ribbon featured a hand with the palm labeled "Protective Policy" and fingers "Commerce," "Mechanic Arts," "Agriculture," "Manufactures," and "Internal Improvements." Tokens (one with the legend "The Wealth of a Nation Is Indicated by Its Industry") bore coastal scenes with clipper ships and smoking factories. Another token read "Henry Clay and Protection of All Our Enterprises" surrounding a barrel, crates, anvil, plow, and sheaf of wheat. A ribbon featuring a likeness of Clay on a cloudy hilltop (inspiring one authority to liken it to "Moses on the Mount") reading "The Working Man—He Is to Society What the Main-Mast Is to the Ship" and a token stating "Protection to the Working Class Is an Assurance of Success" attest to Whig efforts to enhance the blue-collar appeal of the American System.

To a great extent, the heavy emphasis placed on economic issues was prompted by the Whig realization that the key to a Clay victory was a strong showing in the industrial Northeast. Because Polk was deemed especially vulnerable in this hotbed of protectionism for his free-trade beliefs, "Clay and the Tariff" became the central theme of the campaign and the items it engendered. Brass shells urged "Protection to American Industry" and "Protection & Union" and identified Clay as "The Noble & Patriotic Defender of Protection." Parade flags used in Pennsylvania demanded protection, and ribbons (a majority printed in Philadelphia for use in New Jersey and Pennsylvania) insisted "Henry Clay and a Protective Tariff," "Protection to American Industry," and "Clay and Tariff." Tokens pledged "A Tariff for Protection," "A Tariff for Reform," and "Protection to American Industry" and proclaimed Clay "Champion of a Protective Tariff," "Protector of Home Industry," and "The Noble and Patriotic Defender of Protection." Banners developed the theme in various ways, an especially handsome hand-painted cotton one (fig. 52) portraying the "Effects of

Figs. 48 and 49. With their designs of playful raccoons atop slogan balls or thumb-ing their noses at the moon and "The Same Old Coon" slogan, these 1844 Clay parade flags epitomize Whig attempts to give Clay a folksy, down-home identity through exploitation of his "Old Coon" nickname. (Smithsonian Institution)

a High Tariff" by depicting a well-dressed man riding on a cart laden with manufactures. Another colorful banner featured Clay thrashing Polk above this verse:

> Thus Polk the scoundrel tries
>   Our tariff low to lay
> While to the rescue flies
>   Our gallant Henry Clay.

Portraying Polk shackled by a leg-iron to a ball labeled "Texas," this banner was one of very few 1844 Clay campaign objects to make reference to annexation, not surprising in light of his opportunistic waffling on the Texas question.[24] The others were all ribbons issued locally in New England and up-state New York, bastions of opposition to Cotton Kingdom expan-sion where Liberty party nominee James G. Birney threatened to siphon off many antislavery Whig votes. A Lynn, Massachusetts, variety pro-claimed, "The Locos Go for Polk, Texas & Slavery; We Go for Clay, the Union and Liberty." Others insisted, "No Annexation," "No Extension of Slavery," "Union without Texas," and "No Annexation of Texas! No Exten-

THE SAME OLD COON

HENRY CLAY
AND
FRELINGHUYSEN

sion of Slavery!!" The latter ribbon also featured the ill-fated poetic
prophecy:

> With Henry Clay
>   We'll win the day
> And Home Industry defend;
>   With Polk and Dallas
>   We'll to the gallows
> Free Trade and Texas send.

In general, the presidential elections immediately following 1844 were
characterized by an abrupt decline in the material culture inspired and the
functions it served. This was unquestionably due in part to the nature of
the 1848 and 1852 elections, both apparently waged on all sides with little
of the demonstrative exuberance that epitomized the contests of 1840 and
1844. Virtually absent from reference volumes, major collections, and scholarly accounts of 1848 and 1852 are such visual devises as balls, parade flags,
banners, transparencies, and floats, a strong indication that campaigning
for the presidency was maturing into a much more sedate phenomenon.[25]

Figs. 50 and 51. This elaborate cigar case and "Dayton Barbecue" silk ribbon, featuring the same poetic tribute to Clay, identify him as "The American Statesman." (Fig. 51, Smithsonian Institution)

Relics from the 1848 and 1852 campaigns consist almost entirely of individual badges and souvenir memorabilia, nearly two hundred known varieties from 1848, and perhaps one-fourth that number from the moribund 1852 contest. Even taking into account some matched sets of items produced for retail distribution, Whigs Zachary Taylor and Winfield Scott were featured on much larger and more diverse arrays of material culture than were their opponents Lewis Cass and Franklin Pierce. Pewter hand mirrors (figs. 53, 54) introduced in 1848 and again marketed in 1852 seem to have been the only significant innovation in type, unless an ornate cast-iron Taylor parlor stove (fig. 55) in the collection of the Smithsonian Institution was campaign-inspired.

A breakthrough of a different sort occurred in 1848, however, when the Free Soil ticket of Martin Van Buren and Charles Francis Adams became the first third-party effort to inspire a significant material dimension. More

Fig. 52. Portraying the bountiful effects of a protective tariff is this hand-painted 1844 Clay–Frelinghuysen cotton campaign banner. (Smithsonian Institution)

than a dozen different Free Soil campaign items are known, including three types of coins counterstruck into tokens, a pair of shell badges, four Currier prints, a ceramic cup, and a trio of ribbons.[26] All but the Currier prints were ideological in nature. The cup was inscribed "Vote the Land Free," as were counterstruck Bolivian silver pieces, American copper cents, and Mexican two-real coins. The shell badges bore the legends "Free Soil and Free Labour" and "Free Soil/Free Labor/Free Speech." Ribbons urged "Free Soil, Free Men/No More Extension of Slavery" and "Free Soil and Freedom of the Public Lands to Actual Settlers," the latter legend prophetic of Abraham Lincoln's 1860 Republican campaign.

The only known relics of the 1848 Democratic campaign of Cass and William Butler are a half dozen varieties of medalets, two pewter and one silvered brass shell lapel pins, and a few ribbons and prints.[27] These objects attest to a campaign that never really developed a clear focus. A ribbon and two medalets insisted upon "The Freedom of the Seas," another medalet demanded "The Subtreasury & the Tariff of Forty Six," and another proclaimed, "Liberty, Equality & Fraternity, the Cardinal Principles of True Democracy." A ribbon insisted that "The Union Must Be Preserved" and another featured a Cass quotation pledging to "cling to this Constitution as the mariner clings to the last plank when night and the tempest close about him." Facing the most celebrated hero of the Mexican War in Taylor, the Democrats apparently felt compelled to stress the military background of

Figs. 53 and 54. These pewter hand mirrors, featuring the likenesses of 1848 Whig nominee Zachary Taylor and 1852 Democratic nominee Franklin Pierce, were among the few new types of campaign items introduced in either of these campaigns. (Smithsonian Institution)

Fig. 55. This functional cast-iron parlor stove honoring Zachary Taylor and his exploits at Palo Alto, Monterey, and Buena Vista is now in the political collection of the Smithsonian Institution. (Smithsonian Institution)

their man Cass, for one ribbon saluted him as "Gen. Lewis Cass, the Hero and Statesman," another presented him as "General Cass" against a backdrop of cannon, ramrods, drums, and battle flags, and a medalet was inscribed with his stirring words "While I Am Able to Move I Will Do My Duty." All other medalets identified him by military rank. The futility of trying to best "Old Rough and Ready" by battlefield one-upsmanship, however, was perhaps expressed with unconscious irony on a token that read "Gen. Lewis Cass/Principles, not Men."

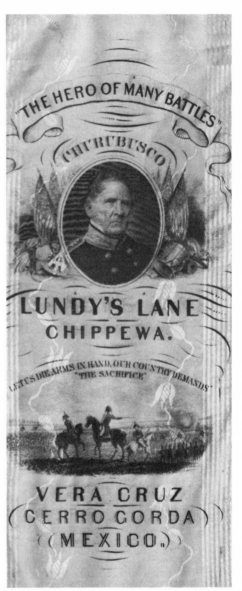

Fig. 56. 1852 silk ribbons promoting the military exploits of rival candidates Franklin Pierce and Winfield Scott. Although Scott was by far the more celebrated of the two as a war hero, Pierce won the presidential contest handily.

Defeated by one Mexican War hero in 1848 and confronted with another in 1852, the Democratic ticket of Franklin Pierce and William King inspired a few ribbons, prints, medalets, and other items,[28] many of which sought to present Pierce as a military marvel. A pair of medalets featured him in uniform by rank, as did a brass shell lapel pin. Two civilian bust medalets identified him as "The Statesman & Soldier," and a ribbon (fig. 56) read

"We Honor the Citizen and Soldier General Franklin Pierce." No known Pierce–King campaign items reflected their positions on the deteriorating sectional crisis or other key issues.

Whig campaign items were much more numerous, but hardly more explicit in 1848 and 1852. After losing with "Clay and Tariff" in 1844, the Whigs reverted in 1848 to their successful 1840 formula of exalting military heroics and ignoring substantive issues. Zachary Taylor was featured on 150 or more varieties of items, the great majority so singularly devoted to promoting his identify as a Mexican War hero that it is impossible to determine whether they were created in 1848 for political purposes or made and marketed earlier simply to exploit the popularity of a new national icon. In addition to the aforementioned parlor stove, Taylor objects included thirty-seven varieties of flasks, nearly that many types of clothing buttons, many plates and other ceramic pieces, eighteen styles of medalets, and several varieties of ribbons, bandannas (fig. 57), and pewter and brass shell lapel pins, plus snuff boxes, cigar cases (fig. 58), razors, clay figural pipes, song sheets, prints, and mirrors.[29]

Taylor's military exploits were promoted in various ways. Military busts (invariably identified by rank) adorned every flask, snuff box, cameo, and mirror, the parlor stove, and a majority of Taylor tokens, cigar cases, shell medalets, bandannas, clothing buttons, and ceramics. Other garment buttons, cigar cases, yard goods, plates, bandannas, prints, and silk ribbons portrayed Taylor in equestrian poses, either mounted with sabre drawn or standing next to his trusty steed. Many items proclaimed him "Hero of Buena Vista," "Hero of Palo Alto & Resaca de la Palma," even (where space permitted) "Hero of Palto Alto, Resaca de la Palma, Monterey and Buena Vista." Other items carried long lists of these encounters and more. A few larger objects, primarily bandannas and cotton chintzes, featured artistic renditions of battle scenes. Nearly all of the garment buttons and some flasks, snuff boxes, bandannas, and ceramics promoted Taylor as "Old Rough and Ready." Many tokens and flasks and a few clothing buttons bore the legend "General Taylor Never Surrenders," and other tokens and flasks reiterated his famous battlefield edict "A Little More Grape, Captain Bragg." His remark "I Have Endeavored to Do My Duty" was featured on other flasks.

The military theme was so pervasive that it even dominated most of the few Taylor items that also carried political content. Tokens read "Gen. Taylor the People's Choice," "The People's Candidate Gen. Zach. Taylor," and (in military bust with list of victories on the reverse) "Zachary Taylor, Whig Candidate for the Presidency, 1848." Only three known Taylor campaign items, two ribbons and a shell medalet, were free from military thematics altogether. One of the ribbons, which read "Taylor Fillmore & Johnston/Protection to American Industry," appears to have been the only 1848 Whig object to make reference to an authentic issue. This ribbon is

Figs. 57 and 58. Among the many campaign items exploiting Zachary Taylor as a war hero was this colorful bandanna and these lacquered wooden cigar cases. (Edmund B. Sullivan)

also a bit unusual in highlighting vice-presidential nominee Millard Fillmore. Remarkably few Taylor artifacts did so, a radical departure from the party's 1844 strategy of featuring Theodore Frelinghuysen prominently on campaign items, especially those distributed in his Middle Atlantic region. The lack of political references on Taylor trinkets was apparently no accident, for two items—a bandanna insisting "Neither Faction nor Party, nor Individual Interest, but the Common Welfare of Every Man in the Union" and a token declaring Taylor "Untrammelled with Party Obligations"—offer evidence that the basic tenor of the Taylor campaign was not merely nonpolitical, but essentially anti-political.

In 1852 the Whig effort to promote Winfield Scott, the last of their presidential standard-bearers, resembled a feeble echo of 1848. No more than three dozen known campaign objects promoted the Scott–William A. Graham effort, nearly all devoted wholly or primarily to exploiting the Mexican-killing abilities of yet another war hero. Included were more than a dozen types of medalets, a few ribbons, ceramics, prints, and bandannas, a yard-goods pattern, and a parade flag.[30] Scott was depicted in military bust portraits or equestrian poses, proclaimed "The Hero of Lundy's Lane" and (fig. 56) "The Hero of Many Battles," and portrayed routing Mexicans at Vera Cruz and deploying his troops after being wounded at Lundy's Lane. A medalet declared him "First in War/First in Peace," and bandannas read "Triumphant in War, yet the constant advocate of Peace. Ever victorious over his country's foes, his courage has only been exceeded by his humanity." Given a notoriously dour personality (his nickname, "Old Fuss and Feathers," was considered a political liability and not exploited) and complete lack of nonmilitary achievements, the designers of these objects were certainly laboring under a decided handicap. Perhaps the best commentary upon the 1852 Whig campaign and its material culture was a cartoon circulated by the Democrats. It featured Scott in parade finery perched atop a pyramid of skulls and was captioned "An Available Candidate/The One Qualification of a Whig President."

In 1854 the Whig party fell prey to discord between its free-state and proslavery wings over the Kansas–Nebraska Act. Its legacy to our political process was enormous, especially in the transformation of material culture into a key feature of American presidential campaigning. From 1834 through 1852 Whig candidates and causes inspired the vast majority of all campaign items created. They pioneered the whole phenomenon of visual devices for mass public events and introduced many new types of individual keepsake objects as well. In the process, they added new dimensions to the art of trinketry by inspiring items that went beyond elementary candidate identification to embrace the politics of personality, symbolism, and issue exploitation. It was a legacy of some significance, as the Whigs who found a new home in the Republican party would demonstrate in 1860, when they used material culture brilliantly to send Abraham Lincoln to the White House as the "Prince of Rails."

NOTES

1. See Robert Gray Gunderson, *The Log-Cabin Campaign* (Lexington, Ky., 1957), 1–11, 108–72.

2. Apparently taunted by Thomas Hart Benton's boast that he had "started the ball rolling" on the Senate's 1837 decision to expunge its earlier censure of Jackson for removing federal deposits from the Bank of the United States, Whigs in many areas built enormous balls covered with buckskin and painted with partisan slogans, which they rolled in Harrison processions or on great journeys. The ball represented in fig. 25 was rolled from Cleveland to Clay's Lexington and another, reportedly ten feet in diameter, survived the journey from Baltimore to Philadelphia before breaking apart during a parade down Chestnut Street. See Albany *Daily Argus*, May 12, 1840; Gunderson, *Log-Cabin Campaign*, 129–30; and Schlesinger, *Age of Jackson*, 291. This practice was continued by the Whigs during the 1844 Clay campaign and then apparently died out until 1888, when it was briefly revived (along with such other 1840 nostalgia as the log cabin and the slogan "Harrison and Reform") for the presidential campaign of Tip's grandson, Republican Benjamin Harrison.

3. Galena (Ill.) *North Western Gazette and Galena Advertiser*, March 27, Oct. 2, 16, 1840.

4. For a survey of 1840 Harrison material culture, see Sullivan, *Political Badges and Medalets*, 55–83; Fischer and Sullivan, *Political Ribbons and Ribbon Badges*, 27–49; Hake, *Political Buttons*, *III*, 23–32; Collins, *Threads of History*, 88–106; Klamkin, *Patriotic and Political China*, 105–12; Lee and Rose, *Glass Cup Plates*, 41–42, 309, 315, 321–25; Lindsey, *American Historical Glass*, 281–85; and Albert, *Uniform and Historical Buttons*, 425–31.

5. Quoted in Albany *Daily Argus*, June 26, 1840.

6. See Heale, *The Presidential Quest*, 114–17.

7. Galena *North Western Gazette and Galena Advertiser*, Oct. 16, 1840.

8. For a splendid account of the incident and the Whig transformation of it into the dominant theme of the 1840 campaign, see Gunderson, *The Log-Cabin Campaign*, 74–75.

9. Quoted in the Galena *North Western Gazette and Galena Advertiser*, June 5, 1840.

10. Gunderson, *The Log-Cabin Campaign*, 75–76.

11. Albany *Daily Argus*, June 9, 1840.

12. Galena *North Western Gazette and Galena Advertiser*, June 19, 1840.

13. Gunderson, *The Log-Cabin Campaign*, 228, 233.

14. See Sullivan, *Political Badges and Medalets*, 45–47, 84–89; Fischer and Sullivan, *Political Ribbons and Ribbon Badges*, 50–53; Hake, *Political Buttons*, *III*, 21–22; and Albert, *Uniform and Historical Buttons*, 424.

15. During the campaign, Democratic newspapers circulated accounts that as a young officer in the Northwest Territory during the late 1790s Harrison had been an active Federalist and had appeared at public events sporting the Federalist "black cockade," while Whig journals countered with "eyewitness" testimony of their own that Harrison had been a loyal disciple of Jefferson. As an Ohio state senator, Harrison had purportedly supported a bill enabling sheriffs to rent out the services of indigent prisoners until their fines had been worked off. To the Washington

Globe, which pointed out that under this scheme white convicts could be leased to free Negroes, Harrison had thus endorsed the principle of "selling white men as slaves." See Washington *Globe,* Jan. 8, Feb. 21, July 10, 1840; and Gunderson, *Log-Cabin Campaign,* 226.

16. The expression "OK" apparently began as an abbreviation of Van Buren's nickname, "Old Kinderhook," and appeared on a few 1840 Van Buren campaign items, although its absorption into the vernacular as a general term of approval was evidently so rapid that it was also used on 1840 Harrison banners and cider-barrel parade standards.

17. See Heale, *The Presidential Quest,* 83–132.

18. Jackson to Van Buren, July 13, 1840, as quoted in Gunderson, *Log-Cabin Campaign,* 109.

19. Albany *Daily Argus,* June 26, 1840.

20. Quoted in Ward, *Andrew Jackson,* 97; and Heale, *The Presidential Quest,* 107.

21. Collins, *Threads of History,* 111, 120.

22. See Fischer and Sullivan, *Political Ribbons and Ribbon Badges,* 69–73; Hake, *Political Buttons, III,* 33–34; and Sullivan, *Political Badges and Medalets,* 91–97.

23. See Collins, *Threads of History,* 110–21; Lee and Rose, *Glass Cup Plates,* 40–41, 307–8, 312–15; Fischer and Sullivan, *Political Ribbons and Ribbon Badges,* 74–90; Hake, *Political Buttons, III,* 35–40; Sullivan, *Political Badges and Medalets,* 97–116; Albert, *Uniform and Historical Buttons,* 432–34; and Sullivan, *Collecting Political Americana,* 103–6, 114–15, 129–31, 134, 151–52.

24. In 1842, Clay and Van Buren, his probable 1844 opponent, had agreed to keep annexation (which both opposed as likely to foment a needless war with Mexico) from becoming an issue in the forthcoming campaign. When Van Buren lost the Democratic nomination to the avid expansionist Polk, however, Texas became the dominant issue in the campaign. Aware of the popularity of annexation in the South and West, Clay in July wrote for publication two "Alabama letters," the first one very ambiguous on annexation and the second accepting it if it could be achieved "without national dishonor, without war, with the general consent of the States of the Union, and upon fair and reasonable terms" (conditions Clay believed impossible to meet). This ploy did little to win the hearts of the expansionists, but it had a marked effect in the anti–Texas northeastern states, where antislavery voters switched to Liberty party candidate Birney in sufficient numbers to narrowly deprive Clay of the presidency.

25. The 1848 and 1852 Democratic campaigns on behalf of Cass and Pierce were both very low key "mute tribune" affairs, while Whig efforts to rekindle the excitement of the Harrison and Clay campaigns were largely unsuccessful. Taylor remained at his military post through the 1848 campaign, and his penchant for writing letters that angered the Whig faithful deprived his campaign of the element of party loyalty necessary for staging participatory events. In 1852 Scott traveled extensively, but his vacuous speeches and stuffy personality and the disintegration of the Whig party dampened participatory enthusiasm. See Heale, *The Presidential Quest,* 102–4, 124–29.

26. See Fischer and Sullivan, *Political Ribbons and Ribbon Badges,* 52–53; Hake, *Political Buttons, III,* 236; and Sullivan, *Political Badges and Medalets,* 138–39. The 1844 Liberty party campaign of James G. Birney produced posters and a Currier

print, but the 1848 Free Soil effort was the first minor-party campaign to utilize material culture to a meaningful degree.

27. Hake, *Political Buttons*, III, 46; Sullivan, *Political Badges and Medalets*, 134–37; Fischer and Sullivan, *Political Ribbons and Ribbon Badges*, 96.

28. See Fischer and Sullivan, *Political Ribbons and Ribbon Badges*, 98; Hake, *Political Buttons*, III, 47; and Sullivan, *Political Badges and Medalets*, 141–43.

29. See Collins, *Threads of History*, 124–28; Sullivan, *Political Badges and Medalets*, 119–34; Hake, *Political Buttons*, III, 41–45; Fischer and Sullivan, *Political Ribbons and Ribbon Badges*, 92–95; Albert, *Uniform and Historical Buttons*, 434–37; McKearin and Wilson, *American Bottles and Flasks*, 481–84; and Sullivan, *Collecting Political Americana*, 89–90, 102–3, 115, 151–53.

30. See Fischer and Sullivan, *Political Ribbons and Ribbon Badges*, 99; Hake, *Political Buttons*, III, 48–49; Sullivan, *Political Badges and Medalets*, 144–50; and Collins, *Threads of History*, 123, 137–38.

3

Liberty and Union 1856–72

During the 1856 presidential election and the four that followed, the sectional crisis over slavery dominated political material culture as it did the attention of the American public. With the very survival of the Union at stake, voter interest and involvement revived quickly from the doldrums of 1848 and 1852, along with such rituals of participatory politics as rallies and parades. This upsurge in activity led to a corresponding increase in campaign items, both mass visual devices and individual curios. Such old standbys as medalets, ribbons, prints, banners, and parade flags remained in vogue, but two-piece brass clothing buttons and shell badges and ceramic and glass objects of all sorts almost died out as political artifacts during this period. Replacing shell medalets and buttons as popular lapel devices were ferrotype[1] disks in holed or looped brass casings (fig. 59), introduced in more than 160 known varieties in 1860, gilt or enameled metal pins worn alone or used to fasten ribbons, and in 1868 and following campaigns brass badges with albumin paper photographs (fig. 60) attached. Innovations in public visuals, prompted by the great popularity of political torchlight parades, included customized torches, illuminated transparencies, and various styles of glass (fig. 61) and paper (fig. 62) lanterns.

Given the extraordinary gravity of the times, a much greater proportion of items reflected serious issues than had been the case during the 1840–52 canvasses. This was particularly true of the first Republican presidential venture, the 1856 campaign on behalf of John C. Frémont and William L. Dayton. Still a rather uneasy coalition of northern Whigs, Free-Soilers, and a few antislavery "conscience Democrats," the early Republicans were really united only in their wholehearted hostility to the spread of slavery into the western territories. While the new party inherited its penchant for high moral purpose primarily from the Free Soil movement, it also fell heir to the Whig tradition of material culture. The result in 1856 was a rather

Fig. 59. Ferrotype lapel pins made their political debut in 1860, with more than 160 styles featuring candidates Abraham Lincoln, Stephen Douglas, John C. Breckinridge, and John Bell.

sizeable number of campaign visuals and personal curios with an extraordinarily ideological tenor. A remarkably large portion of Frémont objects (at least two-thirds of those found in reference works and major collections, a ratio rivaled among major-party candidacies only by the 1896 free silver and sound money efforts of William Jennings Bryan and William McKinley) echoed the strident single-issue thrust of the campaign, opposition to the southern "slave power conspiracy," usually expressed in rhetoric derived from the litany "Free Speech, Free Press, Free Soil, Free Men, Fremont and Victory."[2] Seldom—if ever—in two centuries of American presidential politics has a candidate been so eclipsed by a cause.

The Republicans certainly had other options. Whatever his shortcomings in experience and ability as a statesman or a profound student of the political process, Frémont had qualities that made him a singularly attractive

Fig. 60. By 1868 ferrotypes were being replaced by the more durable and less costly badges with paper photographs like these Ulysses Grant–Schuyler Colfax and Horatio Seymour–Frank Blair varieties. (Edmund B. Sullivan)

candidate. His highly publicized exploits as a western explorer had brought him a reputation throughout the nation as a man of vigor and courage, much in the mold of Washington and Jackson, and widespread public recognition as "the Pathfinder," a considerable political asset in a period in which such nicknames as Tippecanoe, Old Hickory, and Old Rough and Ready had enhanced the presidential prospects of three similar men of action. A rather dashing, handsome young man, the Californian had made a brilliant marriage to Thomas Hart Benton's lovely daughter, Jessie. Very few candidates for the presidency have offered such compelling raw material for the politics of personality.

Yet very few known Frémont campaign items utilized this approach, and most of those that did bore ideological slogans as well. A banner made by pasting paper cutouts of a man and a woman on horseback onto linen read "Fremont and Jessie." A small campaign medalet identified Frémont as "Jessie's Choice," another declared him "The People's Choice," and a third variety portrayed three surveyors and a mountain range and the legend "Honor to Whom Honor Is Due." A larger token bore the slogan "The Rocky Mountains Echo Back Fremont," but also such maxims as "Constitutional Freedom" and "Free Soil." A beautiful parade banner from Pequannoc Township, New Jersey, (fig. 63) featured a scene of several explorers raising

Figs. 61 and 62. Among the many visual devices created for the lavish torchlight parades that were so popular during Civil War–era political campaigns were this 1864 Abraham Lincoln glass lantern and this ornate 1872 Ulysses Grant paper variety. (Edmund B. Sullivan)

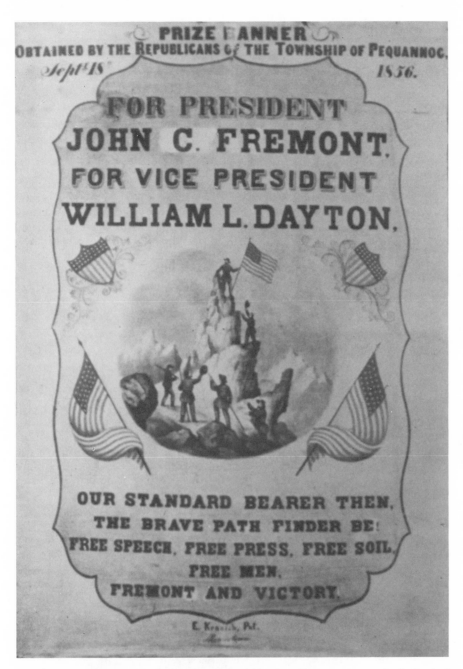

Fig. 63. Combining the campaign themes of John C. Frémont as "Path Finder" and militant free-soil ideology was this magnificent 1856 Pequannoc, New Jersey marching banner. (Smithsonian Institution)

Old Glory on a mountain peak with a verse demanding "Free Speech, Free Press, Free Soil, Free Men, Fremont and Victory." A silk ribbon (fig. 64) featured Frémont placing the flag atop a mountain, but also the demand "Free Speech, Free Men, Free Territory," while another ribbon depicted a mounted Frémont as "Pathfinder," but also insisted (in decidedly bolder lettering), "Free Soil, Free Speech, Free Press."

With few such exceptions, the Frémont items that were thematic in any sense were purely ideological. Tokens was struck with such legends as "Free Soil & Free Speech," "Free Speech, Free Men," and "Free Soil, Free Pres [sic]." Another echoed the era's boundless faith in the inevitability of progress as well as 1856 Republican dogma with the sentiments "Free Soil, Free Speech, Free Labor, and Eternal Progression." Probably the most issue-laden of all known Frémont tokens featured an obverse reading "Free Kansas and the Union" and a reverse insisting "No More Slave States, Free Speech, Free Press, Free Labour, Fremont and Dayton."

Silk ribbons worn by Frémont enthusiasts exhibited similar characteristics. Of the nearly four dozen known varieties, slightly more than a third merely portrayed or identified Frémont, while the majority were inscribed with 1856 Republican ideology. Typical were such slogans as "Principles not Party," "Free Kansas," "The Champion of Liberty," "Free Labor," "Freedom," "Fremont & Freedom," and such variations on the basic 1856 litany as "Free Speech, Free Press and Free Kansas" and "Free Soil, Freedom and Fremont." One ribbon inscribed "Republican Candidate John C. Fremont" also demanded "Free Soil, Free Speech, Free Press, Freemen, Fremont & Liberty." The *ne plus ultra* in this regard, however, was probably a silk ribbon containing two elaborate designs, a portrait, and the legend "The Union Shall Be Preserved/Col. Fremont/Free Speech! Freemen!! Free Kansas!!/Stand for the Right/Freemen! Remember November 4th 1856."

Much larger than ribbons, cotton kerchiefs or bandannas provided correspondingly greater opportunities for ideological bombast. A trio in the Smithsonian collection resemble broadsides printed on cotton instead of paper. One (fig. 65) featured an attack on the proslavery press titled "The Satanic Dodge" and three campaign songs that characterized the opposition—whether in national politics or in the guerilla fighting in Kansas was unclear—as "ruffians," "a cowardly crew," even "vultures now basely retreating." Another variety bore editorials denouncing as "a simpleton or hypocrite" anyone who would vote for Democrat James Buchanan, refrain from voting, or assert that Republicanism was "negro-worship," plus two songs lauding Frémont and one (to the tune of "Oh Susannah") denouncing Know-Nothing nominee Millard Fillmore as "a statesman true to filthy slav'ry's throne." On the third bandanna or kerchief were featured a pair of diatribes titled "The True Issue," one portraying the Democrats as the party of "barbarism, brutality, ignorance, vice, and crime," and the other denouncing them for conspiring "to rivet upon us the chains of slavery,"

Fig. 64. Also exploiting Frémont's renown as an explorer while giving equal or greater emphasis to ideological imperatives were these 1856 Republican silk ribbons.

plus three singularly bloodthirsty ditties (one of which was to be sung to the altogether incongruous melody of "Believe Me, If All Those Endearing Young Charms").

Other 1856 Republican campaign items evinced a similar singlemindedness on the issues. Parade floats and transparencies depicted the sufferings of free-soil settlers in Kansas. Evangelist Lyman Beecher (never one for subtle understatement) used a massive chain with two large padlocks to dramatize the Kansas issue.[3] Currier and Ives "grand national banner" prints of Frémont and Dayton bore the motto "Free Labor, Free Speech, Free Territory." A sampler embroidered during the campaign by a girl of eleven read "Fremont and Freedom '56." A Newport, Rhode Island, banner made by Ackerman and Miller of New York (apparently the first known example of a professionally produced silk parade banner in American politics) bore

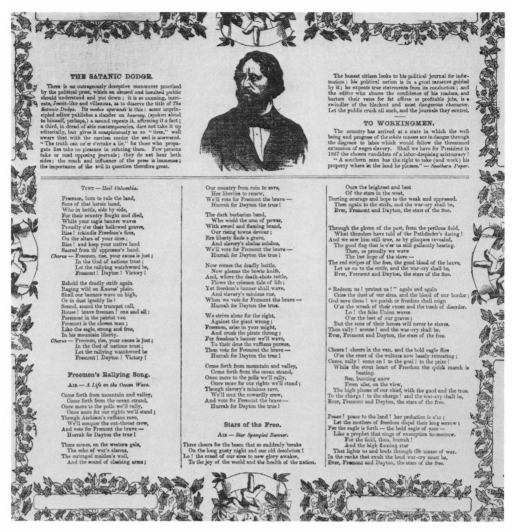

Fig. 65. One of a set of three 1856 Frémont cotton bandannas in the collection of the Smithsonian Institution that rank among the most strident textile items ever produced during an American political campaign. (Smithsonian Institution)

the litany "Free Speech, Free Soil, Free Men, Fremont and Victory." A splendid satiric banner featured a manacled slave riding a mountain goat and the caption "Buck & Breck/Border Ruffian/Democracy & Slavery." According to historian Allan Nevins, banners that read "Kansas Will Be Free" and "No More Rule of Nigger-Drivers" waved in the breeze as Frémont–Dayton parades passed beneath them.[4]

If the Republicans made any real effort to soften their message to win greater support among a frightened electorate, Frémont campaign items do not show it. Only one known 1856 Republican artifact, a ribbon containing a Frémont pledge to govern "According to the True Spirit of the Constitution, as It Was Interpreted by the Great Men Who Framed and Adopted It, and in Such a Way as to Preserve Both Liberty and the Union," paid homage to constitutional restraints and the sanctity of the Union. Otherwise, Frémont items very stridently implied a "damn the South and damn the consequences" philosophy that served the Republicans quite well in the eleven solidly free-soil states of the upper North but led to political doom further south.

The much smaller number of known campaign items inspired by the Democratic ticket of James Buchanan and John C. Breckinridge provide ample evidence that the Democrats alertly exploited the opportunities presented.[5] They used two diverse approaches to do so, blatant racism and high-minded devotion to national unity. A trio of ribbons, one captioned "Black Republican" (fig. 66) featured a running fugitive slave and a skull and crossbones with the legend "Fremont and Dayton." Another ribbon (fig. 67) printed in Baltimore, most likely a postelection item, portrayed fugitive slaves fleeing to Frémont's Rocky Mountains under the caption "Fremont! Free Niggers!" Created to play on white fears over threats to their property and safety, such ribbons were unquestionably put to effective use in the slaveholding states and those regions of the lower North settled primarily by southerners.

More common, however, were items portraying Buchanan as the champion of national harmony. Ribbons featured the legend "The Union It Must Be Preserved" with a scene portraying two men (apparently Buchanan and Breckinridge) with Old Glory standing on the "Democratic Platform" resting firmly upon the "Constitution." Another ribbon proclaimed "Our Union–Our Destiny: In the Lexicon of Buchanan There Is no Such Words as North or South." Tokens urged "James Buchanan/No Sectionalism," "Constitution and Union," "United We Stand, Divided We Fall 1856," and "Buchanan, the Crisis Demands His Election/The Union One and Indivisable [*sic*]." Two objects, a token reading "The Union Must & Shall Be Preserved/Jackson" and a paper electoral ticket with a hickory tree and the slogan "Jackson and Liberty," embraced both traditional American verities and the legacy of Andrew Jackson. Another electoral ticket read "Constitution & Laws." Few Buchanan items tried to exploit the politics of personality or whimsy, but a ribbon proclaimed the nominee "The Sage of Wheatland," at least two others featured stag designs to play upon his "Old Buck" nickname, and several other styles of ribbons offered up this pun-filled prediction:

> We Po'ked 'em in '44,
> We Pierced 'em in '52,
> And we'll 'Buck 'em' in '56.

Figs. 66 and 67. Excellent examples of 1856 Democratic exploitation of blatant racism against John C. Frémont and the Republicans were these "Black Republican" and "Frémont! Free Niggers!" silk ribbons featuring vignettes of fugitive slaves.

In their attempt to portray Buchanan as the apostle of national unity, the Democrats faced stiff competition from ex-President Millard Fillmore, running in 1856 as the nominee of the American (or Know-Nothing) party. Formerly a militant splinter group devoted to saving the land from Catholic immigrants, by 1856 the Americans had been largely taken over by conservative Whigs unable to accept Republicanism and unwilling to become Democrats. Hoping to hold Whig votes with Fillmore while appealing to

Democrats with running-mate Andrew J. Donelson (Jackson's nephew, namesake, and longtime aide), the Americans mounted a vigorous campaign that inspired more than two dozen varieties of items, most devoted to the theme of national solidarity. Ribbons and badges (figs. 68, 69) featured Fillmore's statement "I know nothing but my Country, my whole Country, and nothing but my Country" and such legends as "The Union Forever" and "National Union." Tokens demanded "The Union Now, the Union Forever" and "No North No South but the Whole Country," and another warned "Be Vigilant and Watchful, that Internal Dissensions Destroy not Your Prosperity." A Maryland electoral ticket featured a flag and the motto "Our Country," and a Currier and Ives "grand national banner" print proclaimed "The Constitution and the Union." The only variations from this theme were a token ("Americans Shall Rule America") and two handmade silk banners ("Put None but Americans on Guard" and "Americans Must Rule America!") attesting to the sordid origins of the party. One of these banners also denigrated Buchanan by claiming "We Can't Go Ten Cent Jimmy" and "James Buchanan Is an Unreliable Man!—Genl. A. Jackson" (a remark prompted by Buchanan's alleged role in the Adams–Clay "corrupt bargain" thirty-one years before).

Material culture played an even greater role in the 1860 presidential race, that tense yet oddly festive prologue to civil war. With four credible candidates—Republican Abraham Lincoln, national Democrat Stephen Douglas, southern Democrat John C. Breckinridge, and Constitutional Unionist John Bell—and the Union itself at stake, voter interest was intense. All four campaigns were rather well organized at the grass-roots level, generally into such paramilitary volunteer corps as Lincoln's Wide-Awakes and Rail Splitters, Douglas's Little Giants, Little Dougs, and Chloroformers (a Brooklyn club named for its boast to "put the Wide-Awakes to sleep"), Breckinridge's National Democratic Volunteers, and Bell's Union Sentinels and Bell Ringers. Altogether their ranks numbered nearly a million, more than one for every five votes cast. These corps staged an unusual number of public events, especially spectacular torchlight parades witnessed by millions more. All of the anxiety and activity created an enormously fertile environment for material culture. Several hundred varieties of campaign items survive, intact or in illustrations and narrative accounts, from the four 1860 candidacies.

At least half of these were Republican. Tempered by defeat in 1856, strengthened by a broadened party base, and motivated by excellent chances of seizing the White House from the hopelessly divided Democrats, the Republicans approached 1860 much differently than they had 1856. With victory riding on a strong showing in the rather conservative tier of states across the lower North, where a strident single-issue crusade like Frémont's could once again be a kiss of death, the Republicans sweetened

Figs. 68 and 69. Promoting 1856 Know-Nothing nominees Millard Fillmore and Andrew Jackson Donelson as apostles of national union were this silk ribbon and unusual paper badge, a distant ancestor of the modern sticker.

their idealism with a generous measure of opportunism. One party leader described the perfect nominee as "the man who can carry Pennsylvania, New Jersey, and Indiana, with this reservation, . . . the candidate must be alive, and able to walk, at least from parlor to dining room."[7] When they met in Chicago they fashioned a platform that restated their views on slavery in a more subtle manner and added tariff and homestead planks written with an eye to the doubtful states, then nominated Abraham Lincoln, the most electable if not the most illustrious of their lot. Physical objects played even more of a part in Lincoln's campaign than they had in the Frémont effort for several reasons. Republicans were much more successful at fund-raising in 1860, allowing them to purchase and distribute a greater volume and variety of giveaway items. The new mania for torchlight parades created exciting new opportunities for political visuals. Perhaps most important of all, the whole thrust of the Lincoln campaign—its emphasis on personality and symbolism rather than moral imperatives—was tailor-made for trinkets and visuals. Whatever the reasons, Lincoln's 1860 campaign inspired an abundant variety of tokens, ferrotypes, ribbons, posters, prints, and such parade items as transparencies, banners, torches, flags, floats, and wooden axes.[8]

Their dominant theme was the projection of Lincoln as a human being, a man of the people with whom ordinary Americans could identify and in whom they could take pride. A key step was the promotion of Lincoln as "Old Honest Abe" (or such variants as "Honest Old Abe," "Old Abe," and "Honest Abe"). This nickname served Lincoln well, establishing his identity in millions of minds as a down-to-earth, homespun pillar of personal integrity. After failing to properly exploit Frémont as the Pathfinder in 1856, Republicans would not waste such political capital again. A transparency carried by the Wide-Awakes (fig. 70) bore the legend "Honest Old Abe," and a triangular one now in the Smithsonian collection (fig. 71) urged a vote for "Old Abe." A silk marching banner read "Our Candidate Abe Lincoln," and an elaborate cotton banner depicting Lincoln galloping to the White House predicted "Honest Old Abe Is Bound to Win." Tokens saluted "Honest Abe." Ribbons portrayed him as "Honest Old Abe" and "'Honest Abe' Lincoln, the Hope of Our Country."

The heart of the Republican effort to market Lincoln as a man of the people was their development of his identity as a rail-splitter. A brainstorm of longtime Lincoln friend Richard Oglesby of Decatur, Illinois,[9] the split rail was superb political symbolism, dramatizing at once Lincoln's heroic rise from humble origins, the mystique of the frontier, and the essential dignity of free labor. In the six months from its debut at a party gathering in Decatur through election day, it developed into perhaps the most compelling of all American political icons, helping transform a relative unknown with little popular appeal into a rather attractive candidate in his own right. Few opportunities were missed to work the concept into the cam-

Fig. 70. From Maine to Minnesota, members of Lincoln's "Wide Awake" units like these revelers added a generous measure of color and excitement to the 1860 Republican campaign. (Smithsonian Institution)

paign. Split rails became regular decorations in local Republican "wig-wams," and a Lincoln campaign weekly in Chicago became *The Rail Splitter*. Local Lincoln clubs called themselves Rail Maulers or Rail Splitters. Several campaign songs exploited the theme. Some local Wide-Awake units even performed a special zig-zag march to imitate a split-rail fence.

A host of campaign objects also utilized this theme. Republican parades invariably featured split rails, carried bare or adorned with banners or bunt-ing. A transparency (fig. 71) proclaimed Lincoln "Prince of Rails." Many varieties of wooden axes (fig. 72; see also fig. 70), some handmade and others marketed commercially, were used as parade visuals carried on the shoulders of marchers, often bearing such legends as "Old Abe," "Rail Splitter," "Lincoln & Hamlin 1860," even in one instance "Fear not Old Abe Is Our———, Good Times Coming Soon Boys." Stationery and en-velopes featured Lincoln's bust and "The Fence that Uncle Abe Built." At least a dozen varieties of medalets echoed the theme, several of which displayed scenes of a young Lincoln splitting rails in a pioneer farmyard above such captions as "The Rail Splitter of 1830" and "Progress 1830." One medalet proclaimed Lincoln "The Man that Can Split Rails or Guide the Ship of State." Designers of other tokens worked the concept into their creations with such centerpieces as crossed rails or an axe embedded in a log. Other medalets were bordered by split-rail fences, a motif also used on a cotton "Lincoln and Hamlin" banner made for a parade in Painesville, Ohio. A "Rail Splitter's Badge," at thirteen cents per ribbon, or five cents apiece in quantities of sixty, was advertised weekly in *The Rail Splitter*.[10]

Closely related to the rail-splitter theme was the promotion of Lincoln as a westerner, shrewd politics not only because of the critical importance of the western vote, but also because of the enduring fascination with the frontier and new mania over the Wild West among easterners. One of the most popular of all 1860 Republican campaign songs was "Honest Abe of the West." A token bore the plea "The Great Rail Splitter of the West Must & Shall Be Our Next President." Others promoted Lincoln as "Honest Abe of the West," "The Rail Splitter of the West," and "Honest Abe of the West, the Hannibal of America."

Given the tense national situation and the antislavery fervor of so many rank-and-file Republicans, the Lincoln campaign would have found it impossible to avoid issues totally and didn't try to do so. Two dozen or more tokens, many banners and ribbons, a few ferrotypes, and several posters and parade floats were wholly or primarily issue-oriented, echoing party dogma on slavery in the territories, the tariff, a homestead law, and the Union. In contrast to 1856, these objects reveal an ideological approach that was multifaceted, tailored carefully to regional sensibilities, and—except in hot-beds of free-soil sentiment carried by Frémont—anything but strident in tone.

More items reflected Republican hostility to the spread of slavery west-ward than any other issue. For the most part, these objects were created

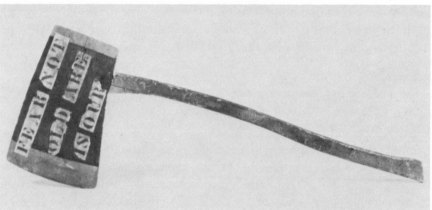

Figs. 71 and 72. Among the many campaign artifacts inspired by Lincoln torchlight parades in 1860 were this "Prince of Rails" triangular transparency aimed at German-American voters and this handmade rail-splitter's axe parade standard. (Smithsonian Institution)

very early in the campaign, before its focus had been clearly established, or produced and used in strongly free-soil regions. In October 1859, the Scovill Manufacturing Company of Waterbury, Connecticut, was commissioned to produce medalets that read "Success to Republican Principles— Millions for Freedom, not One Cent for Slavery" by young William Leggett Bramhall of New York, an avid collector of political medalets and equally enthusiastic abolitionist.[11] Several "Abram" Lincoln items, manufactured before many easterners made the discovery that the 1860 Republican nominee's given name was really Abraham, included a ferrotype inscribed "Free Speech, Free Soil and Free Men" and medalets that read "Free Land, Free Speech & Free Men" and "Free Territory for a Free People; Let Liberty Be National & Slavery Sectional."

Militantly antislavery items produced later in the campaign all seem to have been created in areas carried overwhelmingly by Frémont in 1856. A pair of medalets reading "No More Slave Territory" was made by Joseph Merriam of Boston, while two others urging "Freedom National, Slavery Sectional" were produced by Charles Lang of Worcester, Massachusetts. Handmade or custom-ordered parade banners were even more indicative of regional campaign characteristics. A silk banner borne by the "6th Ward Rail-Splitters Club" of Detroit echoed 1856 with its "Free Soil, Free Speech, Free Men" inscription. A cotton banner (fig. 73) handmade for the Dorchester, Massachusetts, "Rail Splitter's Battalion No. 1" insisted, "Resistance to Tyrants Is Obedience to God." A handmade Derry, New Hampshire, banner read "Lincoln & Liberty Forever, Brekenridge [sic] & Slavery Never," and a Belfast, Maine, marching banner (fig. 74) proclaimed "Lincoln and Hamlin Sure in November for Justice Will Triumph."[12]

Many free-soil items combined that issue with other 1860 party concerns to provide a more balanced statement of Republican principles. A paper ribbon printed in Philadelphia featuring "Abram" Lincoln insisted "Union and Liberty," and a token read "Liberty Union and Equality." Another token linked the territorial issue with Republican support for federal homestead legislation, urging "Free Homes for Free Men, No More Slave Territory." Several objects made in Philadelphia and most likely used primarily in Pennsylvania and New Jersey worked in the party's support for a protective tariff, a key issue in the two industrial states where Frémont had done badly in 1856. A token struck by Robert Lovett urged "Liberty & Protection," and two others read "Protection to American Industry, Free Homes for Free Men." A paper ribbon was inscribed "Liberty/Protection to American Industry." A splendid jugate poster (fig. 75) printed by W. H. Rease managed to cover every base, combining "Free Speech, Free Homes, Free Territory" with "Protection to American Industry" and "The Union Must and Shall Be Preserved." A poster advertising a Republican rally in the heart of Pennsylvania Dutch country with speakers in English and German read "Free Labor, Free Territories, Free Homes, Protection to American Industry."

Other items dealt exclusively with the tariff or homestead issues. One token was inscribed "Protection to All at Home and Abroad." Another token and matching pin-on badge urged "Protection to Honest Industry" above a log with an axe embedded in it, all surrounded by a split-rail fence. A ribbon depicting Lincoln splitting rails demanded "A Home for the Homeless," and other ribbons sought "Free Homes for the People." A prime attraction in the spectacular Wide-Awake torchlight parade in New York on October 3, 1860, was a large log-cabin float with banners reading "Uncle Sam Has Land Enough to Give Us Each a Farm."

Many 1860 Lincoln items proclaimed Republican reverence for the Union and Constitution, sound politics for a party attempting to enhance its appeal to old-line Whigs in the teeth of constant charges from the three opposing camps that Republicanism remained a divisive, disruptive force. Tokens, ribbons, banners, ferrotypes, and parade standards were all used to identify Lincoln's candidacy with Unionist sentiments. If a few of these— tokens and ferrotypes reading "The Constitution 1860," "The Union Must and Shall Be Preserved," and "The Constitution and the Laws 1860," for example—were produced for all four 1860 candidates, others were uniquely Republican. A handmade banner stated, "We March Under the Banner, and Keep Step to the Music of the Union." A ribbon printed by Merrill and Son of Concord, New Hampshire, urged "Union and Victory!" A token made by John D. Lovett of New York warned "United We Stand, Divided We Fall," and one created by Smith and Hartmann of the same city recycled an old Fillmore token reverse to admonish "Be Vigilant and Watchful that Internal Dissensions Destroy not Your Prosperity." A token struck by Jensch and Meyer of Chicago insisted "Our Policy Is Expressly the Policy of the Men Who Made the Union, no More, no Less," while one produced by William H. Key of Philadelphia read simply "The Union." A standard carried in the October 3, 1860, Wide-Awake parade in New York bore the legend "1776/The Union/1860." A ferrotype made by Ellis and Read of Springfield, Massachusetts, demanded "The Constitution and Union Forever."

Replete with rhetoric dear to the hearts of such Henry Clay Whigs as Lincoln himself, these unionist items and 1860 Lincoln objects generally provide compelling evidence of the dramatic transformation in image accomplished by the Republicans just four years after their shrill, single-issue debut in presidential politics. Many 1860 Lincoln items unabashedly celebrated the politics of personality and symbolism, substituting split rails and homespun nicknames for ideological imperatives. When Lincoln's campaign objects did focus on issues, their general tenor was multifaceted, reflective of regional priorities, and rather subdued in style except in safe free-soil constituencies. Few campaigns in our history have used material culture so astutely or effectively.

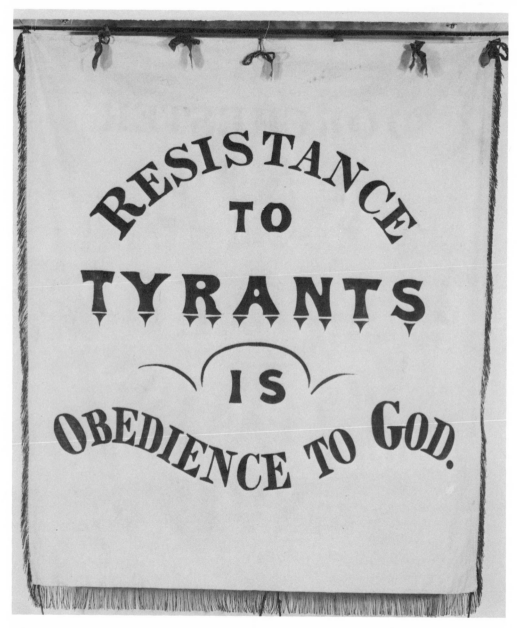

Fig. 73. Such militant sentiments as expressed by this Dorchester, Massachusetts, marching banner were representative of the 1860 Lincoln campaign only in staunchly antislavery constituencies. (Smithsonian Institution)

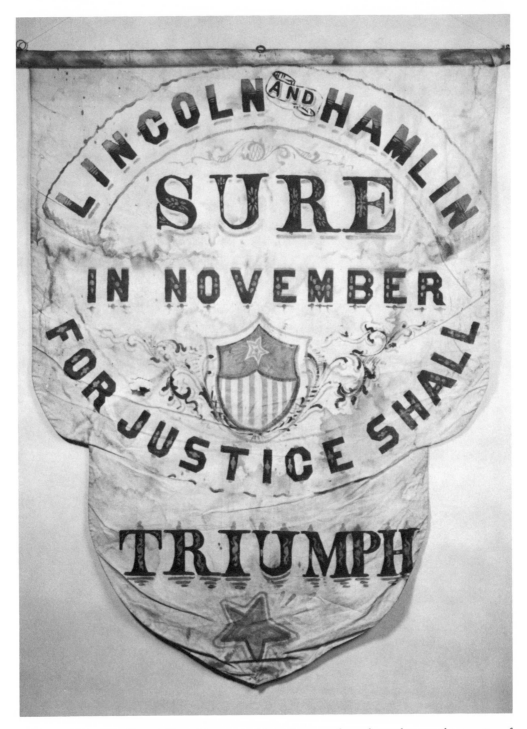

Fig. 74. This Belfast, Maine, marching banner also echoes the moral intensity of the 1860 Lincoln campaign in fervently free-soil northern New England.

Fig. 75. This attractive Lincoln–Hamlin jugate poster published by W. H. Rease of Philadelphia cleverly combined such 1860 Republican campaign themes as preservation of the Union, opposition to the spread of slavery, support for homestead legislation, a protective tariff, and Lincoln's rail-splitter image. (Library of Congress)

If devotion to the Union was a major tenet of Lincoln's campaign, it was virtually the sum total of John Bell's Constitutional Union effort. The Bell–Edward Everett ticket inspired more than sixty known varieties of campaign items, including at least three dozen different ferrotypes, a dozen or more medalets, and a few parade flags and lithographed prints.[13] Aside from a few rebus campaign objects picturing a bell instead of naming the nominee, 1860 Constitutional Union items that went beyond simple identification invariably proclaimed the party's basic reason for being, a desire to preserve the Union through compromise on the slavery question. Tokens urged "The Constitution and the Union/Now and Forever," "Union Forever/Freedom to All," "Constitution and Union," and "Union, Constitution & Enforcement of the Laws." A ribbon (fig. 76) insisted "The Union and the Constitution/One and Inseparable." Bell–Everett ferrotypes read "The Constitution and the Laws 1860" and "The Constitution 1860/Union of the States 1860," as they did for all of the tickets, but one unique to the Constitutional Union campaign read "John Bell and the Constitution/Ed-

Fig. 76. These 1860 silk ribbons, promoting the candidacies of Constitutional Union nominee John Bell and Democrat Stephen Douglas, echo the emphasis put by both campaigns upon preservation of the Union.

ward Everett and the Union." A Virginia electoral ticket proclaimed, "The Union, the Constitution & the Enforcement of the Laws."

As devout a Unionist as any man alive, Stephen Douglas did not abandon the theme of national solidarity to Bell and Lincoln, although not it but "popular sovereignty"—his belief that the voters of a territory should settle the status of slavery within that territory, thus removing the conflict from the federal arena and virtually nullifying the possibility of disunion—was the major thrust of the more than six dozen known items inspired by the 1860 Douglas–Herschel Johnson national Democratic campaign. Four dozen varieties of ferrotypes, half that many medalets, several silk ribbons and cotton parade flags, and a few lithographed prints were produced for the "Little Giant's" final bid for public office.[14] Many of them expressed unionist sentiments. In addition to the standardized ferrotypes and some tokens made for several candidates with such slogans as "The Union Must and Shall Be Preserved," "Union and Equality," and "Liberty Union and Equality," Douglas ribbons (fig. 76) proclaimed "The Union Now and Forever," a flag insisted "Peace/Peace/Constitution & Union," and an envelope or "cachet" saluted Douglas as "True to the Union and the Constitution." Other items, including three ribbons and a pair of tokens, promoted Douglas as the "Little Giant." One of these tokens, rather surprisingly the only known 1860 campaign item to do so, paid tribute to his distinguished legislative career with the plea "Support 'The Little Giant' Who Has Proved Himself the Greatest Statesman of the Age."

Even more Douglas items made the case for popular sovereignty. Tokens admonished "Intervention Is Disunion 1860/M. Y. O. B." ("mind your own business"), insisted "Popular Sovereignty/National Union," and named Douglas "The Champion of Popular Sovereignty." A ferrotype demanded "Nonintervention/Popular Soverty [sic]." Two tokens created by S. D. Childs of Chicago were much more explicit. One proclaimed "Popular Sovereignty/Non Intervention by the General Government in Any of the States or Territories of the Union/Let the People of Each Rule." The other insisted "Vox Populi, Vox Dei/The Voice of the People Is the Voice of God/Let It Be Heard & When Heard Let All Obey/With These Political Maxims for Our Guide, the Union of the States Will Be Perpetual." A rational solution to an emotional dilemma, popular sovereignty died with the guns of Sumter, and its author followed suit just months later.

Alone among the 1860 campaigns, the southern Democratic effort of John C. Breckinridge and Joseph Lane did not engender a multitude of items proclaiming the sanctity of the federal Union. Their canvass inspired more than sixty known objects, including more than three dozen ferrotypes, ten medalets, and a few ribbons, flags, and prints.[15] Most were altogether nonthematic. Except for the standard unionist tokens and ferrotypes produced for all four 1860 campaigns, the only Breckinridge items to even pay lip-service to the Union gave equal billing to southern "rights." Tokens read "Our Rights, the Constitution and the Union" and "Our Country and Our Rights." More in keeping with the truculent tenor of this extremist effort, however, was another token urging "No Submission to the North." Appropriately enough, this reverse was later paired with a reverse of another Breckinridge token celebrating "The Wealth of the South/Rice Tobacco Sugar Cotton" to make a very popular memento for Confederate enthusiasts.

After nearly four years of civil war, it was only natural that items inspired by both camps in the 1864 contest between Lincoln and General George B. McClellan, the Democratic candidate who had once headed the Army of the Potomac, essentially echoed the theme of preserving the Union through military victory. Although the level of campaign activity was diminished considerably from 1860 by the war and by two fewer factions in the race, 1864 was a rather good year for political items. At least 250 known pieces have survived, about two-thirds of them promoting the National Union ticket of Lincoln and Andrew Johnson.[16] It was an especially fertile year for ferrotypes, tokens, and metal stickpins, leading one to wonder whether the war possibly might have been shortened by at least a few days if such large quantities of brass had been devoted to artillery rather than trinketry.

Very few 1864 items attempted to exploit the politics of personality or symbolism. In fundamental contrast to the material culture inspired by his first race, Lincoln's identity as "Old Honest Abe, Railsplitter of the West" was featured in 1864 on only two campaign tokens, one portraying an axe embedded in a fence rail with the legend "Good for Another Heat" and the other (fig. 77) proclaiming Lincoln "Honest Old Abe." Two other tokens made oblique reference to this nickname with the plea "Abraham Lincoln/An Honest Man/The Crisis Demands His Re-Election 1864." A token reading "Little Mac for President/Spades Are Trumps" and a Doylestown, Pennsylvania, poster promoting the McClellan–George H. Pendleton ticket as "Little Mac and the Buckeye Boy" seem to have been virtually unique among 1864 Democratic objects for indulging in this sort of folksy banality.

Instead, the campaign items of both parties focused primarily upon Union and victory. Of forty-five known McClellan tokens, forty (fig. 78) portrayed him in military bust style, and two others in equestrian poses. Some of these urged "One Flag and One Union Now and Forever," "The Constitution as It Is/The Hope of the Union," and "Union & Constitution One & Indivisible," while their Lincoln counterparts bore such sentiments as "Our Country and Our Flag Now and Forever," "Lincoln and Union," "Our Union," and "May the Union Flourish." Tokens demanding "The Union Must and Shall Be Preserved" were struck for both candidates, as were some featuring designs consisting of drums, flags, stacked muskets, and cannon. Lincoln ferrotypes proclaimed him "Firm to Defend and Maintain the Union" or urged "Union & Laws," while McClellan ferrotypes bore such maxims as "The Constitution as It Is" and "Union/Constitution/Laws & Flag." A Delaware County, Pennsylvania, Lincoln poster exhorted "Rally Around the Flag!/Union." A cotton McClellan–Pendleton broadside insisted upon "The Union at All Hazards." Indulging in a little heavy-handed irony, some "The Union Forever" ribbons (fig. 79) added to the Lincoln-Johnson ticket as "peace commissioners" the names of Generals Grant, Sherman, and Sheridan and Admiral Farragut.

Figs. 77 and 78. The "Honest Old Abe" medalet represents a rare echo on 1864 Lincoln campaign items of the 1860 personality politics that put him in the White House, while the "Foe to Traitors" variety and military medalets of Democrat George B. McClellan reflect more accurately the prevailing preoccupation with Civil War themes that dominated the 1864 campaign.

Another major theme on 1864 Lincoln items was that of human rights, a potent political weapon at a time when the war was engendering an idealism over emancipation that temporarily outweighed our longstanding tradition of white racism. A Lincoln token struck by Frederic B. Smith of New York pledged "If I Am Re-Elected President Slavery Must Be Abolished with the Reunion of States." Other tokens read "Proclaim Liberty Throughout the Land/Lincoln," "Freedom," "Lincoln and Liberty,"

"Freedom/Justice/Truth," and "Liberty for All 1864." Several Lincoln items combined this theme with unionism. Ferrotypes and ribbons (fig. 79) demanded "Union and Liberty." Medalets produced by William H. Key of Philadelphia urged "Freedom to All Men/War for the Union" and "Freedom to All Men/Union." A McClellan shield-shaped lapel pin bore the motto "McClellan & Liberty," but the Democrats made no real effort to wrest the humanitarian vote from the Great Emancipator. More indicative of the prevailing Democratic attitude on the race issue was a poster (fig. 80) predicting that a victory for Lincoln's "Black Republican Ticket" would "Bring on Negro Equality" and other dire results.

In one respect, McClellan trinkets provided a seriously flawed image of his presidential campaign by their nearly absolute silence on the Democratic proposal for peace without victory through sectional compromise. Dismissing the war effort as "four years of failure to restore the Union by the experiment of war," the party platform called for an immediate cease-fire followed by a convention of the states to restore peace. During the campaign that followed, Democrats opportunistically castigated Lincoln simultaneously for the war and for his failure to win it. Only one known McClellan object, however, directly exploited this line of attack, a token produced and distributed in very small numbers that urged "The Union and the Constitution to Be Preserved/No More Arbitrary Arrests/A Cessation of Hostilities and a Convention of States with a View to Peace and Re-Union." This theme was echoed by implication on the aforementioned "Black Republican . . . Negro Equality" poster (fig. 80) with the assertion that a McClellan victory would "re-establish the UNION! In an Honorable, Permanent and happy PEACE."

The Republican response to this proposal was reflected on a host of Lincoln items. Medalets (fig. 78) proclaimed him "A Foe to Traitors" and truculently demanded, "No Compromise with Armed Rebels" and "No Compromise with Traitors." A poster welcomed to a Brandywine Manor, Pennsylvania, Lincoln–Johnson rally "All Who Desire Peace through Victory over Rebels in Arms Against Their Government; All Who Rejoice in the Successes of Grant, Sherman, Sheridan, and Farragut; and All Who Are Opposed to a DISGRACEFUL ARMISTICE with Traitors." A blunt expression of Republican principles, this reaction became a blueprint for political success as well when the Union military fortunes improved dramatically during the final weeks of the campaign.

Union through the sword remained political magic for the Republicans in 1868, when their standard-bearer Ulysses Grant won the presidency in a 214–80 electoral-vote landslide over Democrat Horatio Seymour. Grant eclipsed Seymour almost as decisively in campaign objects as he did in electoral votes, with better than two hundred known varieties to less than half that number for his Democratic adversary.[17] The great majority of 1868 Grant and Seymour campaign items were small, rather standardized, and

Fig. 79. 1864 Lincoln campaign items seeking to capitalize upon the impending Union victory over the Confederacy included these "Union and Liberty" and "Union Forever" ribbons. The "Peace Commissioners" variety indicates that the Civil War had not deprived Americans of a sense of humor.

generally nondescript mass-produced trinkets, primarily medalets, ferrotype badges and disks, little brass shell pins, garment buttons, and lapel studs and badges (fig. 60) combining cardboard or paper photographs and ornate brass casings. The campaign also produced many ribbons and such diverse memorabilia as bandannas, prints, and cigar cases, as well as such mass visual devices as parade flags, transparencies, paper lanterns, and cloth banners. Especially among the latter category, used in grass-roots activities rather than purchased in stores, Grant items predominated over Seymour varieties by a wide margin.

These 1868 Grant campaign items reflect a rather one-dimensional appeal to the voters, exploitation of his renown as the architect of the Union

Fig. 80. One of the few known 1864 Democratic campaign objects to exploit the racist backlash against the "Great Emancipator" Lincoln, this McClellan poster warned that a "Black Republican" victory would result in "Negro Equality" and other grim results.

triumph over the Confederacy. Grant was portrayed in military attire (nearly always identified by rank) in Currier and Ives prints and on bandannas, cigar cases, parade flags, paper lanterns (fig. 62), printed and woven ribbons, small metal tins, a most unusual figural ceramic whatnot box (fig. 81), clothing buttons, and nearly every known variety of medalet and lapel pin. Woven ribbons recalled such military milestones as Fort Donelson, Shiloh, Vicksburg, Richmond, and Appomattox. Items proclaimed Grant "Freedom's Defender," "His Country's Friend in the Hour of Danger/Protector of American Liberty," "First in the Hearts of His Soldiers," "The Hero of Appomattox," and "Serene Amidst Alarms/Inflexible in Faith/Invincible in Arms." A token hoped "May He in Wisdom Rule the Country He Has Saved." Variations of his famous declaration "I intend to fight it out on this line if it takes all summer" appeared on ribbons, tokens, and lapel pins, while his statements "I propose to move immediately on your works," and "We will all act together as one army until it is seen what can be done with the enemy" graced other items. One of the most imaginative 1868 Grant trinkets was a hinged brass pin in the shape of an army knapsack that opened to reveal a military bust portrait of the general.

Fig. 81. This unusual figural ceramic box was used as a receptacle for jewelry, pins, or other small objects or merely as a decorative piece of bric-a-brac so popular in the post–Civil War period. (Edmund B. Sullivan)

In light of the enormous importance of the civil rights issue in the 1868 impeachment controversy and subsequent presidential race, it is rather surprising that the material culture of the Grant campaign was virtually silent on the subject (with the possible exception of some objects bearing the word "liberty"). Grant items were much less evasive on another Republican passion, reminding northern voters of white southern (and by implication, Democratic) treason through what has come to be known as the politics of the bloody shirt.[18] Although few Grant items really belabored this theme overtly, many suggested that Republicanism and loyalty to the Union were synonymous entities. Tokens insisted "Loyalty Shall Govern What Loyalty Has Preserved" and "Loyalty Shall Govern the Nation," while other tokens and Currier and Ives prints were inscribed "Liberty and Loyalty." Much more blatant was a cloth transparency handmade for an Indiana parade. One side read "Seymour and Gray Uniform Aristocracy/Blair Rebel Champion" and another "Democracy Sold Out Cheap/Gone Down with Rebel Colors Flying." Such strident items were more than offset, however, by tokens, shells, ribbons, and banners bearing Grant's conciliatory edict "Let us have peace." The best of these from a thematic standpoint was a large white metal token (fig. 82) with a reverse featuring stacked muskets, a scene of a former Confederate plowing a field, and the legend "The Men Will Need Their Horses to Plow With/Appomattox."

In striking contrast, most 1868 Seymour campaign items ignored thematic legends and symbolism altogether, in part perhaps because such a large majority of them were designed and produced purely for commercial purposes. The few exceptions exhibited no unifying focus. Monetary reform, the Union, an end to military Reconstruction, and white supremacy were each promoted on small numbers of Seymour items. An unusual parade flag (fig. 83) featured a "greenback" dollar promoting Seymour, equal taxation, and paper money, a harbinger of the great currency wars ahead, and a medalet read "General Amnesty/Uniform Currency/Equal Taxes & Equal Rights." Other medalets were inscribed "Union & Constitution/Preservation of the Rights of the People" and "No North, No South/The Union Inseparable," and a Currier and Ives print picturing Seymour and running-mate Frank Blair read "Peace and Union, and Constitutional Government." The pervasive racism that characterized Democratic campaigns at every level during the late 1860s was echoed on a few Seymour items. On a medalet was the legend "White Men to Govern/The Restoration of Constitutional Liberty," an oval brass lapel pin read bluntly "This Is a White Man's Government," and a ribbon bore the inscription "Our Motto: This Is a White Man's Country; Let White Men Rule." A "5th Ward White Boys in Blue" ribbon (fig. 84) parodied the traditional Grand Army of the Republic "the boys in blue are for . . . " endorsement of Republicans.

Grant's overwhelming re-election in 1872 over "Liberal Republican"[19] challenger Horace Greeley generated something less than a bumper crop of campaign items on either side.[20] Barely one hundred varieties of 1872 presidential items have been documented altogether, for once rather evenly divided between the two major parties. Apart from a few banners, prints, lanterns, ribbons, and chintzes, a handsome matched set of hand-blown crystal goblets, and a clever pair of figural iron matchboxes (fig. 85) designed for mounting near stove or fireplace (the matches were stored in Grant's cap and Greeley's hat), 1872 campaign items consisted almost exclusively of such small trinkets as medalets, sundry lapel devices, and tiny imported telescopes (known as "Stanhopes") made of ivory with portraits of Greeley or Grant inside.

With little but a seemingly endless succession of embarrassing scandals as a first-term legacy, Grant was again presented on at least half of his 1872 items as a military hero. Half of the tokens and badges portrayed him in uniform (often identified by rank), as did the goblet, matchbox, and little ivory telescope. A token proclaimed him "Patient in Toil/Serene amidst Alarms/Inflexible in Faith/Invincible in Arms" and another commemorated Lee's surrender to him at Appomattox. A shield-shaped brass lapel pin read "1864 on to Richmond/U.S. Grant for President 1872." Echoes of the

Figs. 82 and 83. The 1868 Grant campaign medalet, with its design and quotation recalling his magnanimous treatment of the conquered Confederates at Appomattox, is an excellent example of Republican exploitation of the "Let Us Have Peace" theme on Grant's behalf, while the unusual Horatio Seymour parade flag was one of the very few 1868 Democratic objects to exploit issues of any sort, in this instance paper currency and equal taxation.

Fig. 84. This "White Boys in Blue" ribbon was one of several 1868 Horatio Seymour campaign items to echo white resentment over the range of civil and political rights being conferred upon black Americans by the Radical Republicans.

bloody shirt were apparently limited to an "1861 Liberty/1872 Loyalty" liberty cap lapel pin, while the Republican commitment to racial justice seems to have surfaced only on a token "In Honor of the 15th Amendment." A "Grant Wilson & Prosperity" token represented the sum total of known 1872 Republican efforts to exploit pocketbook issues through material culture. A splendid Currier and Ives "Workingman's Banner" (fig. 86) sought to win working-class votes by identifying Grant and his running-mate Henry Wilson, dressed appropriately, as "The Galena Tanner" and "The Natick Shoemaker." This theme was also developed on an unusual "The Natick Cobbler/The Galena Tanner 1872" jugate disk of leather.

Greeley items posed a real challenge for designers, for the absurdity of an essentially Democratic effort headed by a lifelong gadfly of Radical Republican causes made a thematic focus all but impossible. Strangely, the lone unifying link between the Democrats and the idealistic Republican defectors—outrage over the shabby scandals of Grant's first term—was not exploited on a single known Greeley campaign object (with the possible exception of a "Reform 1872" brass badge). Instead, 1872 Liberal Republican items primarily exploited the politics of personality. Greeley was identified as "The Honest Old Farmer of Chappaqua" and "The Sage of Chap-

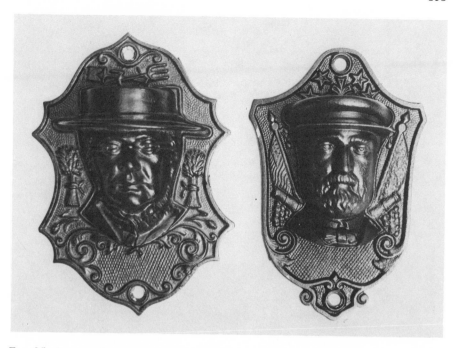

Fig. 85. Among the more unusual campaign items ever produced for an American election were these Ulysses Grant (right) and Horace Greeley figural iron match-boxes, made to be mounted near stove or fireplace. The matches were stored in Grant's cap and Greeley's hat. (Edmund B. Sullivan)

paqua" on tokens and portrayed on badges, chintzes, ferrotypes, and the aforementioned match safe and inside the ivory telescopes wearing his personal trademark, a distinctive parson's hat. Greeley's identity as an editor was reflected by badges (fig. 87) resembling quill pens bearing the adage "The Pen Is Mightier than the Sword" and by brass shells depicting Greeley as "Our Later Franklin." Currier and Ives prints insisting on "Liberty Equality & Fraternity/Universal Amnesty/Impartial Suffrage," and tokens urging "Universal Amnesty & Impartial Suffrage" attempted to tie together the reform Republican belief in Negro suffrage with the southern Democratic yearning to restore the civil rights of former Confederates. Tokens reading "Greeley Brown & Amnesty" and brass lapel pins featuring a Greeley hat hanging from clasped hands (a popular symbol of sectional reconciliation) made the case for an end to Radical Reconstruction.

Although these Greeley items were nearly five years premature in their plea for an end to Reconstruction, they were—in a direct sense, at least— the last of a generation of presidential campaign items reflecting our preoccupation with the politics of sectional conflict. In 1876, none of the more than one hundred known objects inspired by the campaigns of Rutherford B. Hayes and Samuel J. Tilden exploited sectional themes. After 1872, former generals would be occasionally portrayed in military attire, "Boys in

Fig. 86. Reflecting awareness of the growing importance of the blue-collar vote was this Currier and Ives "Workingman's Banner" depicting Grant as "The Galena Tanner" and 1872 Republican vice-presidential nominee Henry Wilson as "The Natick Shoemaker."

Fig. 87. Shaped like a quill pen and bearing the quotation "The Pen Is Mightier than the Sword," this 1872 Democratic badge paid tribute to Horace Greeley's renown as an editor while obliquely denigrating his opponent, Civil War hero Ulysses Grant.

Blue" banners (fig. 88) and ribbons made for Grand Army of the Republic groups would imply a Republican monopoly on patriotism, and the colors of Old Glory would be utilized to excess (especially on Republican items), but the sectional themes that dominated our presidential material culture through five elections would be replaced by new approaches to the hearts of the electorate.

NOTES

1. These tintype portraits of candidates, usually set into casings of brass, derived the name *ferrotype* from the thin iron plate treated with a wet collodion solution to produce the photograph. Sold at prices ranging from twenty to fifty cents each, ferrotypes were gradually supplanted as political lapel devices by the less expensive (and much less fragile) brass shell badges with albumin paper photographs.

2. For a good representation of Frémont campaign items, see Fischer and Sullivan, *Political Ribbons and Ribbon Badges*, 113–19; Collins, *Threads of History*, 140–41, 143–48; Sullivan, *Political Badges and Medalets*, 156–60; Hake, *Political Buttons*, *III*, 52–53; Sullivan, *Collecting Political Americana*, 61, 90, 115–16, 129, 134; and the illustrations accompanying Michael Kelly, "John C. Frémont and the Founding of the Republican Party," *APIC Keynoter* 85 (Summer 1985): 4–15. For a more detailed analysis of Frémont campaign material and its importance to historical

scholarship, see Roger A. Fischer, "The Republican Presidential Campaigns of 1856 and 1860: Analysis through Artifacts," *Civil War History* 27 (June 1981): 125–30.

3. George H. Mayer, *The Republican Party, 1854–1964* (New York, 1964), 45.

4. Allan Nevins, *Ordeal of the Union*, II (New York, 1947), 503.

5. See Sullivan, *Political Badges and Medalets*, 151–55; Hake, *Political Buttons, III*, 50–51; Sullivan, *Collecting Political Americana*, 64, 72–73, 82, 114–16, 129; and Fischer and Sullivan, *Political Ribbons and Ribbon Badges*, 110–13.

6. See Collins, *Threads of History*, 142–43; Sullivan, *Political Badges and Medalets*, 161–63; Fischer and Sullivan, *Political Ribbons and Ribbon Badges*, 119–22; Hake, *Political Buttons, III*, 54–55; and Sullivan, *Collecting Political Americana*, 3, 115–16, 146, 152.

7. Fitz-Henry Warren, quoted in William E. Baringer, "The Republican Triumph," in *Politics and the Crisis of 1860*, ed. Norman A. Graebner (Urbana, Ill., 1961), 93.

8. An outstanding contribution to the literature of Lincoln material culture is Harold Holzer, Gabor S. Boritt, and Mark E. Neely, Jr., *The Lincoln Image: Abraham Lincoln and the Popular Print* (New York, 1984). Another useful recent contribution is James W. Milgram, *Abraham Lincoln Illustrated Envelopes and Letter Paper, 1860–1865* (Northbrook, Ill., 1984). For an attempt to place 1860 Lincoln material culture within the context of the campaign, see Fischer, "Republican Presidential Campaigns of 1856 and 1860," 130–37. A comprehensive representation of 1860 Lincoln campaign items may be found in Fischer and Sullivan, *Political Ribbons and Ribbon Badges*, 122–30; Collins, *Threads of History*, 150–61, 163; Sullivan, *Political Badges and Medalets*, 171–213; Hake, *Political Buttons, III*, 56–63; Sullivan, *Collecting Political Americana*, 27–29, 61, 71, 73–74, 78, 82–83, 90–91, 95, 108–9, 111, 114, 116–19, 123–24, 129–31, 134, 146–48, 150, 153, 161–62, 190–91; and Herbert R. Collins, "Huzzah! Huzzah! Lincoln Torchlight Parades," *APIC Keynoter* 79, 4 (Winter 1979): 9–11.

9. After learning from old pioneer John Hanks that Lincoln had helped him split rails west of Decatur thirty years before, Oglesby procured a pair of rails identified (incorrectly, it appears) split by the pair, hid them in his barn until the Illinois Republican convention opened on May 8, 1860, then had Hanks and another grizzled pioneer march into the hall carrying the rails, decorated with banners proclaiming them as Lincoln's handiwork. The enthusiastic response assured the use of rails as Lincoln icons during the Republican national convention in June and in the subsequent general election effort. See Fischer, "Republican President Campaigns of 1856 and 1860," 132–33, William E. Baringer, *Lincoln's Rise to Power* (Boston, 1937), 181–85; Allan Nevins, *The Emergence of Lincoln*, vol. 2 (New York, 1950), 244–46; Rufus R. Wilson, ed., *Intimate Memories of Lincoln* (Elmira, N. Y., 1945), 240–47; J. M. Davis, *How Abraham Lincoln Became President* (Springfield, Ill., 1909), 63–67; and Jesse W. Weik, *The Real Lincoln* (Boston, 1922), 276–77.

10. *The Rail Splitter* (Cincinnati), Aug. 1, 8, 15, 22, 29, Sept. 5, 12, 19, 26, Oct. 3, 10, 17, 1860.

11. Charles McSorley, "The Earliest Lincoln Campaign Medalets," *Political Collector* (York, Pa.) 14 (March 1985): 1, 6, 11, 13. See also Sullivan, *Political Badges and Medalets* 191–92.

12. These banners and other objects provide persuasive if fragmentary evidence of a geographic diversity on major issues that has not been explored adequately in any of the excellent studies of the campaign since Reinhard H. Luthin, *The First Lincoln Campaign* (Cambridge, Mass., 1944).

13. See Sullivan, *Political Badges and Medalets*, 233–47, 260; Collins, *Threads of History*, 158, 161; Fischer and Sullivan, *Political Ribbons and Ribbon Badges*, 148–49; Hake, *Political Buttons, III*, 67; and Sullivan, *Collecting Political Americana*, 27, 116–17.

14. See Fischer and Sullivan, *Political Ribbons and Ribbon Badges*, 144–46; Collins, *Threads of History*, 157, 159, 161; Sullivan, *Political Badges and Medalets*, 214–32, 260; Hake, *Political Buttons, III*, 65–66; and Sullivan, *Collecting Political Americana*, 27–28, 73, 116.

15. See Sullivan, *Political Badges and Medalets*, 247–58, 260; Fischer and Sullivan, *Political Ribbons and Ribbon Badges*, 147; Hake, *Political Buttons, III*, 68; Sullivan, *Collecting Political Americana*, 27, 116, 125; and Collins, *Threads of History*, 163.

16. Comprehensive representations of 1864 Lincoln and McClellan campaign items may be found in Sullivan, *Political Badges and Medalets*, 271–328, 630; Collins, *Threads of History*, 167–72; Hake, *Political Buttons, III*, 56–64, 69–71; Fischer and Sullivan, *Political Ribbons and Ribbon Badges*, 130–32, 151–52; and Sullivan, *Collecting Political Americana*, 5, 71–72, 75, 78, 110, 134, 147.

17. For thorough representations of the material culture generated by the 1868 Grant–Colfax and Seymour–Blair campaigns, see Sullivan, *Political Badges and Medalets*, 341–400, 631–32; Fischer and Sullivan, *Political Ribbons and Ribbon Badges*, 153–56, 161–62; Hake, *Political Buttons, III*, 72–79; Collins, *Threads of History*, 175–81; and Sullivan, *Collecting Political Americana*, 29, 74–75, 83, 102, 107–8, 111, 117–18, 121, 125, 129, 134, 147–49, 152, 154, 160–61, 163, 168, 171.

18. Deriving its name from the lurid but effective tactic of inciting Republican crowds with blood-soaked shirts allegedly belonging to Union soldiers slain in battle, "waving the bloody shirt" developed into a Republican campaign staple during the incredibly bitter 1866 congressional elections and remained a useful campaign tactic for Republicans (especially in obscuring issues or blunting scandals) into the 1890s.

19. Although the Greeley–B. Gratz Brown ticket was entered in some states under the Democratic rubric (and even as "Conservatives" in some southern states), the "Liberal Republican" label was used widely in 1872 to attract the support of Republicans alienated by the Grant scandals but hesitant to cast a Democratic ballot.

20. See Sullivan, *Political Badges and Medalets*, 401–24; 632; Collins, *Threads of History*, 181, 183–86; Fischer and Sullivan, *Political Ribbons and Ribbon Badges*, 155–56, 162–63; Hake, *Political Buttons, III*, 72–77, 80–81; and Sullivan, *Collecting Political Americana*, 19, 29, 74–75, 91, 129, 139, 154.

4

Lapels Festive and Flamboyant 1876–92

Waged with uncommon enthusiasm and intensity, especially at the grass-roots level, the succession of presidential races from 1876 through 1892 provided a natural environment for the proliferation of political material culture, both in form and function. Although many historians have summarily dismissed the political wars of the period as inconsequential and irrelevant (primarily because they did not promote the modern general welfare state a half century before the voters might have accepted it),[1] the people who waged or witnessed these contests shared no such misgivings. In an era of fervent partisanship, voter turnouts were exceptionally high; the major parties were nearly equal in strength, and it mattered greatly to most Americans whether a Republican or Democrat occupied the White House. In a time of limited recreational opportunities, mass meetings, torchlight parades (fig. 88), ox-roasts (fig. 89), and the like provided millions with both entertainment and the chance to reaffirm traditional values and renew their sense of solidarity. Local political clubs—often bearing such grand names as the Utica Republican Continental Club, Young Italian Democratic Legion, and Republican Invincibles of Philadelphia—flourished as never before and never since, testimony to both the era's affinity for group organization and the pervasive localism of late nineteenth-century politics. Whatever the merits or shortcomings of the administrations they produced, these campaigns demonstrated an extraordinary element of grass-roots vitality.

A natural result was a bountiful harvest of campaign objects, especially during the close, well-funded, and vigorously contested 1884 and 1888 races. Local political clubs begat hundreds of distinctive badges, and the parades and rallies they staged begat even more plus a host of banners, standards, lanterns, customized torches, and other visual devices. In turn, the enthusiasm engendered a lucrative market for an almost infinite variety

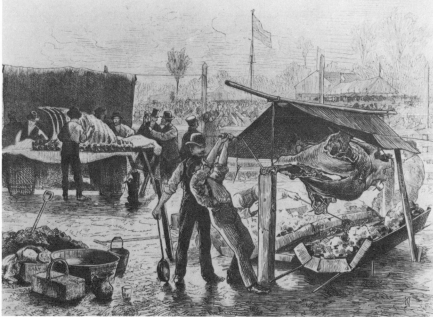

Figs. 88 and 89. Torchlight parades and ox-roasts, like these Rutherford B. Hayes celebrations in Brooklyn illustrated in *Harper's Weekly*, November 11, 1876, added a colorful participatory dimension to the political culture of late nineteenth-century America. (Smithsonian Institution)

of personal mementos. An inventory of reference volumes and major collections reveals more than two thousand varieties of campaign objects from the five elections, slightly more than three-fifths of them promoting Republican candidates. Although the Democrats continued to be generally out-trinketed, as they had been since the days of Jackson and Van Buren, the three campaigns of Grover Cleveland in 1884, 1888, and 1892 at long last established essential parity in material culture between the major parties. During the period third-party badges and other items, issued by such groups as the Prohibitionists, Greenbackers, Populists, and Equal Rightists, became a regular campaign phenomenon for the first time.

The ribbon, with more than six hundred 1876–92 varieties documented and new ones still surfacing regularly, enjoyed its greatest vogue in American politics during this period, its popularity enhanced in part by major innovations in structure and design. Pioneered as simple strips of printed cloth during the Jacksonian era, ribbons were fastened with ordinary household pins for wear as political badges and were often utilized later as bookmarks. During the sectional crisis of the 1860s it became increasingly common to use small brass or enameled patriotic lapel pins with ribbons as fasteners and ornaments. Beginning in 1880 and increasingly thereafter, however, many ribbons were manufactured with built-in pins or hangers, a few of the more elaborate celluloid or brass varieties (figs. 102, 111) even more distinctive than the ribbons themselves.

In keeping with this metamorphosis, ribbons generally became much more colorful and often much more ornate during the period. Most earlier political ribbons had featured black lithography on white or light pastel fabric, with bright coloration limited to the most part to the beautiful multicolor woven silks produced by Thomas Stevens of Coventry, England and his many imitators. In the 1880s, festive colors became the rule rather than the exception, with silver and gold inscriptions and designs on vivid reds and blues nearly as common as black on white had been a generation earlier. Purple and wine-red plush fabrics, usually trimmed with metallic gold braided fringes and tassels (fig. 90), made some of the more flamboyant ribbons of the period resemble the heavy velvet draperies and upholstery found in the more pretentious Victorian homes. Often nearly a foot in length and more than three inches wide, such ribbons were not for the excessively self-conscious. Other varieties featured such hanging attachments as brass tops and bells and tin top hats, relics of an age noted more for its partisan enthusiasm than for its conservative aesthetics.

Rivaling ribbons in popularity were the various types of smaller lapel devices (fig. 91) marketed commercially throughout the period, including several hundred different varieties of metal pin-on badges. Nearly half of these featured albumin paper or cardboard photographs of candidates set into shells stamped from thin sheets of brass or other metals. Easier and

Fig. 90. A foot or more in length and weighing several ounces each, with metallic gold inscriptions, fringes and tassels, and rich red, blue, and burgundy plush fabric, such ribbon badges as these James G. Blaine and Benjamin Harrison varieties were not for the politically self-conscious. (Kenneth J. Moran)

Fig. 91. These imaginative varieties represent only a small portion of the vast array of lapel ornaments worn by supporters of the 1880–92 presidential candidates.

less expensive to produce than ferrotypes and much more ornate, they became so popular that ferrotypes virtually became extinct as campaign devices after 1880. Introduced during the 1880 campaign, lapel studs (affixed through the buttonhole on suitcoat lapels) soon rivaled the pin-on badges in popularity. Political clothing buttons enjoyed a modest revival as well. Studs, pins, and buttons were produced in a variety of metallic finishes—some shaped like miniature flags, pistols, log cabins, brooms, knights, top hats, and bust likenesses—as well as fabric-covered and truly handsome enameled and mother-of-pearl designs. Perhaps the most distinctive lapel pieces from the period were pins featuring 1888 nominees Grover Cleveland and Benjamin Harrison, alone or with running-mates Allen Thurman and Levi Morton, carved from smoky quartz or "moonstone." Surely the most ingenious were a few mechanical brass shell badges marketed as novelties during the 1880–92 campaigns (fig. 92), including nose-thumbers appearing in 1880 and 1884 and flip-up presidential chairs produced in 1892.

Such innovative lapel ornaments had a predictable effect upon metal tokens with holes, which had been worn as badges since the 1820s. Although more than one hundred different varieties were struck for the campaigns of the period, most surviving specimens do not have holes, a strong indication that the political medalet had evolved essentially into a pocket lucky piece. In addition to the metal tokens, disks made of rubber, leather, solid celluloid, and wood (for checkers sets in some instances) were created bearing the busts of presidential candidates. Other small political trinkets included inscribed horseshoe nails and a few charms with photographs inside, among them plastic or ivory Stanhope miniature telescopes, ceramic "little brown jugs" with see-through bottoms, even rather risque little metal pigs with pictures of Cleveland, Harrison, Winfield Scott Hancock, and other luminaries visible through the anus.

Political handkerchiefs, kerchiefs, and bandannas,[2] formerly of real significance only during the 1840 and 1848 Whig campaigns of William Henry Harrison and Zachary Taylor, truly came into vogue in the late nineteenth century. This was particularly the case during the 1888 Cleveland–Benjamin Harrison "battle of the bandannas," when these gaily decorated textiles developed into a major campaign theme in their own right.[3] Although nearly 150 varieties from the 1876–92 races have been documented, the total was certainly much greater, because one retailer alone carried one hundred different styles in its 1888 catalogue. They ranged from tasteful black decoration on white linen and silk handkerchiefs, purchased by fastidious gentlemen for as much as a dollar apiece, to the flamboyantly colorful cotton bandannas (fig. 93) favored by blue-collar workers and farmers, "rattling ten-centers" that wholesaled for as little as four cents each.

Fig. 92. Among the more creative and amusing political lapel pins ever created were this 1880 James A. Garfield mechanical "nose-thumber" and an 1892 mechanical presidential chair, with a lever-activated flip-up seat featuring photographs of rivals Benjamin Harrison and Grover Cleveland.

Produced by block printing or lithography onto prehemmed squares of cotton, linen, or silk or by roller printing onto continuous lengths of fabric, handkerchiefs were perhaps the most versatile of all political objects. In addition to their obvious hygienic function (particularly essential for snuff-dippers), they could be worn by women as kerchiefs or shawls, or by men or women around the neck as scarves or cravats, but they were most commonly worn as men's pocket accessories: white linen or silk handkerchiefs were tucked neatly into breast suitcoat pockets, and bandannas usually dangled from the hip pockets of overalls or the knee-length Sunday coats of farmers and industrial workers. Political bandannas were often used directly as campaign devices. To exhibit support at conventions, parades, and rallies, they were waved by hand or attached to poles or walking-sticks. In parts of the Midwest, they were flown from buggy whips (the distant ancestors of our modern antenna flags) and were used to decorate front porches, platforms, storefronts, and campaign trains. Banners and bunting, as well

Figs. 93 and 94. During the 1880–92 presidential campaigns, colorful bandannas like the 1880 Winfield Scott Hancock variety were popular political devices, and uncut bolts of bandanna cloth were used for banners, bunting, and even parade uniforms like this 1888 Benjamin Harrison variety. (Edmund B. Sullivan)

as aprons, parasols, and even whole uniforms (fig. 94) for parade participants, were fashioned from single bandannas sewn together or from uncut
bolts of bandanna cloth. To accommodate such improvisation, one firm
marketed uncut bolts of cotton cloth containing six dozen identical patterns
to use as "flags and decorations."

In addition to the ubiquitous bandanna, a variety of other visual devices
was made and used for public events during the period. Handmade cloth
transparencies continued to see use in parades, as did the great hand-
painted banners that helped make the political procession one of the premier attractions of the age. According to a newspaper account, a parade of
Democratic veterans in Indianapolis in 1876 featured several such banners,
including a Samuel Tilden–Thomas Hendricks jugate specimen executed
by artist M. A. Fischer of Louisville distinguished by "illuminating colors,
fine golden finished lettering, and to crown it all, remarkable portraits of
both candidates that were wagered to be the handsomest in the parade."[4]
Increasingly, however, such outstanding folk art was supplanted by standardized visuals mass-produced for an Industrial Revolution electorate. Banners, bunting, and flags with black portraits or slogans on red, white, and
blue fields became the rule. Accordion-pleated paper lanterns, replaced
gradually by the hexagonal expanding variety (fig. 110), were produced very
inexpensively in enormous quantities in a few designs for use in nearly
every torchlight parade. Parade canes and noisemakers (including rattles,
horns, whistles, and ratchets) were also mass-produced to use in public
demonstrations. Although many varieties of political torches also became
rather standardized, an element of individuality managed to survive in this
genre of objects. Harrison high hat torches and James G. Blaine varieties
resembling pine cones and battle axes (figs. 150, 114) are excellent cases
in point.

Late nineteenth-century Americans appear to have had an almost insatiable appetite for decorative ornamental objects. No middle-class Victorian
home was considered fully furnished without its bric-a-brac cabinet, and
empty space on shelves or walls was regarded as a frontier to be conquered.
A host of opportunistic entrepreneurs responded with an enormous array
of glass and ceramic campaign mementos. At least one hundred known
varieties of ceramic plates were produced, most of them common household
earthenware with black or brown transfer candidate likenesses added,
although a few pieces transcended such drab aesthetics. Many ceramic
pitchers were marketed, including a handsome pink glazed variety (fig. 95)
portraying Harrison and 1888 running-mate Levi P. Morton. Portrait tiles,
used as tea-set trivets or purely as decorations, featured several candidates.
Some of these were striking "intaglios" (fig. 96) molded below tile level and
filled with a colored glaze to create attractive highlights and shadows "almost like a photograph in clay." Other political ceramic objects marketed
during this period included bread plates, bowls, creamers, mugs, pin trays,
bust and figurine statuary, even a bisque china matchbox (fig. 97) featuring

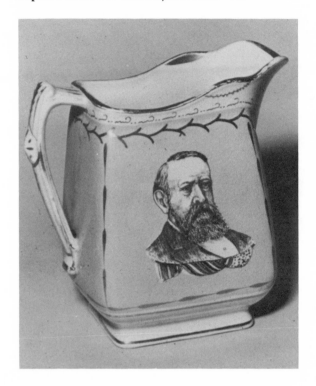

Fig. 95. One of the most distinctive and aesthetically pleasing late nineteenth-century political ceramics is this 1888 pink glazed pitcher portraying Benjamin Harrison and, on the reverse side, Levi P. Morton. (Smithsonian Institution)

a droll caricature of the era's most colorful political gadfly, Benjamin F. Butler.

Political glass bric-a-brac from the period included an assortment of tumblers with etched likenesses and legends or intaglio busts, clear and light amber mugs and cups, frosted (fig. 98) and clear plates, attractive lamp chimneys, paperweights, the first political flasks to appear in more than a generation, and such novelty items as Harrison top hat toothpick holders (fig. 113). Milk glass objects included plates, trays, wall plaques, and a most unusual Garfield shaving mug (fig. 99) with attached brush holder. Frosted figural bust likenesses (fig. 100) of many of the era's presidential candidates were marketed. In 1880, a matched set of Hancock and Garfield figural bust cologne bottles with bottom openings appeared, followed eight years later by a pair of Cleveland and Harrison pedestal bust bottles produced both in clear and extremely attractive frosted varieties.

Other political novelties created during the period included figural clay and briar pipes, brass belt buckles, portrait bridle rosettes, umbrellas, razors, a Garfield–Chester A. Arthur tin cup, and painted lead equestrian figurines of Garfield and Hancock. Several intriguing political toys and games were marketed, including an 1884 checkers set with Democrats Cleveland and Thomas Hendricks featured on the natural pieces and Republicans Blaine and John A. Logan on the black ones and an 1888 or 1892 toy (fig. 101) of Harrison and Cleveland wrestling. A few campaign lithographs were produced early in this period by Currier and Ives and other printmakers,

Figs. 96 and 97. Among the ceramic objects inspired by an almost insatiable Victorian appetite for political bric-a-brac was this Grover Cleveland intaglio tile and this Benjamin F. Butler matchbox. (Edmund B. Sullivan)

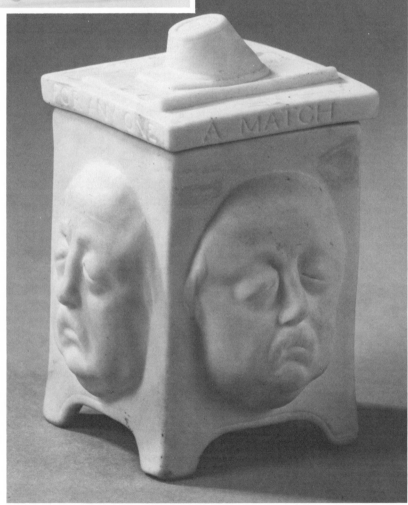

Figs. 98 and 99. These handsome frosted-glass plates featuring Cleveland and John A. Logan (matching varieties pictured 1884 running-mates Thomas A. Hendricks and James G. Blaine), and this unusual James A. Garfield milk-glass shaving mug with attached brush holder were among the many examples of political glass produced during this period. (Edmund B. Sullivan)

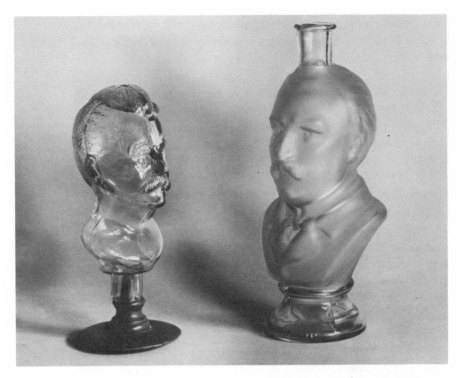

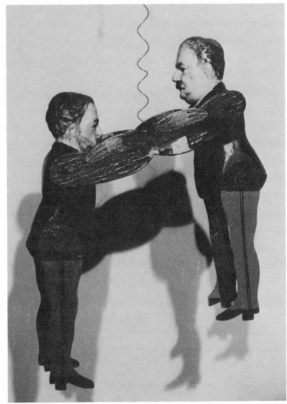

Figs. 100 and 101. Among the political novelty items available to Gilded-Age political partisans were these 1880 Hancock and 1888 Cleveland figural glass cologne bottles and an ingenious 1888 or 1892 toy featuring Harrison and Cleveland wrestling for the presidency. (Edmund B. Sullivan)

but during the 1880s such items were almost completely supplanted by inexpensive "cabinet photos" and other items made possible by the development of commercially manufactured gelatin "dry" plate.

Awesome in quantity, almost infinite in variety, and frequently unrestrained in color and design, the campaign memorabilia of the late nineteenth century provides cogent insights into the political process that inspired it. Like the ornate architecture of Victorian America, characterized by one authority as having been "founded on the rock of superb confidence,"[5] the era's equally flamboyant political material culture bears witness to the assurance and enthusiasm with which this generation waged its elective wars. A people short on faith in its political system would have been most unlikely to decorate its torsos with vivid red bandanna cloth, its lapels with tasseled and fringed ribbons a foot long, or its bric-a-brac cabinets with glass and ceramic images of its partisan idols. A generation riddled with doubts over the ability of this nominee or that one to provide able leadership would have provided a poor market for Garfield and Hancock cologne bottles, Cleveland and Blaine checkers sets, and Harrison high hat toothpick holders. In stark contrast to our modern "era of lowered expectations," when trinkets and regalia exhibiting such gaudy exuberance are common only at conventions and other gatherings of the true believers at the top of their party hierarchies, Victorian relics suggest a political grassroots untainted by cynicism or apathy. A frequent utilization of the theme and symbols of modernization provides evidence that political self-assurance was only one manifestation of a pervasive faith in American's mission.

These items may also provide some insights into the role of women in late nineteenth-century politics. At a time when only a relative handful of women enjoyed voting rights, a surprisingly large number of campaign mementos seem to have been wholly or primarily feminine in appeal. Although appreciation for decorative ceramics, glass, textiles, and other ornamental household objects may have come from men and children as well, such items were probably produced primarily to please women, for the Victorian "cult of domesticity" clearly conceded to wives' authority over home furnishings. In addition to the silk and linen handkerchiefs popular during the period, in large part as women's items, campaign objects intended solely for women included necklaces, pendants, bracelet charms, compact mirrors, and pin cushions. The wives of candidates began to appear on campaign memorabilia. In 1888, Frances Folsom Cleveland was featured on posters, plates, handkerchiefs, playing cards, table napkins, tokens, ribbons, song sheets, and advertising cards hawking fabric, tonic, and "The Thread that Binds the Union." Whether or not one accepts Edith Mayo's interesting and rather convincing hypothesis that both parties appear to have wooed women more before they received the vote than afterward,[6] there is no question that these artifacts indicate that women were widely regarded as an influential factor in determining how their husbands would vote (thus lending a measure of integrity to the argument advanced by anti-suffragists that women already voted indirectly).

In one important respect campaign relics provide a fundamentally flawed reflection of late nineteenth-century presidential politics, for they convey very little of the basic meanness that characterized these campaigns. At a time when opposition standard-bearers were almost routinely portrayed as philanderers, thieves, or unpatriotic slackers (even closet Roman Catholics), only a relative handful of campaign objects resorted to character assassination. The few that did were invariably pocket trinkets, ribbons, or parade visuals, not items manufactured for household decoration (in keeping with the prevailing concept of the Victorian home as a wholesome sanctuary from the unpleasantries of public life).

Abusive or genteel, barely more than a hundred varieties of campaign items—primarily lapel badges, tokens, and ribbons—survive from the spirited but poorly financed 1876 contest between Republican Rutherford B. Hayes and Democrat Samuel J. Tilden.[7] The objects that did appear in this depression year were rarely thematic, for the public was growing weary of Reconstruction, both parties were split internally on economic policy, and both nominees were so widely associated with honest government that neither party could advantageously usurp the mantle of reform. Several items saluted a century of independence by promoting both tickets as the "Centennial Candidates," although neither slate could really claim much credit for that national milestone. Attempts to exploit the reform issue were largely limited to an "Honest Money/Honest Government" Hayes token, one proclaiming Tilden "The Aggressive Leader of Reform," and a satiric silk banner carried by a group of Greenfield, Indiana, Democratic veterans in an Indianapolis parade bearing the alliterative reminder of many Grant scandals "Republican Reformers—Blaine, Belknap, Babcock and Shepherd."[8] Fervent Republican efforts to wave once more the bloody shirt resulted in a few veterans' "Boys in Blue" ribbons and parade banners (fig. 88), but for the first time in a generation the sectional crisis failed to dominate the material culture of a presidential election.[9]

Although the Hayes–Tilden contest was characterized by a generous measure of mudslinging, the only known items to reflect such nastiness are a trio of satirical postelection "Shammy" Tilden tokens produced by George H. Lovett for fellow New Yorker Isaac F. Wood. One pronounces the Democratic party dead of "Tildenopathy." Another portrays a coffin atop a bier inside the epitaph "Here Lies Our Little Tilden Dear/He Died of Reform 'Loquendi-Rhoea' [verbal diarrhea]." The third exults that Tilden has been "Ciphered Out" (perhaps an echo of Tammany's "Honest John" Kelly's celebrated allusion to Tilden as "the old humbug of Cipher Alley") because "Shammy the Shameless Cheats Uncle Sam on His Income Tax," a reference to an August 1876, *New York Times* allegation that Tilden had submitted a falsified 1863 federal tax return.

The 1880 race between Republican James A. Garfield and Democrat Winfield Scott Hancock engendered a volume of lapel ornaments and medalets similar to 1876 but a much more copious array of textile objects and ceramic, glass, and miscellaneous memorabilia (figs. 92, 93, 99, 100),[10] perhaps a reflection of an improving economy. With Hancock a stranger to civilian politics and Garfield compulsively eager to please everyone (he "could not face a frowning world," Hayes complained), 1880 was a rather lean year for meaningful issues. Only five known relics of the campaign—an "Equality All Men" Garfield chintz, a "Union/Freedom/Education" Garfield ribbon, two Garfield ribbons promoting a protective tariff, and a torch portraying Hancock with the motto "The Subordination of the Military to the Civilian Power"[11]—can be characterized as truly issue-oriented, and three of those looked primarily to the past.

The odd phenomenon of savage campaigns that did not beget equally nasty material culture occurred again in 1880. An anti–Garfield token urging that he be sent up the "Salt River" on the "Chinese Line"[12] may well have been the really negative object produced. No known badges, trinkets, or bric-a-brac denigrated Hancock's dubious qualifications, south-ern treason, Garfield's alleged $329 profit from the Credit Mobilier scheme, or his running-mate Chester Arthur's reputation as a spoilsman, although oratory and literature from both camps reeked of character assassination and "329" scribbled on fences and out-houses helped pioneer the art of America political graffiti.[13] As a matter of fact, the only two known 1880 campaign items to make reference to the $329 were both Republican rib-bons seeking to make light of the affair, a "Norwich Garfield Rockets/329" club badge and an unusual cartoon ribbon depicting Hancock and running-mate William H. English on a Cuyahoga River canal barge being low-bridged by a wooden bridge decorated with "329" graffiti.

At least in terms of its material culture, 1880 was more than anything else the year of the generals. Hancock was portrayed in uniform and iden-tified by rank on badges, bandannas, and tokens (one saluting him as "A Superb Soldier"). A token utilized the cloverleaf symbol of Hancock's 2nd Army Corps, as did the "Little Gem Corps Badge" and "Hancock Army Corps Pin" wholesaled by Gaynor and Fitzgerald of New Haven at prices ranging from two cents apiece for brass pins to six cents each for gold-plated ones. Garfield was identified by rank on ribbons, lauded as "Farmer/Scholar/ Soldier/Statesman" on bandannas, and acclaimed as the "Soldier's Friend" on lapel pins. Another pin featured the acorn symbol of the 14th Army Corps. Painted lead statues of both candidates on horseback portrayed them in military regalia and identified them by rank. Among the items promoting the third-term aspirations of Ulysses Grant were some military bust ribbons and medalets, one proclaiming him "Grant the Preserver," and a "Let Us Have Peace" ribbon.[14]

The most creative thematics on any 1880 campaign objects reflected Garfield's rags-to-riches rise from a log cabin and a poverty-stricken boyhood spent as a canal boy along the Cuyahoga River. Medalets bearing such inscriptions as "Canal Boy 1845/President 1881" and "From the Tow Path to the White House" featured vignettes of a lad on horseback towing a

Figs. 102 and 103. Among the more cleverly designed 1880 campaign badges were this Garfield "Cuyahoga" ribbon hanger, commemorating his Horatio Alger rise from Cuyahoga River canal boy, and the Hancock ("hand-cock") rebus puzzle lapel pins below.

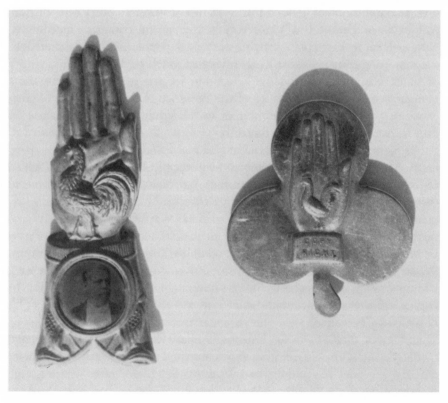

barge. One ribbon presented the Garfield–Arthur slate as the "Towpathers' Ticket," and another (fig. 102) came suspended from a creative brass "Cuyahoga" hanger in the shape of a canal barge. The closest that Demo-cratic campaign items could come to such personality politics was a medalet describing Hancock somewhat grandiloquently as "A Combination and a Form Indeed Where Every God Did Seem to Set His Seal to Give the World Assurance of a Man." The most imaginative of all Hancock items were an unusual clay pipe, some brass pins (fig. 103), and other curios that utilized a hand and a rooster to create a hand-cock rebus puzzle of his name, the first political rebus items since 1856 and 1860, when the names Buchanan and Bell provided similar opportunities.

The year 1884 was a vintage one for the politics of material culture in quantity, variety, design, and thematics alike. With the Republicans depart-ing from a tradition of bland compromise candidates by turning to the dynamic and controversial James G. Blaine, the Democrats enjoying their best chance in a quarter-century to regain the White House with Grover Cleveland, some colorful splinter-party entries, intense public interest, and a healthy economy, the 1884 contest provided a natural environment for campaign badges and other regalia, visuals, trinkets, and bric-a-brac. With more than five hundred varieties known, 1884 apparently inspired a harvest of campaign objects greater than any American presidential race since the "great commotion" of 1840. More varieties of virtually every type of cam-paign object appeared in 1884 than in the several contests preceding it, with ribbons in particular enjoying enormous popularity. Full pocketbooks and campaign war chests on both sides had much to do with the quantity of items manufactured and marketed, but for the most part, 1884 was a banner year for objects because of the presence of Blaine, a man of great charisma and controversy of whom it was said that "men went insane over him in pairs, one for and one against."

His detractors[15] may have thought him flashy and corrupt, but to support-ers he had been the "Plumed Knight" ever since Robert G. Ingersoll's fabled 1876 nominating speech in Cincinnati, an identity that helped give to 1884 Republican material culture an element of personality lacking in re-cent campaigns.[16] According to historian H. Wayne Morgan, "The Blaine marchers were spectacular. One of their parades featured hundreds of men in white papier-mache suits of armor, complete with tall plumes and swords. When it rained, marchers donned suitably embossed capes and high hats, adding a touch of the debonair to the charmingly absurd."[17] Plumed knight parade canes (fig. 104) were produced, as were battle-axe torches (fig. 105) designed to be carried over the shoulder instead of held upright. Plumed knight lapel pins, clothing buttons, ribbons and hangers, badges, and medalets (including a striking variety featuring a knight on rampant charger and the legend "We Will Follow Where the White Plume Waves") were marketed, as were handsome enameled metal lapel pins shaped like a

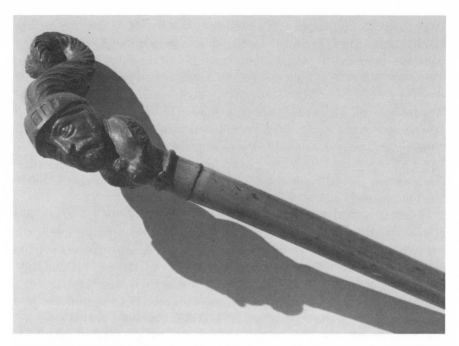

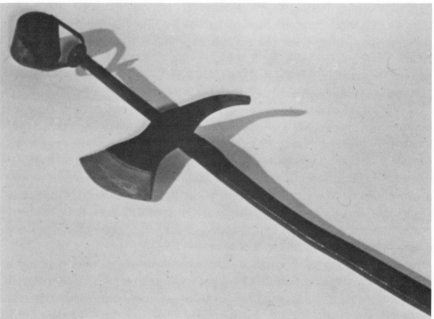

Figs. 104 and 105. This "Plumed Knight" figural Blaine parade cane and battle-axe parade torch (cleverly designed to be carried over the shoulder without dripping hot oil on the marcher) were among the many 1884 Republican objects used in demonstrations to salute Blaine's identity as the Plumed Knight. (Edmund B. Sullivan)

knight's shield. Plumes waved by hand or attached to sticks or canes became familiar sights in rallies and along Republican parade routes. Not since the Abraham Lincoln split rail in 1860 had a political symbol been exploited with such creativity. Other Blaine campaign items featured the pinecone symbol of his state of Maine, sometimes accompanied by the motto "The Woods Are Full of Them." Running-mate John A. Logan, a Civil War general and Grand Army of the Republic mainstay immensely popular with Union veterans, was symbolized on campaign ribbons by the symbol of Logan's Corps, an ammunition pouch inscribed "40 Rounds U. S.," virtually the only 1884 Republican items to attempt to exploit the sectional crisis in any way.[18]

Blaine campaign items were not wholly given over to pinecones and plumes and the like, however. An avid disciple of tariff protection as the key to industrial growth and job opportunities, his energetic efforts to build a new Republican urban-industrial constituency by turning his campaign into a referendum on tariff policy were not entirely successful, but did inspire the first substantial body of campaign objects to address the new economic issues of the industrial age. Tokens and ribbons read "Protection to American Industry," a bunting was printed "Blaine and Protection," and a pearl clothing button urged "Reciprocity/Blaine/Protection." A ribbon featured a scene of merchants and sailors loading cases and barrels on a busy pier, symbolizing the prosperity that would result from a protectionist Blaine presidency, and a medalet struck by G. B. Soley of Philadelphia featured a hammer and muscular arm and the uncompromising inscription "Protection/No British Pauper Wages for Americans."

With ample campaign funds for the first time in memory (in large part because their parsimonious "gold-bug" standard-bearer presented no threat to eastern business conservatives) and popular support sufficient to eke out a narrow victory in November, the 1884 Democratic canvass on behalf of Cleveland and running-mate Thomas Hendricks inspired the greatest variety and volume of campaign objects in the long history of the Democratic party up to that time.[19] From a thematic standpoint, however, all but about a dozen of the more than two hundred documented 1884 Cleveland campaign items were as dull as the nominee himself, limited exclusively to legends and images providing primary identification. A stodgy, pompous man known as "Uncle Jumbo" to his nieces and nephews, Cleveland could not compete with the Plumed Knight in personality politics; an essentially negative statesman (dubbed by opponents in Albany the "Veto Governor" and "His Obstinacy") heading a party trying to paper over internal economic conflicts, he could not vie with Blaine in the arena of substantive issues. Apart from a "Free Trade" lapel pin, all known thematic 1884 Cleveland objects sought to exploit his reputation for integrity (and, by implication at least, Blaine's for corruption) with such legends as "Reform" and "Public Office a Public Trust."

Although the 1884 race was extraordinarily vicious and personal, the material objects it inspired were once again polite to a fault. Cleveland's gift of a bastard child to one Maria Halpin may have produced chants of "Ma, Ma, Where's My Pa?," but no echoes on Republican campaign items. Disclosure that he had personally hanged two Irishmen during a stint as a county sheriff inspired only a Boston pamphlet dubbing him "The Hangman Candidate."[20] Allegations that Blaine had enjoyed sexual relations with his wife before their marriage, that he was a clandestine Catholic, and that he was dying of palsy, leprosy, or Bright's Disease did not find their way onto Democratic badges, trinkets, or visuals. Even the "Mulligan letters" controversy that may have cost Blaine the presidency in 1876 when it broke, and again in 1884 when it was conveniently revived by the persistent Mulligan, apparently inspired only a defiant "Don't Care a DAMN for the Mulligan Letters" Republican ribbon from Ohio. An "I Told You So!" Democratic ribbon bore the bust of the Reverend Samuel Burchard, the Presbyterian divine whose snide characterization of the Democrats as the "party of rum, Romanism, and rebellion" proved deadly to Blaine in Irish constituencies, and a satiric token mocked both Blaine for his silence on the "rum, Romanism, rebellion" slur and Cleveland as the "United South/ Renegade Press/Free Traders" candidate. Both were clearly postelection pieces, however, and not campaign items.

Although third-party candidacies with broad-based public support had engendered many material objects before this time, 1884 was really the first presidential election to experience a significant volume of campaign items produced on behalf of (or in opposition to) splinter-party movements. Generally unrestrained in enthusiasm for the cause and never inhibited by a need to ignore or straddle issues to avert defeat, such objects were commonly much more expressive than the major-party campaign items of the period. The 1884 Prohibitionist ticket of John P. St. John and William Daniel inspired ribbons, various trinkets, and a few lapel pins, the most creative of which featured the names of the candidates across an upside-down wine glass. The National Greenback Labor party candidacy of perennial lost-cause gadfly Benjamin Butler inspired several lapel pins and ribbons (including one urging "Equal Rights/Equal Burdens/Equal Powers/And Equal Privileges for All People Under the Law"). His penchant for unpopular causes and a face magnificently prone to caricature (fig. 97) inspired a host of satiric creations, among them a soap figure accenting his droopy eyelid, an iron bank portraying him as a frog,[21] and a number of cartoons and cards presenting him in various absurd situations and costumes (fig. 106). Two pro–Butler lapel pins utilizing spoon motifs (fig. 107), a parody on his identity as "Silver Spoons Butler" for allegedly leaving his occupational command in New Orleans during the Civil War with a coffin full of silver spoons, demonstrates a capacity for self-deprecation rare among public figures. The Equal Rights candidacy of feminist Belva Ann Lockwood

Figs. 106 and 107. This droll card depicting political gadfly Benjamin Butler as an unlikely cherub and these lapel pins, using silver spoons to evoke memories of his days as "Silver Spoons Butler," scourge of occupied New Orleans, were inspired by Butler's 1884 campaign as presidential nominee of the Greenback Labor party.

inspired a rebus ribbon and some creative satire items, including a card with a pop-up skirt with Butler (also a suffragist) hiding beneath it.

With the colorless Cleveland (paired with the aged and infirm Allen Thurman) running against Republican Benjamin Harrison, a man so dour and remote he was nicknamed "the human iceberg," producers of campaign items in 1888 might well have surrendered in dismay and simply rested for four years. They did not, however, and the result was an enormous outpouring of material culture that surpassed even 1884 in volume, variety, and creativity.[22] More than seven hundred varieties of 1888 campaign items are known, at least two-thirds of them inspired by the $3,300,000 Republican effort on behalf of Harrison and Levi Morton. Not since the 1840 "great commotion" sent Harrison's grandfather to the White House had a campaign engendered such a variety of material objects, and the total inspired by all 1888 entries surpassed even that of 1840. More than half of all known 1888 items are textiles, primarily ribbons and handkerchiefs, but 1888 was also a productive year for lapel studs and pins, glass and ceramic bric-a-brac, and such miscellaneous geegaws as caneheads, umbrellas, pocket watches, toys, razors, and clay pipes. Never in the long history of political material culture have the men and women who design campaign objects done so much with so little.

Although the majority of 1888 Cleveland items were as unimaginative as most of his 1884 ones had been, a larger number sought to exploit substantive issues and personality politics than had been the case four years earlier. Several tokens and bandannas echoed the 1884 honest government theme, either with the maxim "A Public Office Is a Public Trust" or the symbolism of crossed brooms (fig. 108). A cloth stud carried a plea for civil service reform, the only known 1888 Cleveland item to do so despite the importance of the issue in winning over Republican and independent "Mugwump" reformers in 1884. Bandannas, ribbons, and studs proclaimed the virtues of tariff reduction with such phrases as "Tariff Reform," "For Revenue Only," "No Surplus," and "Low Taxes," carefully avoiding the "Free Trade" slogan Republicans were seeking to saddle the Democratic donkey with. Cleveland items engaging in the politics of personality wisely excluded the nominee, with the exception of a jugate bandanna proclaiming the president and Thurman "Our Study Leaders," a singularly unfortunate choice of words in light of Cleveland's massive girth. His marriage to the appealing Frances Folsom provided better opportunities; she was an attractive woman in her own right, and her presence helped counteract the "Ma, Ma, Where's My Pa?" image of Cleveland as a profligate whoremonger. In 1888, "Frankie" appeared on song sheets, posters, playing cards, handkerchiefs, ribbons, trade cards, napkins, plates, and several varieties of tokens (identifying her as "The Nation's Favorite Belle") and might have become even more of a campaign icon if her husband had not objected vigorously to this as undignified.[23]

Figs. 108 and 109. During the "Wave High the Red Bandanna" campaign of 1888, this crossed brooms (symbolizing a "sweeping clean the stables" of government reform theme) Cleveland–Allen Thurman variety and this patriotic and protectionist Harrison–Levi P. Morton variety were just two of hundreds of designs marketed.

The primary inspiration for 1888 Democratic personality politics, however, was provided by a rather unlikely source, Cleveland's tottering septuagenarian running-mate, Allen Thurman. A renowned snuff-dipper, Thurman was rarely seen in public without the ubiquitous red bandanna that became his trademark to such an extent that his nomination prompted supportive delegates to tie bandannas to Cleveland standards and a critic to grumble, "You have nominated a pocket handkerchief!" Essentially by default, the red bandanna—both the plain style immortalized by Thurman and many patterns with portraits and slogans printed expressly for political use—soon developed into the dominant symbol of the Democratic campaign, utilized in more diverse ways than any other type of political artifact before or since. A favored form of campaign activity was "bandanna dancing," in at least one instance an inspiration for cloth invitations resembling miniature bandannas. Banners, bunting, and several ribbons featured bandannas as symbols. Issue after issue during the campaign, the fervently anti–Cleveland humor weekly *Judge* featured multicolored cover and centerfold cartoons by Bernhard and Victor Gillam and other artists utilizing red bandannas as satiric devices—a sinking Cleveland dinghy featuring a red bandanna sail, Cleveland auctioning American jobs to John Bull under a "Cleveland and Thurman Auctioneers" red bandanna, Cleveland and other party leaders drying their eyes with red bandannas over a Democratic donkey dying from the strain of pulling a "Free Trade" wagon, and Cleveland lying dazed in a ravine with a "Free Trade" red bandanna pinned to his rump, to mention only a few. Never before or since has political material culture played a role so prominent in the cartoon art of a presidential campaign.

Saddled with a less colorful vice-presidential candidate and a glacial presidential nominee married to a rather sedate woman far less glamorous than "Frankie" Cleveland, the Republicans might have been forced to forgo personality politics altogether in 1888 if their "human iceberg" had not been the grandson of the legendary William Henry Harrison. As a result, the 1888 Republican campaign inspired an orgy of nostalgia unrivaled in American politics before or since. Log cabins were erected as Harrison headquarters in many communities, many of them equipped with barrels of hard cider. Tippecanoe clubs sprouted up throughout the land, often made up of men who had participated in the 1840 "great commotion." One such club in Harrison's Marion County, Indiana, composed of men from 75 to 101 years of age, marched through a rainstorm on July 4 in review for "Old Tip's" grandson to celebrate the official Notification Day. The practice of rolling huge parade balls (fig. 25) enjoyed a modest revival, with a steel-ribbed specimen fourteen feet in diameter and forty-two feet in circumference—decorated with such slogans as "Tippecanoe and Morton Too"—rolled from Cumberland, Maryland, to Harrison's home in Indianapolis and then another five thousand miles through the Midwest.[24]

This log-cabin revival inevitably found expression in a host of 1888 Republican campaign items. Ribbons, lanterns (fig. 110), bandannas, and studs urged "Tippecanoe and Morton Too!" Medalets, bandannas, ribbons (fig. 111), studs, brass shell lapel pins, and charms featured log-cabin motifs. One such medalet featured an obverse struck from the die of an 1840 "The Log Cabin Candidate/The People's Choice" token and a reverse calling attention to the fact. A brass log-cabin Benedict and Burnham clothing button was identical to one created by the firm in 1840 except for the legend "1840/1888." "Our Country's Hope" ribbons (fig. 112) duplicated a popular 1840 pattern, only with Benjamin's face substituted for his grandfather's. Other ribbons proclaimed him "A Chip Off the Old Block." Porcelain cider-barrel studs were marketed. "Tippecanoe and Morton Too" ribbons were made with hangers featuring log cabins, cider barrels, and coonskins.

One result of Democratic protests that their opponent in 1888 was not a long-dead folk hero but his grandson was their campaign song, "His

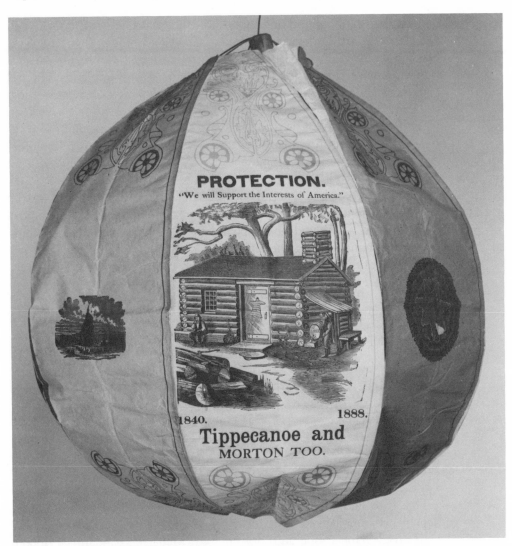

Fig. 110. Typical of many 1888 Republican campaign items, this hexagonal paper log-cabin lantern almost makes it seem as if the candidate were the long-dead William Henry Harrison instead of his grandson Benjamin. (Smithsonian Institution)

Grandfather's Hat," gibing that it was too big for Benjamin to fill. Republican songsmiths quickly came back with "The Same Old Hat," insisting on a perfect fit, and producers of campaign trinkets and curios responded with a variety of "Same Old Hat" objects that added a new dimension to 1888 Republican personality politics. Many varieties of hat-shaped toothpick holders made of clear, amber, and milk glass (fig. 113) and other materials made their appearance, as did ornamental little hats made of brass, terra cotta, papier mache, porcelain, and macerated currency. Several

Figs. 111 and 112. Excellent examples of the exploitation of 1840 nostalgia on 1888 Benjamin Harrison campaign items are this "Tippecanoe and Morton Too" ribbon with superb brass log-cabin hanger authentic down to the cider barrel, coonskin, and dangling latchstring, and this "Harrison & Reform" ribbon, a copy of an 1840 variety with Benjamin Harrison's bust substituted for his grandfather's.

varieties of lapel pins and studs were shaped like hats or utilized hat designs, as did a glass paperweight. Among the many types of lighting devices used to illuminate Harrison–Morton torchlight parades were figural hat torches (fig. 114).

Republican material culture in 1888 was not all log cabins, cider barrels, and beaver hats, however, for the Harrison effort was more than anything else a crusade for the protective tariff. Bandannas, tokens, lapel pins, studs, ribbons, posters, and other objects prompted the issue with such slogans as "Protect Home Industry" (fig. 109), "Tippecanoe and Tariff Too," "Protection to American Homes," "Harrison and Protection," or simply "Protection." Use of the issue to court blue-collar support was reflected by "Protection for American Labor" ribbons, studs, bandannas, and clay pipes and by tokens with pie-shaped wedges removed that read "Your Wages Under Free Trade/What Matters if Prices Are Reduced if Wages Drop to Free Trade Levels?" Posters and ribbons contrasted scenes of industrial prosperity under "Protection" with scenes of industrial desolation under "Free Trade." The protectionist impulse inspired a handmade satiric three-sided transparency (fig. 115) depicting Cleveland fishing in "Salt River" for "Defeat" with "Free Trade" bait and a postelection leather disk with an urn bearing "Free Trade" ashes. One of the few other known 1888 put-down objects was a marching banner (fig. 116) copied from a *Judge* cartoon by F. Victor Gillam gibing Cleveland's vetoes of veterans' pension bills.

The Republican campaign and many items that it inspired sought to equate protection with patriotism and tariff reduction with subservience to British interests. Late in the campaign Harrison reviewed a parade of business clubs featuring a man riding a bull with a banner that read "John Bull Rides the Democratic Party and We Ride John Bull"[25] Tokens again insisted "No British Pauper Wages for Americans." "True blue Republican" cotton bandannas demanded "Protection & Prosperity/Home Markets for Home Industries/American Wages the Highest/No Competition with Half Paid Labor." Red, white, and blue handkerchiefs featuring flag designs proclaimed "The Stars and Stripes Will Always Wave for Protection." A Grand Army of the Republic handkerchief insisted upon "The Old Flag and Protection." Like this Civil War veterans' momento, the enormous number of trinkets and textiles exploiting Old Glory or myriad design variations symbolized the Republican attempt to perpetuate a patriotic image in the transition from the sectional crisis to an era of new economic concerns.

Ironically, the 1888 campaign item best utilized for this purpose was not a Republican variety, but rather a little woven Cleveland ribbon, produced by the W. H. Grant Company of Coventry, England, that cleared customs in New York on June 5, 1888, a day before Cleveland was formally nominated in St. Louis for another term. Conveniently ignoring the facts that Cleveland was virtually unopposed within his party in 1888 and that Grant had produced the ribbons for general retail distribution rather than for the

Figs. 113 and 114. Among the many top hat 1888 Benjamin Harrison items exploiting the "Same Old Hat" theme were these glass toothpick holders and this figural torch.

Democratic party, *Judge* on its October 6 cover (fig. 117) "exposed" (accompanied by snippets from British newspapers lauding Cleveland's antiprotectionist policies) this "Pauper Labor Badge" as damning evidence that the "English knew whom they wanted!"[26]

With Ben Butler on the sidelines and Belva Ann Lockwood's second Equal Rights party presidential bid a symbolic gesture at best, 1888 was not the year for creative splinter-party objects that 1884 had been. The Lockwood candidacy apparently inspired only an updated version of her

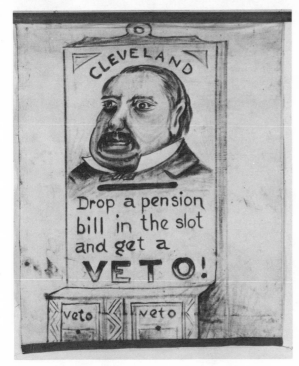

Figs. 115 and 116. Two of the few known essentially negative 1888 campaign items, this unusual triangular transparency and parade banner, both handmade, poke fun at Cleveland's tariff ideas and use of the presidential veto. The banner represents a copy of F. Victor Gillam's *Judge* cartoon "A Campaign Medley." (Smithsonian Institution)

earlier rebus ribbon. The United Labor party effort of Alson J. Streeter produced a jugate shell badge, a stud, and a token. More prolific were the Prohibitionists, with nominee Clinton Bowen Fisk featured on several ribbons, tokens, lapel pins, and studs and a "Dare to Do Right" stickpin.

The 1892 Harrison–Cleveland rematch produced almost none of the excitement of 1888. Harrison seemed immobilized by his wife's impending death, Cleveland fished in Buzzard's Bay, and the voters dozed. One result was an array of campaign objects considerably diminished from 1884 and 1888,[27] especially organizational ribbons, visual devices, and other sorts of items generally inspired by participatory activities. Political material culture of 1892 was even more limited in creativity than in volume, with most objects either duplicating 1888 thematics or avoiding them altogether. With

VOL. 14 NO. 364   OCTOBER 6 1888.   PRICE 10 CENTS.

Judge

ENTERED AT THE POST OFFICE AT NEW YORK AS SECOND-CLASS MATTER.   COPYRIGHT 1888 BY THE JUDGE PUBLISHING CO.

AWARDED 7 HIGHEST PRIZE
MEDALS & DIPLOMAS.

London, 1885.

W. H. GRANT,
Sole Inventor and Manufacturer.
FOLESHILL, COVENTRY.

INVOICE RECEIVED JUNE 5TH
CLEVELAND NOMINATED JUNE 6TH

AWARDED 7 HIGHEST PRIZE
MEDALS & DIPLOMAS.

London, 1885.

W. H. GRANT,
Sole Inventor and Manufacturer.
FOLESHILL, COVENTRY.

INVOICE RECEIVED JUNE 5TH
CLEVELAND NOMINATED JUNE 6TH

WHAT ENGLAND THINKS OF IT.

The main question at issue is English free trade against the continental system of protection.—*London Sunday Times, July 15.*

The American election is infinitely more important to Englishmen than their own internal politics just at this juncture.

The result of the American election will help to decide many important issues in Great Britain.—LONDON SUNDAY TIMES, JULY 15.

FROM "THE LONDON DAILY NEWS."

President Cleveland shows that he is the Free-Trade candidate in everything but name. The reservation is an important one for American party purposes. The President feels compelled to characterize the attempt to brand him as a Free Trader as deception, but for all that THE ELECTORAL CONFLICT NOW IN PROGRESS IS A CONFLICT BETWEEN FREE TRADE AND PROTECTION AND NOTHING ELSE.

Haddingtonshire Courier: We may look to an impetus being given to our home trade that will go far to make up for the depression of late years.

London Globe: Mr. Cleveland has taken his stand on free trade. * * * And on that broad question Mr. Cleveland's candidature naturally and necessarily carries English sympathy.

London News: The electoral conflict now in progress is a conflict between free trade and protection and nothing less. The stone now set rolling will not stop until it has broken the idol of protection to pieces.

It may be admitted that large reductions in the duties on imported manufactured goods would produce great distress in many parts of the United States. The free importation of iron, coal and wool would be a great boon to British producers. * * * If once the United States finds herself on the road to free trade she will hardly know where to stop.—*The Scotsman, Dec. 10.*

If President Cleveland should be able to carry out his plan for admission into America free of duty, one of the first effects which would be produced on the English iron trade would be the transference of much of the enormous stocks of pig iron in the Scotch and Cleveland markets to United States ports. Shipments of hematites from Scotland and from the west coast of England would also increase. The iron-ore mines of Lancashire and West Cumberland would be certain to do a greatly enlarged trade with the United States. The future course of events will be watched with considerable interest by the British iron trade.—*London Colliery Guardian, December 16, 1887.*

THE PAUPER LABOR BADGE!
Enormous quantities of this English Silk Badge passed the Custom House, June 5th.—Cleveland was nominated June 6th.
The English knew whom they wanted!

Fig. 117. On its October 6, 1888, cover, the pro-Harrison humor weekly *Judge* used this Cleveland "Pauper Labor Badge" imported from Coventry, England, as "proof" that Cleveland was a pawn of the sinister British mercantile interests. (Edmund B. Sullivan)

Harrison's incumbency militating against another nostalgia craze, the known 1892 Republican items featuring hats or 1840 symbols or slogans could be counted on one hand. With Adlai Stevenson replacing Thurman as Cleveland's running-mate, bandanna mania appears to have followed its inspiration into retirement. In 1892, the designers of campaign regalia and souvenirs finally ran out of ways to promote the human iceberg and His Obstinacy through the politics of personality.

Harrison items echoed the call for tariff protection with such slogans as "Protect Home Industry," "Protection and Reciprocity," and "Republican Protection." Ribbons with sheep-shaped brass hangers that read "Home Market" promoted Harrison and woolen duties. Protection for American tin plate was urged by "Protection/American Tin/Reciprocity" ribbon badges featuring hanging "American Tin" high hat attachments and by miniature tin plates demanding "American Tin/Our Country First Protect Home Industries." Two million miniature tin plates, produced for the American Protective Tariff League, promoted the APTL's pet cause with this verse:

> Protection's banner guards our land
> From England's greed and pauper pay;
> And when I play Great Britain's hand,
> Please take me for a blooming jay.

In response, the Cleveland campaign commmittee distributed tin rectangular cards pointing out that "American" tin plate was made with British steel, Australian tin, and African oil on British machines by illegal British aliens.[28] Other Democratic items reiterated the party's traditional economic priorities with such slogans as "Tariff Reform," "Tariff for Revenue," and "Government Economy." Several Cleveland items again exploited the integrity issue with broomstick symbolism or the familiar maxim "Public Office a Public Trust." A clever 1892 Democratic trinket was an enameled stud, inspired by Republican efforts to enact legislation enforcing the civil rights of southern Negroes, depicting a Harrison high hat in a soup kettle inscribed "No Force Bill."

On the whole, however, neither Cleveland nor Harrison objects were nearly as imaginative as those produced for 1892 hopeful and third-party candidacies. James G. Blaine's final flirtation with the presidency inspired "The People's Choice" ribbons, helmeted and plumed convention standards, and other items during the brief interval between his "shotgun resignation" as secretary of state on June 4, 1892, and Harrison's renomination in Minneapolis six days later. Blaine's refusal to disavow a presidential draft inspired perhaps the most interesting of all 1892 campaign pieces, a "'Blocks of Five' or the Administration Puzzle" game issued by the *New York World* that offered $100 to the player who solved the "Blaine Is In. How Can Harrison Get Him Out?" puzzle in the shortest time.[29] Democratic hopefuls

David Hill and Horace Boies were promoted on ribbons worn at the party's Chicago convention. The Prohibitionist candidacy of John Bidwell inspired some cloth-covered studs, one a clever rebus design, and a few ribbons. Several ribbons were printed for supporters of the People's party ticket of James B. Weaver and James G. Field. Some of them reflected the Populist ideological imperatives and "raise less corn and more hell" spirit with such legends as "Equality Before the Law," "Homes for the Toilers," "Equal Rights to All Special Privileges to None," and "The Issues: Money, Land and Transportation." Like the crusade they represented, these ribbons were harbingers of a new era dawning in American elective politics. One in particular, demanding "Free & Unlimited Coinage" of silver, prophesied the great "Battle of the Standards" just ahead.

NOTES

1. The consensus indictment of Gilded-Age politics as "an era of evasion, avoidance, and postponement, glazed over with a mix of flamboyant rhetoric and sterile purposes" may be in retreat at long last, due in large part to the insistence of such scholars as H. Wayne Morgan and Geoffrey Blodgett that we judge the period in terms of its own priorities and problems rather than imposing the yardstick of post-New Deal hindsight. For an excellent analysis of this trend, see Blodgett, "A New Look at the Gilded Age: Politics in a Cultural Contest," in *Victorian America*, ed. Daniel Walker Howe (Philadelphia, 1976), 95–108.

2. Although textile specialists have argued that only Turkey red handkerchiefs with patterns of white diamonds or squares, evolving from the tie-died *bhandas* of the Coromandle Coast of India, may be considered true bandannas, I use the term in its nineteenth-century vernacular sense to encompass all brightly colored handkerchiefs. Because bandannas were handkerchiefs, and handkerchiefs, when worn as such, were kerchiefs, scarves, and cravats, some flexibility in nomenclature is unavoidable.

3. For an outstanding account of this phenomenon, see Otto Charles Thieme, "'Wave High the Red Bandanna:' Some Handkerchiefs of the 1888 Presidential Campaign," *Journal of American Culture* 3 (Winter 1980): 686–705, reprinted in *American Material Culture: The Shape of Things Around Us*, ed. Edith Mayo (Bowling Green, Ohio, 1984), 92–111. See also Collins, *Threads of History*, 7–17.

4. Indianapolis *Sentinel*, quoted in John D. Pfeifer, "Ballots, Beerwagons and Buzzards: The Great Veterans' Rally of 1876," *APIC Keynoter* 81 (Spring 1981): 20.

5. John Maass, *The Gingerbread Age: A View of Victorian America* (New York, 1957), 14.

6. Edith P. Mayo, "Campaign Appeals to Women," *Journal of American Culture* 3 (Winter 1980): 722–42; reprinted in *American Material Culture*, ed. Mayo 128–48.

7. See Sullivan, *Political Badges and Medalets*, 425–46: Sullivan, *Collecting Political Americana*, 29–30, 32–33, 91, 94, 121, 129, 135, 142, 152, 168; Hake, *Political Buttons, III*, 82–85, 238; Collins, *Threads of History*, 211–15; and Fischer and Sullivan, *Political Ribbons and Ribbon Badges*, 163–68.

8. Indianapolis *Sentinel*, quoted in Pfeifer, "Ballots, Beerwagons and Buzzards," 20. In 1876, James G. Blaine was reaping notoriety from the "Mulligan letters"

allegation that he had been bribed with railroad stock, Secretary of War William W. Belknap had just resigned after a unanimous House vote to impeach him for pocketing a $24,450 bribe. Babcock, Grant's personal secretary, was a key figure in the "Whiskey Ring" attempt to defraud the government of liquor revenues, and Grant crony Alexander Robey Shepherd was being accused of engineering a series of kickback schemes on District of Columbia construction projects.

9. The dearth of 1876 bloody shirt items may be explained in part by the fact that it was not until late summer when the Republicans, at the insistence of Hayes, really resorted to the theme to divert voter attention from scandals and hard times. As Hayes insisted in a letter to Garfield on August 5, 1876, "Our main issue must be *It is not safe to allow the Rebellion to come into power*," mainly because, as he candidly admitted to Blaine, "It leads people away from 'hard times,' which is our deadliest foe." Quoted in Keith Ian Polakoff, *The Politics of Inertia: The Election of 1876 and the End of Reconstruction* (Baton Rouge, 1973), 115.

10. See Sullivan, *Political Badges and Medalets*, 447–72, 633; Collins, *Threads of History*, 216–28; Fischer and Sullivan, *Political Ribbons and Ribbon Badges*, 179–84, 189–92; Hake, *Political Buttons, III*, 86–91; and Sullivan, *Collecting Political Americana*, 29–30, 56–58, 61, 75, 91–94, 107–12, 118, 129–30, 135, 146, 152–53.

11. The Garfield "Equality All Men" chintz and "Union/Freedom/Education" ribbon were most likely printed early in the campaign and the two tariff ribbons after September, when stunning defeats in elections in Maine prompted a dramatic shift in emphasis away from Civil War-related themes to the tariff issue. See H. Wayne Morgan, *From Hayes to McKinley: National Party Politics, 1877–1896* (Syracuse, 1969), 116–17. The inscription on the Hancock torch echoed a statement he had made in 1867 in New Orleans, after replacing the heavy-handed Philip Sheridan as Fifth District military commander, that made him very popular among white southerners.

12. "Salt River" was a popular nineteenth-century vernacular expression for oblivion that appears on many satiric political items. "Chinese Line" made reference to an alleged letter from Garfield supporting Chinese immigration as a source of cheap labor for employers that might have cost him the support of West Coast workers had it not been exposed as a patent fraud. See Morgan, *From Hayes to McKinley*, 118–19.

13. See Herbert J. Clancy, *The Presidential Election of 1880* (Chicago, 1958), 226–31; and Morgan, *From Hayes to McKinley*, 113–15.

14. Although two of the tokens were struck as postconvention mementos for the "faithful 306" delegates who held firm for Grant through all thirty-six ballots, the other medalets, two clothing buttons, and a few ribbons were pre-nomination campaign objects. While they were not unique in this respect, items promoting hopefuls for major party nominations were quite unusual until the 1890s.

15. Reform Republican Carl Schurz remarked that Blaine had "wallowed in spoils like a rhinocerous in an African pool" (inspiring Thomas Nast to draw a series of vicious 1884 cartoons depicting him as a rhino), and when asked that year to campaign on Blaine's behalf, Roscoe Conkling replied, "Gentlemen, you have been mis-informed. I have given up criminal law." See Morgan, *From Hayes to McKinley*, 67–70, 202–4, 215–17, 223.

16. For a representation of 1884 Blaine campaign items, see Sullivan, *Political Badges and Medalets*, 489–514, 633–34; Hake, *Political Buttons, III*, 109–18; Fischer

and Sullivan, *Political Ribbons and Ribbon Badges*, 213–23; Collins, *Threads of History*, 229–31, 233–34, 236–45; and Sullivan, *Collecting Political Americana*, 29, 32, 55–58, 62, 75, 94, 104, 107, 120, 129, 131, 145, 149–50, 155, 162.

17. Morgan, *From Hayes to McKinley*, 230.

18. Although Cleveland had avoided military service during the Civil War by hiring a substitute, the Republicans were not able to exploit this embarrassing situation because Blaine had done likewise—and to make matters worse, Blaine's substitute was later imprisoned for selling forged deferment papers. See John M. Dobson, *Politics in the Gilded Age: A New Perspective on Reform* (New York, 1972), 153–54. Apart from the Logan "40 Rounds U. S." ribbons, only a medalet with a "Union" shield and the inscription "The Republicans Have Ruled Since 1860 and with Blaine & Logan Are Good for Another Term" gave any evidence of an effort to rekindle sectional emotions for political advantage.

19. See Sullivan *Political Badges and Medalets*, 473–89; Collins, *Threads of History*, 230, 234–39, 241–42, 244, 246–47; Fischer and Sullivan, *Political Ribbons and Ribbon Badges*, 193–95, 200–3, 206; Hake, *Political Buttons, III*, 92–93, 96–108; and Sullivan, *Collecting Political Americana*, 29, 33, 55, 62, 95, 104, 106, 130, 147, 155.

20. See Charles McSorley, "Cleveland the Hangman," *Political Collector* 9 (Aug. 1980): 1.

21. During this period Greenbackers were commonly referred to as "frogbacks" or simply "frogs." On the bank, Butler's left arm reads "For the Masses," and his right arm "Bonds and Yachts for Me," an allusion to his ownership of the famous racing yacht *America*. See Sullivan, *Collecting Political Americana*, 160.

22. For a good selection of the massive number of campaign objects promoting the 1888 presidential candidates, see Fischer and Sullivan, *Political Ribbons and Ribbon Badges*, 195–98, 200–3, 205–7, 226–34, 236–41, 246–53; Collins, *Threads of History*, 251–83; Sullivan, *Political Badges and Medalets*, 515–82, 634–36; Hake, *Political Buttons*, 92–108, 119–27, 239–40; and Sullivan, *Collecting Political Americana*, 6, 29, 31–32, 54–57, 91, 94, 98–99, 106–8, 110–12, 118, 134–36, 144–49, 154–57, 163. See also Thieme, "'Wave High the Red Bandanna," in *American Material Culture*, ed. Mayo, 92–111.

23. Morgan, *From Hayes to McKinley*, 302.

24. Ibid., 307, 316.

25. Ibid., 307.

26. *Judge*, Oct. 6, 1888. See also Fischer and Sullivan, *Political Ribbons and Ribbon Badges*, 175–77.

27. See Sullivan, *Collecting Political Americana*, 31–32, 54, 72, 75, 93, 111–12, 118–19, 121, 131, 135, 148, 150–51, 158; Hake, *Political Buttons, III*, 96–99, 101–2, 104, 107–8, 123–25, 130–32, 135, 137; Fischer and Sullivan, *Political Ribbons and Ribbon Badges*, 198–202, 204–9, 235–36, 243–46, 253–55; Collins, *Threads of History*, 288–98; and Sullivan, *Political Badges and Medalets*, 583–613, 636.

28. See Charles McSorley, "Tin Plates and Sardine Cans," *Political Collector* 9 (May 1980): 1–2.

29. Despite declining health and the recent deaths of two of his children, Blaine did not flatly rule out a presidential bid until Harrison sent him a curt message to renounce his candidacy or resign from the Cabinet a week before the

1892 Republican convention convened. The "blocks of five" reference was inspired by an incident during Harrison's 1888 campaign, when a scandal developed after publication of a letter from Republican national party treasurer W. W. Dudley to Indiana operatives urging the deployment of paid "floaters" on election day in "blocks of five." See Morgan, *From Hayes to McKinley*, 311–12, 395–402. The game is pictured in Hake, *Political Buttons, III*, 119.

5

What Hath Amanda Wrought? 1896–1916

If the changes in campaigning for the presidency that occurred from 1896 through 1916 were of fundamental importance, the transformation in political material culture during this period was little short of revolutionary. Before 1896, significant changes in campaign objects and their use had been more or less simple applications of existing technology to either new trends in popular tastes or such new forms of campaign activity as the great rallies of 1840 and the lavish torchlight parades of 1860. This was not the case in 1896 and the races that followed, however, despite such important innovations as William Jennings Bryan's frenetic railroad excursions and Mark Hanna's mastery of centralized campaign organization and fund-raising on behalf of William McKinley. These developments influenced political material culture to be sure, but to a much less dramatic degree than did the genesis of the celluloid campaign button.

Motivated by a billiard ball manufacturer's $10,000 prize offered for a substitute for ivory, American inventors John Wesley Hyatt and his brother Isaiah developed celluloid in 1868. The first commercially successful plastic, celluloid was soon utilized in such products as eyeglass frames, piano keys, and dental plates. Early experiments in celluloid campaign objects included solid die-struck disks in 1876 and lapel studs with likenesses printed in ink on celluloid in 1888, but neither idea caught on. Then, on December 3, 1893, a patent was granted to a Boston woman, Amanda M. Lougee, for a clothing button with a textile surface covered with a thin sheet of transparent celluloid. Her patent was soon acquired by the Whitehead and Hoag Company of Newark, New Jersey, which on July 21, 1896, secured patent rights to the celluloid button as we know it today: a printed paper disk under celluloid set into a metal collet with one of several types of fastening devices.

No other innovation in the history of material culture in American politics ever gained acceptance so rapidly or on such a massive scale. In 1896 alone, more than a thousand different varieties of celluloids promoted the various presidential candidates and their causes.[1] The superiority of the celluloid to other types of lapel badges was apparent from the outset. Often wholesaled in quantity for little more than a cent apiece, it was much less expensive than any of its predecessors, and at the same time was much more durable than the easily bent metal lapel badges with paper pictures that peeled off more often than not. Capable of conveying any artwork that could be printed on a small paper disk, the celluloid made possible imaginative designs and colors that were impossible on objects struck from dies or cast in molds. An important consideration at a time when Americans were beginning to retreat from the gaudy ornamentation of the flamboyant Victorian era was the small size of most celluloids, often less than an inch in diameter. All things considered, the legacy of Amanda Lougee and Whitehead and Hoag to our political process has been substantial.

The period from 1896 up to World War I is commonly known as the golden age of the political celluloid, both because of the superb aesthetic qualities of some of the more imaginative designs (especially from the 1900, 1904, and 1908 races), and because they were so extraordinarily plentiful during the era. Millions were made and used in several thousand known varieties in presidential campaigns. They were created for myriad purposes. Most were produced to sell by retailers (often the larger and more colorful styles) at five or ten cents each or to be given out in storefront headquarters or at rallies by campaign organizations. Other varieties were made to give out as endorsement items for various political and nonpolitical organizations. Coattail buttons (fig.118) featuring presidential candidates along with aspirants for lesser office were often produced for local campaigns hoping to benefit from the popularity of a national figure, although in some cases the effect was a "reverse coattail" attempt to transfer some of the popularity of respected local politicos onto a less-fortunate national ticket. Some companies ordered celluloids (fig. 119) to promote a favored presidential candidate and their product simultaneously. Small buttons bearing political slogans were produced and given out as premium items to purchasers of American Pepsin gum and Sweet Caporal and High Admiral cigarettes.

The advent of the celluloid button had predictable effect on the older types of political lapel devices. At least two hundred varieties of campaign studs appeared in 1896 (fig. 120), including a large number of celluloid styles identical in appearance to pinback buttons, some very attractive O'Hara porcelain pieces, and some extremely imaginative metal types. Few were produced for 1900, however, and virtually none after that. The year 1896 was also an exceptional one for metal lapel pins, most notably some rather ingenious mechanical gadgets and the many styles of little gold bugs

Figs. 118 and 119. Celluloid campaign buttons were used for many purposes following their introduction in 1896, including the promotion of coattail candidates for
state or local office and the advertising of products. Pictured with presidents
McKinley, Roosevelt, and Taft are Republican gubernatorial candidates Robert
LaFollette of Wisconsin, Edwin S. Stuart of Pennsylvania, and David Clough,
Samuel Van Sant, and Robert C. Dunn of Minnesota. The producers of Lucas
paint, Hartford Times cigars, and *The American Gentleman* magazine mixed politics
and business on the celluloids pictured below.

Fig. 120. These metal and celluloid lapel studs represent only a fraction of the varieties available to the supporters of McKinley and Bryan during their 1896 and 1900 presidential contests. All but three or four of these are 1896 varieties. (Smithsonian Institution)

and silver bugs (fig. 121) worn to symbolize the currency debate, but after 1896 this type of device declined markedly in popularity. Several varieties of metal shell badges with glued-on paper pictures were marketed in 1896, very few in 1900, and almost none thereafter. Metal tokens, long in decline as lapel devices, now moved closer to extinction. Some attractive varieties appeared in 1896 (along with many so-called "Bryan dollars" poking fun at the Nebraskan's silver crusade) and in 1900 and 1904 as well, but by 1908 most campaign tokens were nondescript brass items, and relatively few tokens and medalets of any sort appeared during subsequent campaigns. Although 1896 was also an extraordinary year for ribbons (especially Republican delegation and sound money demonstration items), ribbons printed for wear as badges appeared in steadily diminishing numbers after 1896. More and more, the use of ribbons was limited to such special events as party conventions, visits by a nominee or a sitting president, or other major celebrations. The most distinctive of these special occasion items were elaborate ribbon badges (fig. 122), often ornate two- and three-piece devices reminiscent of the flamboyance of an earlier day

The celluloid pinback button was by no means the only important innovation in political material culture during this period. Political postcards (fig. 123) enjoyed great popularity during the early years of the new century, as did political watch fobs. Penny postcards, set free from a government monopoly by Congress in 1898, made their political debut in 1900, really caught on in 1904, and reached the peak of their popularity during the 1908 campaign, when several hundred varieties appeared including some truly attractive multicolor designs and some of the wickedest examples of satire (figs. 151, 152) ever inspired by our political process. The return of Theodore Roosevelt from Africa in 1910 engendered many postcards, as did the 1912 election, but after 1912, political postcards declined rapidly in quantity and in the thematic and aesthetic quality of those printed. Whether or not this was a result of the general decline in postcards after the introduction of folded greeting cards mailed in envelopes, few postcards were printed during subsequent elections, and most of those that did appear (with the exception of many 1940 cards protesting Franklin Roosevelt's bid for a third term) were purely pictorial in style.[2] Political watch fobs also made their debut in a minor way in 1900, enjoyed enormous popularity during the 1904 and 1908 campaigns (with as many as one hundred varieties created for each race) and to a lesser extent in 1912, and then were produced in limited numbers into the 1930s, when they increasingly became casualties of the new mania for wristwatches.

Several styles and sizes of metal trays were produced as campaign objects during the 1900–8 period. Large round or oval tin serving trays (fig. 143) promoted the 1900, 1904, and 1908 major party candidates, and a handsome 1908 miniature variety four inches wide, similar to the "tip trays" of the period given out by breweries and distilleries for use in saloons, featured

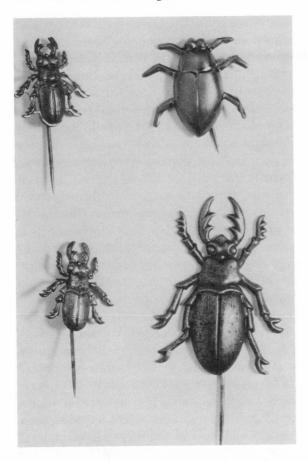

Fig. 121. These little gold bug and silver bug lapel pins, usually produced in both colors and sold side-by-side from salesman's cards on store counters, hatched out in great profusion during the 1896 McKinley-Bryan Battle of the Standards.

Republicans William Howard Taft and James Sherman. Aluminum pin trays (fig. 124) were also produced and marketed in a number of styles and shapes, evidence—along with such other innovations as McKinley pincushions (fig. 125) and Woodrow Wilson buttonhooks and an abundance of the older types of feminine political bric-a-brac—of a continuing interest in winning the allegiance of women before they received voting rights. Other additions to the very eclectic political material culture of this period included campaign stamps, pens, wooden pencils, umbrellas, cigars, bow ties, neckties, aluminum combs, aluminum and celluloid bookmarks, coin purses, and jackknives. Political soap dolls in cardboard boxes proclaiming the merits of free silver and sound money (fig. 126) were marketed in 1896 but never again, perhaps because of their macabre similarity to babies in coffins.

With the advent of such new types of campaign items, many old mainstays of late nineteenth-century memorabilia began to lose much of their popularity. The year 1896 was an excellent one for political handkerchiefs and bandannas, but the next four campaigns inspired fewer than a

Fig. 122. Typical of the intricate and ornate new ribbon badges were these varieties, created to welcome Taft to a Minneapolis reception in 1911, Bryan back to the United States after his 1906 trip to Europe, and Roosevelt to the twin cities of Minneapolis and St. Paul. (Kenneth J. Moran)

dozen varieties each, and the 1916 contest may have produced none at all. The ceramic and glass decorative objects that filled the bric-a-brac cabinets of Victorian partisans remained very much in vogue through the 1908 campaign, declined perceptibly in 1912, and were virtually nonexistent in 1916. Among the glass campaign objects produced during the period were tumblers, flasks, attractive Heisey glass mugs ("sugars") with domed covers (fig. 127), pressed glass plates, and a host of paperweights. Ceramic items included

Fig. 123. Enormously popular during early twentieth-century campaigns were post-cards like these 1908 and 1912 Taft, Wilson, and Bryan varieties. (Kenneth J. Moran)

many plates, the most attractive of which were some Staffordshire blue varieties (fig. 128) featuring Theodore Roosevelt, figural busts, intaglio portrait tiles, and a number of rather droll pitchers and mugs known as "tobies."[3]

The gradual extinction of one whole group of campaign objects was caused neither by new technology nor by changes in popular tastes, but by a basic transformation in the political system itself. Largely as a result of Mark Hanna's herculean efforts in 1896, presidential campaigns evolved steadily into highly centralized operations. One consequence was the inexorable decline of the local political clubs and the campaign activities they traditionally staged, including the political parade. With its sound money and free silver demonstrations, 1896 was an extraordinary year for such events, but after 1896, parades diminished drastically, both in number and in creativity. The last distinctive lighting devices created for torchlight parades were the "full dinner pail" metal lanterns used by the Republicans in 1900. Political parade canes were apparently used for the last time in 1912. With the passing of the marching banners, torches, transparencies,

Figs. 124 and 125. Evidence of a strong interest in winning the minds and hearts of American women at a time when they had voting rights only in a few Rocky Mountain states is this ornate and unusual 1904 Alton Parker–Henry G. Davis aluminum pin tray and this "Put Your Faith in Honest Money" 1896 McKinley–Garret Hobart pincushion. (Fig. 125, Smithsonian Institution)

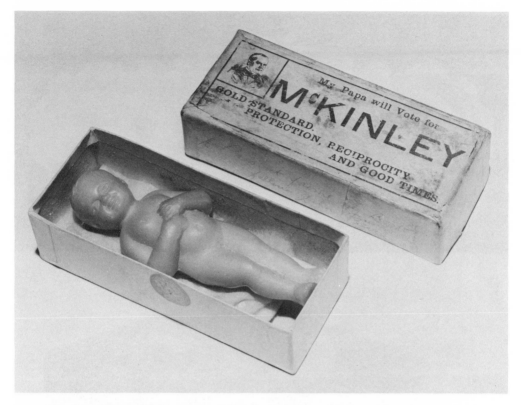

Fig. 126. This 1896 McKinley "soap baby" in woodtone cardboard box bears a chilling similarity to a naked baby in a coffin, explaining perhaps why such objects were not issued in subsequent elections. A matching variety promotes Bryan, free silver, an income tax, and a tariff "for revenue only." (Smithsonian Institution)

lanterns, canes, parade uniforms, floats and the like, the most creative aspect of material culture in American politics came to an end.

Despite the introduction of so many new types of campaign items and the demise or decline of so many others, the succession of presidential elections that began with the first McKinley–Bryan contest represented essential continuity in the use of material culture much more than it signified fundamental change. Like the elections of the 1880s and 1892, the 1896 "battle of the standards" and the first three or four presidential contests of the twentieth century inspired a massive quantity and variety of material objects that bear witness to the enormous vitality of participatory politics in a nation where choosing a chief executive had not yet degenerated into a spectator sport.

This was especially true of 1896, certainly the most emotion-charged presidential contest since 1860, if not ever. The triumph of the insurgent agrarian wing of the Democratic party under the free silver banner at their Chicago convention set loose an extraordinary release of enthusiasm tinged

Figs. 127 and 128. Among the more attractive glass and ceramic political decorative objects produced during this period were the matched set of 1896 Bryan and McKinley Heisey glass sugars and this handsome 1904 Staffordshire blue Roosevelt plate. (Fig. 127, Smithsonian Institution; Fig. 128, Edmund B. Sullivan)

with anger, gave the party a cause much more compelling than civil service reform or tariff reduction, and in William Jennings Bryan gave them a candidate uncommonly blessed with energy and charisma, if not a genius for the politics of consensus. Frightened by the first truly substantive challenge to their fundamental beliefs since the Civil War, the Republicans rallied around William McKinley and the defense of industrial capitalism. While Mark Hanna raised and spent unprecedented sums in a superbly organized Republican campaign, Bryan was forced by a hostile press and an empty till to break with tradition and take his case straight to the electorate, traveling some eighteen thousand miles to give more than six hundred speeches to five million people. On election day, voter turnout in five fiercely contested midwestern states exceeded 95 percent. But many partisans did more than listen and vote. The year 1896 was exceptional for rallies and parades, especially for Republicans, who staged sound money demonstrations in nearly every city and town (and many hamlets) east of the Mississippi and north of the Ohio.[4]

All of this excitement and activity created an extraordinary environment for campaign items of all sorts, and opportunistic producers were quick to respond with an amazing array of wares. Included were more than a thousand celluloid pinbacks and studs, hundreds of different metal lapel devices and cloth ribbons, many banners, handkerchiefs, bandannas, posters, medalets, plates, tumblers, and cane tops—even such exotica as hats, umbrellas, tops, and soap dolls.[5] McKinley items appear to have outnumbered Bryan objects in 1896 by a ratio of roughly three to two, probably because McKinley was more popular than Bryan (especially among middle-class urbanites most likely to buy campaign memorabilia), and because his partisans sponsored more activities and raised more money. The total of at least two thousand varieties of items promoting McKinley, Bryan, and the 1896 splinter party candidates virtually doubled the number of objects inspired by any previous presidential election.

As the several hundred 1896 Bryan items made clear, free silver—the minting of unlimited quantities of silver coinage at a value of one-sixteenth that of gold to increase the money supply and the value of commodities by returning the nation to a bimetallic system established in 1837 but abandoned in 1873—*was* the Democratic campaign. Many items (fig. 129) demanded "Free Silver" or "Free Coinage," and even more (including more than three dozen buttons and studs and nearly half of all ribbons) promoted the magic ratio "16 to 1." Buttons proclaimed "Only Silver," "Silver Is Good Enough for Me," "Silver Should Rule the World," "Silver First, Last and All the Time," "I Am a Silver Man," "The Country Needs Silverization," "I'm Solid Silver," even "I Will Carry Silver if It Breaks My Back." A porcelain O'Hara stud with a silver wheel read "Silver Juggernaut." Buttons with silver dollar designs read "The Money We Want" and "There Is Only One Girl in This World for Me." Silver coloration was used exten-

Fig. 129. Representative of the strident, single-issue preoccupation of the 1896 Bryan presidential campaign with the crusade for free silver at a ratio of 16 to 1 with gold were these expressive items. (Edmund B. Sullivan)

sively on buttons and studs, the more ornate ribbons often featured silver braiding or tassels, and nearly all metal lapel pieces were made of silvered metal. Among the more creative Bryan silver items were buttons using flower and coin motifs to dramatize "16 to 1" and clocks set to 12:44, or "sixteen to one." The silver bug emerged as a ubiquitous symbol of the crusade, with dozens of different lapel pins, buttons, and studs featuring the little creatures.

Items equating the silver issue to larger considerations were few in number. "Free Silver and Prosperity" ribbons and buttons reading "Silver/ Prosperity" and "Silver—Prosperity, Are You with Us?" pledged better times through bimetallism, while "Free Silver/Dollar Wheat" lapel pins and "Free Coinage Means Higher Wages" buttons tailored this argument to farmers and blue-collar workers. "The People's Money" Heisey glass sugars and marching banners with such legends as "Free Silver and Liberty," "Free Silver/A Free People," and "Free Coinage/The People's Rights" hinted at a link between gold money and dictatorship. Buttons insisting "Europe Wants Gold, We Want Silver," "American Money for Americans," and "No English Dictation/1776–1896/The American Policy/We Demand the Money of the Constitution," and a ribbon demanding "Bryan and Silver/National Freedom" equated silver with Americanism itself, a bid to make political capital of Republican opposition to bimetallism unless silver was authorized by international agreement.

With the exception of a set of bandannas reading "Tariff for Revenue Only" (in much smaller letters than "Free Coinage/16 to 1"), no known 1896 Bryan items made reference to issues other than silver. Fewer than one-third of all Bryan objects attributable to 1896 ignored silver altogether, and without exception these items were completely nonthematic. Moreover, no known 1896 Bryan objects made any attempt to exploit the politics of personality, despite the Nebraskan's considerable charisma and many familiar nicknames. This was single-issue protest politics to an extent not practiced by a major party since the free-soil campaign of Republican John C. Frémont forty years before. That it was also the most evangelically strident presidential campaign since Frémont's was reflected by buttons insisting "No Compromise," buttons and lapel pins depicting gold bugs being impaled by pitchforks, spikes, and silver arrows (sometimes accompanied by such threats as "What We'll Do to Gold Bugs"), and by buttons, lapel pins, banners, marching jackets, and ribbons repeating the "No Crown of Thorns, No Cross of Gold" summation from Bryan's celebrated Chicago convention speech, words more appropriate for some sort of spiritual Armageddon than a contest for tenancy at 1600 Pennsylvania Avenue. That the Bryan campaign was not without a measure of Populist paranoia was made clear by the popularity of "Wall Street Demonetized Silver" buttons and porcelain studs featuring "We Are the People" silver bugs wearing "Wall Street" barrels.

In contrast, fewer than half of the 1896 William McKinley campaign items were issue-oriented, and those pieces that were ideological provide clear evidence of a much more subtle, much more diverse effort to win votes. A relatively small number of McKinley objects made a direct appeal for the preservation of the gold standard. A button featured a gold coin and the motto "The Money We Want," a caricature button depicted McKinley and running-mate Garret Hobart cycling to the White House over the promise "Gold Didn't Get There July 7th, but Watch Us Take It There Nov. 3rd," other buttons read "Grand Old Party, Good as Gold" and "I Am for Gold," gold nugget stickpins bore the legend "Gold Basis," and glass tumblers demanded "Gold Standard/No Split Dollars." Gold bugs hatched out in even greater profusion than did their silver cousins. Ribbons, buttons, and studs frequently utilized golden coloration, metal McKinley lapel pins were almost invariably gilded, and some of the more flamboyant ribbon badges featured gold braiding and tassels.

Other McKinley items, however, revealed a strategy of elevating the monetary issue above mere metallurgy by endowing the gold standard with an ethical dimension. A button and an immense gilded shell badge urged "An Honest Dollar." Several ribbons and parade banners bore the motto "Honest Money," one of the banners adding "And National Integrity" to further emphasize the innate nobility of McKinley's monetary philosophy. The ubiquitous rallying cry of Republicans in 1896 was "sound money," a phrase that appeared on literally hundreds of items (fig. 130), many of them produced for the sound money demonstrations staged by the sound money clubs created in many communities, trades, and industries to work on McKinley's behalf.

A large number of McKinley campaign objects show that the Republicans were able to do what Bryan's Democrats were either unable or unwilling to do, diversify their economic appeal beyond the debate over currency. Nearly as many items featured the inscription "Protection" as the slogan "Sound Money," an excellent indication of the importance the Republicans placed on the tariff. This was especially true of McKinley himself, a longtime tariff enthusiast whose fealty to the gold standard was rather recent and somewhat suspect. Many other McKinley pieces more broadly stressed good times through economic expansion. Banners, broadsides, handkerchiefs, ribbons, Heisey glass sugars, and many varieties of buttons and studs bore the motto "Prosperity's Advance Agent."[6] The boxes containing McKinley soap dolls read "My Papa Will Vote for McKinley/Gold Standard, Protection, Reciprocity and Good Times."

Political historians have argued that the most important factor in McKinley's decisive victory over Bryan was his ability to outpoll the Nebraskan among blue-collar voters in eastern and midwestern industrial communities. Many campaign items indicate that this was no accident. While Bryan objects (with the exception of a "Free Coinage Means Higher Wages" but-

Fig. 130. Unlike the opposition items demanding free silver with no compromise, these 1896 McKinley sound money campaign items reflect a more diverse and subtle strategy of linking the gold standard to fiscal integrity, prosperity, and national honor. (Edmund B. Sullivan)

ton) ignored industrial workers, McKinley items courted them vigorously. Ribbons pledged "An Honest Dollar and a Chance to Earn it," and posters pledged "Work for All and 100 Cents on the Dollar." Other posters (fig. 131) featured McKinley's dictum, "I believe it is a good deal better to open the mills of the United States to the labor of America than to open up the mints of the United States to the silver of the World." Buttons echoed "Open Mills Not Mints" and rhymed "It's McKinley We Trust, to Keep Our Machines Free of Rust." Another button proclaimed McKinley the "Leader of Labor in Liberty's Land," and a dinner-pail stud insisted "Protection Fills the Dinner Pail," a rare early use of the essentially blue-collar symbol that would be utilized so effectively in McKinley's 1900 re-election effort.

It was an extraordinary year for put-down political objects, nearly all of them Republican pieces poking fun at Bryan's monetary beliefs or his unorthodox style of campaigning. Buttons in 1896 lampooned free silver as "16 Parts Foam/1 Part Beer" and taunted "In McKinley We Trust, In Bryan We Bust." Buttons reading "In God We Trust/For the Other 47 Cents," and satiric greenbacks (fig. 132) lampooned the notion of a silver dollar worth fifty-three cents at current bullion values, as did one of the many so-called "Bryan dollar" tokens (fig. 133) issued to deride the silver crusade.[7] Other Bryan dollars were pot metal pieces more than twice the size of the standard silver dollar (to demonstrate the size necessary for a dollar to contain its worth in bullion), while the most imaginative of the genre featured "POP," a creature half donkey and half goose, a symbol of the Bryan coalition of Democrats and Populists. Bryan's unprecedented travels and six hundred speeches (while McKinley sat out the campaign in the traditional "above the battle" style at his home in Canton, Ohio) inspired numerous buttons, studs, and lapel pins featuring skeletons, cadavers, and coffins, usually with such legends as "Talked to Death" or "Too Much Politics," although the epitaph "16 to 1 to Death" graced one imaginative pin consisting of a skeleton on a spring.

Although 1896 represented a departure from traditional Republican reliance on bloody shirt demagogy, political historians who maintain that the break was absolute would do well to examine the material relics of the campaign. No Republican objects indicted Bryan (just months old when the guns roared at Sumter) or his party for ancient crimes against the Union, but large numbers of them featured rhetoric or designs portraying McKinley as the candidate of national glory, patriotism, and the Unionist tradition of Lincoln and Grant. Several buttons and studs bore the familiar Grand Army of the Republic endorsement "The Boys in Blue Are for Wm. McKinley." Buttons depicting him as "Maj. W^m McKinley" were suspended from ribbon replicas of Old Glory, reminders of his service in the Union Army ranks. An abnormally large number of buttons and other objects utilized the colors red, white, and blue and flag designs. A host of items featured the motto "Patriotism," and ribbons read "Rally Round the

Fig. 131. An excellent example of the ability of the 1896 McKinley campaign to link sound money with jobs for blue-collar workers is this magnificent poster inspired by an August 12, 1986, McKinley speech. (Robert A. Fratkin)

Figs. 132 and 133. Among the many 1896 anti–Bryan items lampooning the fiscal soundness of coining silver in unlimited quantities at one-sixteenth the value of gold were these satiric "greenbacks" and "Bryan dollar" medalets. The larger coins represented the enormous size necessary to give a dollar one hundred cents worth of silver at current market value, while the smaller token featured "POP," a half donkey, half goose symbol of the union of Democrats and Populists in support of Bryan.

Flag" and "We Will Maintain Our Nation's Honor." Efforts to link McKinley with Old Glory were apparently so successful that his national campaign committee was able to buy and distribute as McKinley campaign badges huge numbers of cloth flag stickpins designed as general patriotic items.[8]

Adding to the material culture of the 1896 campaign were many items promoting unsuccessful candidates for major party nominations and at least five minor party tickets. Democrats William B. Allison, Richard P. ("Silver Dick") Bland, and Horace Boies used celluloid buttons in Chicago, and Boies and Claude Matthews distributed ribbons. Republican hopefuls Thomas B. ("Czar") Reed and Matt Quay each inspired three types of buttons, and Quay a ribbon with the rather puzzling call to arms "Quay and Victory/Things Are Different Now." Perhaps the most interesting 1896 hopeful items were two pieces engendered by the effort of an overwhelmingly outmanned silver Republican minority for Colorado Senator Henry M. Teller, a "Teller Silver Republican/16 to 1 by Uncle Sam Alone" button and a "We Are as Solid for Teller as Teller Is Solid for Silver" ribbon. Minor party items included a button for Nationalist candidate Charles Eugene Bentley; six for Prohibitionist Joshua Levering; a Bryan–Thomas E. Watson button issued by Populists unable to accept Bryan's Democratic running-mate (millionaire shipbuilder Arthur Sewall); "Equal Rights to All" and "Prosperity above Party" buttons for Silver party candidate Joseph Sibley; and "The True Democrat," "For an Honest Dollar," and "Jeffersonian Democrats" buttons for supporters of Gold Democrat John M. Palmer.

The rather anticlimactic rematch between McKinley and Bryan in 1900 inspired only about half the variety of items made for 1896, with many types of lapel devices largely disappearing, and few public demonstrations to beget visuals and badges. Yet in quantity and quality alike (especially in the still developing art of the celluloid button), the material culture of 1900 was much more exciting than the election that inspired it. Several hundred varieties of celluloids exhibited more imaginative uses of color and design and much more creative expression of thematics and symbolism than in 1896, as did many attractive posters. Other 1900 campaign objects included a few studs and metal lapel pins; many ribbons and ribbon badges; some banners and handkerchiefs; many plates and other types of ceramic bric-a-brac; such odds and ends as umbrellas, aluminum combs, glass tumblers, pencils, and figural pipes; and the first few political postcards, watch fobs, tin serving trays, and aluminum pin trays.[9]

Despite the urging of party leaders that his 1896 defeat, combined with rising commodity prices and the discovery of massive deposits of gold in the Klondike, decreed abandonment of the silver issue in 1900, Bryan's stubborn refusal to do so resulted in many buttons and other items featuring this theme. Buttons again proclaimed "16 to 1" and "Free Silver" and portrayed Bryan on a 12:44 clockface, and a 1900 Montana convention ribbon urged "Bryan and Silver." More Bryan buttons utilized silver as a background color in 1900 than had been the case in 1896. Another indication that the Bryan camp was slow to learn from past mistakes was a general failure on his 1900 items to appeal to the blue-collar vote. One exception, however, was a button (fig. 134) depicting Bryan shaking hands with a workingman with pick in hand identified as "Labor" under the legend "United We Stand, Divided We Fall/No Trusts."

Most of the thematic 1900 Bryan items, however, expressed opposition to the twin evils of imperialism and the trusts. A host of buttons (fig. 135) and other items protested McKinley's recent adventures in Cuba and the Philippines with such mottos as "For the Republic/No Dreams of Empire for the Free," "Stand by the Republic," "Republic not Empire," and "Anti-Expansion." A number of buttons and studs insisted "The Constitution Follows the Flag." Another celluloid pictured George Washington (an icon more commonly exploited by Republicans) with the legend "Imperialism! Has the Country I Made Free Come to This? Bryan Will Save It." Like the silver items, these anti-expansion ones reflected Bryan's personal beliefs more than they did a pervasive public sentiment. More potentially profitable politically were the many items (fig. 136) attacking the trusts, for Democratic propaganda and the undeservedly cruel public image of McKinley field marshal "Dollar Mark" Hanna had combined to foster a fairly widespread impression that McKinley was the minion of big business interests. Posters depicting a hideously bloated "Trust Rex" upon his throne asked "Shall the People Rule?," as did buttons and stickpins. Other buttons read "No Trusts," "Anti-Trusts," and "Democracy Stands for People not Trusts," and a stickpin featuring a skeleton on a spring urged "Death to Trusts." An "Equal Rights to All/Special Privileges to None" poster (fig. 137) portrayed the trusts as an octopus wrapping its tentacles around American factories. Agrarian resentment over low wholesale beef prices inspired buttons reading "Down With the Beef Trust" and "We Need Relief From the Trust of Beef."

With McKinley riding the crest of widespread popularity as a result of an improving economy and the jingoistic response to a "splendid little war," and with the addition to the ticket of Rough Rider Theodore Roosevelt, 1900 Republican campaign items rather predictably emphasized the themes of prosperity and patriotism, portraying McKinley as the architect of economic revival and Roosevelt as a war hero. Despite their considerable debt to the gold standard, Republicans confined echoes of 1896 to a few buttons demanding "Sound Money" along with other priorities, the use of gold as a background color on other buttons, and a "Without Sound Currency There Cannot Be Prosperity" banner made for the Coffee Exchange and Lower Wall Street Sound Money Club. In 1900, the Republicans had other, newer symbols to exploit. One was the Rough Rider identity of Theodore Roosevelt. Despite the reluctance of McKinley (and downright revulsion of Mark Hanna) to put the "damned cowboy" on the ticket, the campaign made the most of the opportunity. A number of buttons featured

Figs. 134, 135, and 136. Echoing the three major themes of Bryan's 1900 campaign are these buttons attacking the gold standard, American expansion in the Caribbean, and various business trusts.

Roosevelt in his celebrated uniform or just the ubiquitous Rough Rider hat. A large brass shell depicted an equestrian likeness of "Roosevelt at San Juan," a banner portrayed him, sabre drawn, in Rough Rider dress and seated on a charging mount, and a hinged elephant lapel pin that opened to a drawing of Roosevelt in Rough Rider apparel on a bucking horse was captioned "He Never Was Thrown." Not since Allen Thurman immortalized the red bandanna in 1888 had a vice-presidential candidate attracted so much attention on campaign memorabilia.

The dominant symbol of the 1900 McKinley–Roosevelt campaign, however, was the full dinner pail, an ideal device for dramatizing the theme of prosperity in a manner especially geared to the critical blue-collar voters.[10] Ribbons and at least a dozen styles of buttons (fig. 138) featured dinner pail designs, the most imaginative of them a "Do You Smoke? Yes—Since 1896! That's What McKinley Promised" variety depicting a smoking factory in

Fig. 137. Depicting Bryan as an apostle of free silver and a foe of expansionism and the trusts as an octopus engulfing American farms and factories is this handsome multicolored 1900 Democratic poster.

the shape of a dinner pail. Figural metal dinner pail parade lanterns appeared, one with cut-outs to read "4 Years More of Full Dinner Pail" when the device was lit. Metal lapel pins resembled miniature dinner pails. Included among the bric-a-brac items produced for the campaign were little wooden "Vote for Full Dinner Pail," glass "Full Dinner Pail," and ceramic "A Full Dinner Pail" figurals. Several of the full dinner pail buttons featured the agenda "Employment for Labor/A Full Dinner Bucket/Prosperity/Sound Money/Good Markets." Other objects exploiting the prosperity theme included multicolor buttons with scenes of smoking factories and lush fields or busy wharves and such captions as "Protection/Expansion/Prosperity," "McKinley and Prosperity," and "Commerce and Industry." The hinged elephant label pin with the "He Never Was Thrown" tribute to Roosevelt also portrayed McKinley with the legend "His Policy Brings Prosperity."

With a decisive victory over the Spanish to replace the fading memories of the Civil War, Republican campaign objects made the most of the opportunity. A ribbon exulted "Old Glory Stands Higher Among the Nations than Ever Before," and another depicted Uncle Sam endorsing McKinley with the tribute "William Accept My Congratulations. My Affairs Have Been Looked After Satisfactorily for Four Years and the People Desire a Continuance of the Same Management." To further remove doubts over the comparative patriotic attributes of the two candidates, a particularly vicious Republican button (fig. 139) placed Bryan with Tammany boss Richard Croker (misspelled "Croaker" either from ignorance or for comic effect) and Philippine resistance leader Emilio Aguinaldo over the legend "Three of a Kind." A "Pro-Expansion" button portrayed McKinley with Miss Justice and her scales and Miss Liberty holding a map of Cuba. Another variety featured McKinley with a sword and Uncle Sam with Old Glory advancing upon some rather sinister-looking individuals (apparently Spaniards) inside the text "Is This Imperialism? No Blow Has Been Struck Except for Liberty and Humanity." Many McKinley–Roosevelt buttons and ribbons featured flag coloration and designs.

Several 1900 Republican items combined the themes of patriotism and prosperity. Buttons, ribbons, parade canes, and posters bore such slogans as "Victory and Prosperity," "Patriotism and Protection," "Prosperity and Patriotism," "Prosperity at Home/Prestige Abroad." A ribbon explained, "We Are Prosperity Creators, Flag Defenders and for Honest Money and Expansion." A superb multicolor button (fig. 140) with scenes of a Philippine military cemetery and busy factories promised that Old Glory would forever wave over the bodies of our dead soldiers in the "Sands of the Luzon" and predicted that "Our People Will Not Vote Themselves into the Poor House Twice in Eight Years," a reference to the 1892 Democratic victory followed by the "Panic of 93." A multicolor poster (fig. 141) featured the candidates, the flag, and McKinley's dictum "The American Flag Has not Been Planted in Foreign Soil to Acquire More Territory but for Hu-

Figs. 138, 139, and 140. Among the more creative 1900 Republican campaign buttons were these full dinner pail varieties, and the expansionist celluloids that link Bryan with Philippine rebel Emilio Aguinaldo (and Tammany kingpin Richard Croker) and proclaim "the Sands of the Luzon" hallowed ground.

manity's Sake" amid scenes contrasting Cuba under Spanish and American rule and our economy under Democratic and Republican governance.

Some very creative buttons for supporters of both McKinley and Bryan were inspired by a total solar eclipse in most parts of the nation on May 28, 1900, an event accompanied by enormous public interest and widespread anxiety (much of it caused by religious fundamentalist prophets predicting the end of the world). At least a dozen varieties of buttons (fig. 142) depicted Bryan eclipsing McKinley or McKinley eclipsing Bryan, accompanied by such predictions as "Total Eclipse Nov. 6" or "Partial Eclipse/ Will Be Total in November." A Republican variety inspired by the Kansas City Democratic convention that nominated Bryan read "Imaginary Eclipse/Visible Only at Kansas Cy July 4."

With McKinley unopposed within his own party and Bryan receiving a second Democratic nomination almost by default, 1900 was a thin year for major party hopeful objects. Such splinter parties as the anti-fusionist Populists and the Socialist Labor party used campaign buttons, and the Social Democrats issued a few, including a "No Government by Injunction" variety featuring candidates Eugene Debs and Job Harriman. The effort of Prohibition standard-bearer John Granville Woolley inspired some outstanding thematic pieces, including "The Honor of the Church Is the Issue of 1900" and "In Defense of Home, Sweet Home" buttons and a "pox-on-both-houses" flyer insisting, "A vote for the Republican party is a vote for 'booze' in the dinner pail-A vote for the Democratic party is a vote for a dinner pail full of 'booze.'"

In 1904, another Republican landslide produced a material response much more exciting than the campaign itself. The lopsided victory of Theodore Roosevelt over a virtually catatonic Alton B. Parker (who spent the whole campaign in seclusion at his home in Ulster County, New York, setting an example apparently followed by most of his supporters) and several splinter party candidates inspired as many as a thousand different buttons, nearly a hundred types of watch fobs, many posters, ribbons, and postcards, and several varieties of bandannas, paperweights, plates, serving trays, banners, and pin trays. Also produced were such memorabilia as aluminum and celluloid bookmarks, tumblers, toby mugs, pocket knives, razors, clay pipes, canes, scissors, coin purses, and marbles.[11]

As several 1900 pieces had done, many 1904 Roosevelt items exploited his fame as the war hero who led his Rough Riders up San Juan Hill. He was portrayed in uniform, often astride his galloping charger, on several buttons, a multicolor tin serving tray (fig. 143), cloth broadsides, metal lapel pins, fobs, and a cast-iron figural bank. On the whole, however, Roosevelt objects in 1904 were remarkably free from the militaristic calls to national glory that dominated so many 1900 McKinley items. Apart from a series of five handkerchiefs reading "Protection/Prosperity/Expan-

Fig. 141. Contrasting scenes of economic desolation, fiscal chaos, and Spanish tyranny in Cuba under the Democrats with American prosperity and Cuban liberty under McKinley is this colorful 1900 Republican poster. (Edmund B. Sullivan)

Fig. 142. Inspired by a May 28, 1900, solar eclipse, these ingenious 1900 buttons predicted the "total eclipse" of either McKinley or Bryan in the November election. (Robert A. Fratkin)

Fig. 143. Exploiting Roosevelt's fame as the Rough Rider hero of the Spanish–American War was this superb multicolored serving tray, presumably depicting his celebrated charge up San Juan Hill. (Edmund B. Sullivan)

sion/Sound Money" (a 1900 design used without modification on the 1904 varieties), a "Same Old Flag and Victory" button was the only echo of 1900 jingoism.

Far fewer Roosevelt items exploited personality politics than such economic themes as the continuation of good times under Republican rule, tariff protection, and a "Square Deal" for business and labor alike. A huge canvas banner featuring running-mate Charles W. Fairbanks proclaimed, "Every Republican Vote Aids in Securing Continued Prosperity for the American People," and a multicolor button read "To Assure Continued Prosperity Elect Theodore Roosevelt." The slogan "Prosperity" graced buttons, postcards, razors, handkerchiefs, and posters. A button featured the full dinner pail symbol of 1900. Perhaps to reassure Republican conservatives that the reformist Roosevelt stood firm for at least some party traditions, many 1904 campaign items read "Protection," and a bandanna, "Protection to American Industry." The popular Square Deal slogan was featured on "A Square Deal" buttons, "A Square Deal for Every Man" postcards, and "Give Every Man a Square Deal" coin purses. Special appeals to blue-collar voters included "Justice to All" and "Equal Protection" buttons depicting labor shaking hands with management and coal-scuttle lapel pins symbolic of Roosevelt's widely heralded role in ending the 1902 anthracite strike in a manner that made him something of a hero to the American labor movement.

Other items inspired by the campaign made the issue the Roosevelt record pure and simple, sensible tactics in light of his enormous personal popularity, good times, and some popular policy initiatives. A "Liberty/Protection/Prosperity" poster pointed with pride to such accomplishments as Cuban home rule and the beginning of the Panama Canal. An enormous canvas banner boasted "Republican Policy Needs No Explanation/Acts and Promises Fufilled/Guarantee the Future." The poker expression "Stand Pat" was utilized on a brass badge and some buttons, two of them featuring playing-card motifs, and another button urged "Let Well Enough Alone."

Perhaps the most interesting and least understood of all 1904 campaign items are a trio of "Equality" buttons inspired by Roosevelt's 1901 White House dinner with black educator Booker T. Washington. In 1903, Charles H. Thomas, a white Chicago Republican who hoped to "impress upon the colored brothers that the only way to the higher life was to vote the Republican ticket," commissioned both a lithographed print (fig. 144) and a matching button (fig. 145) depicting the two men at table, with "Equality" inscribed boldly on the tablecloth. According to a September 24, 1903, account in the *Cincinnati Enquirer*, "thousands of the buttons are being worn by colored men in Chicago, and the demand throughout the country is growing." Sensitive over the outraged white supremacist response to the dinner, party leaders not only disavowed the buttons but also apparently sought to counteract them without alienating black supporters by ordering

Figs. 144 and 145. This Charles H. Thomas print above and matching button (center), commissioned in 1903 to strengthen Republican ties among black voters, inspired imitation buttons (left and right) given out in many southern and border states to arouse racist passions against Roosevelt and the Republicans.

another Equality button depicting Roosevelt leading black soldiers up San Juan Hill.[12] Another pro-Negro button issued by the Republican (fig. 146), apparently without causing any controversy, depicted Uncle Sam removing the barriers of "Prejudice," "Lawlessness," and "Injustice" as "President of All the People" Roosevelt looked on approvingly.

Meanwhile, Democratic campaign committees in border and southern states were evidently ordering and distributing large quantities of two vari-

Figs. 146 and 147. This multicolored Roosevelt button and blatantly racist anti–Roosevelt card
were among the many 1904 campaign objects inspired by Roosevelt's 1901 White House dinner
with Booker T. Washington and
the general debate over whether
or not black Americans deserved
a measure of legal, civil, and political rights in twentieth-century
America.

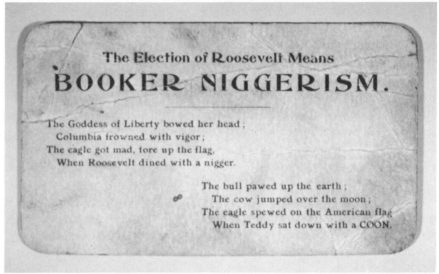

eties of buttons similar to the Thomas originals, only with the positions of
the men reversed, Washington portrayed as blacker and with more gener-
ically negroid features, and "Equality" above the dinner scene. In January
1904, the *Chicago Post* attributed this effort to operatives of Maryland senator and Democratic presidential hopeful Arthur P. Gorman, but Roosevelt
believed that the tactic had been used more widely. A month after the
election, he complained in a letter to Silas McBee, "These campaign buttons were distributed by the Democratic committees not merely in Tennessee but in Maryland, in southern Indiana, in West Virginia, in Kentucky,
and elsewhere where it was believed they could do damage to the Republican cause, and especially to me."[13]

The Roosevelt-Washington White House dinner also inspired some Democratic campaign items much less equivocal in origin and intent, some of them ranking among the most blatantly racist objects ever used in an American presidential election. Surely the poetry of prejudice has seldom been surpassed by the doggerel on a card (fig. 147), believed to have been distributed in Georgia, predicting that "The Election of Roosevelt Means Booker Niggerism." A button caricatured Roosevelt touching heads with a grotesque black man, presumably Washington, over the caption "Two Souls with but a Single Thought." Another button bluntly dramatized the traditional bottom line of white supremacist fears by portraying Democrat Alton B. Parker above a white wedding couple and Roosevelt above a white bride and black groom. The caption read "It's Up to You—Take Your Choice."[14]

With these exceptions and a few others, the items promoting Parker and octogenarian running-mate Henry Gassaway Davis featured only the names and likenesses of the two candidates. This was most likely due to the failure of the Democratic campaign to establish any thematic focus, for neither Parker nor Davis was especially remarkable in appearance. Although they were nominated primarily because eastern conservative Democrats wanted to repudiate Bryan and his agrarian radical wing, a few Parker–Davis items—"Our Country for the Masses not for the Classes/High Tariff Breeds Trusts/Anti-Militarism" postcards, for example—bore distinctly Bryanite rhetoric. More typical of the Parker faction's beliefs (and its desire to win the votes of Republican conservatives alienated by Roosevelt's activism) were many buttons with gold background coloration and such examples of Grover Cleveland's legacy as a "We Favor a Return to Jeffersonian Principles" poster and a "Good Government for the People" bandanna.

The 1904 campaign was a singularly poor one for items promoting major party hopeful candidates and also rather lean for minor party objects. Several buttons, including a "Workers of the World Unite" picture variety, featured Socialist candidate Eugene Debs, and buttons were also produced for Populist Thomas E. Watson and Socialist-Labor nominee Charles Hunter Corregan. Prohibitionist Silas Comfort Swallow inspired nearly a dozen different buttons, including two attractive multicolor styles featuring bird wordplays on his name and another variety urging Swallow supporters to "Use Maple City Soap."

The year 1908 was another outstanding election in terms of the material culture inspired by the candidacies of Bryan and Republican William Howard Taft. Several hundred varieties of postcards and buttons were produced, some of them—especially a number of multicolor buttons imitating the art nouveau style of artist Maxfield Parrish (fig. 148)—exhibiting aesthetic qualities rarely equaled on campaign objects before or since. It was also an excellent year for fobs promoting both candidates and for Republican ceramics. Ribbons, posters, serving trays, pennants, tumblers, caneheads,

Fig. 148. Promoting the 1908 Republican slate of William Howard Taft and James S. Sherman, these buttons reminiscent of the art nouveau style of Maxfield Parrish represent the artistic pinnacle of aesthetics for political lapel devices.

aluminum bookmarks, and handkerchiefs were among other memorabilia created.[15]

On the whole, the items inspired by Bryan's final presidential bid were much less thematic in nature than his 1896 and 1900 pieces, but some of them did echo the anti-big business populist rhetoric of 1900. Buttons and posters asked, "Shall the People Rule?" A "Down with the Trusts" button linked Bryan with Washington, Jefferson, Jackson, and Lincoln as "Enemies of Special Privilege/Upholders of Equality Before the Law." A handmade South Dakota cotton banner urged, "The People who produced the Wealth should have and enjoy what their labor has produced." A "Free Coinage/Prosperity" silk handkerchief represented the only known effort to revive the old silver crusade. Bryan's fondness for apocalyptic religiosity was reflected by a button featuring the Commoner with a dead tree and a thriving one (with ten leaves, each bearing the Roman numeral of a Commandment) and the Biblical admonition "The Tree That Does not Bear Good Fruit, Shall Be Dug Out by the Roots and Cast into the Fire!" A caricature button reading "The Nation/The State/No Twilight Zone" obliquely criticized the drift toward federal activism under Roosevelt. The economic downturn of 1907 gave Bryan a rare opportunity to usurp the full dinner pail issue. Buttons and postcards (fig. 149) proclaimed Bryan and corn "Two of America's Great Essentials to Peace and Prosperity," while other buttons urged, "Vote for Bryan and Prosperity." Buttons with hanging metal ears of corn promised "These Two and Prosperity."

Some 1908 Bryan items exhibited characteristics almost altogether absent from his 1896 and 1900 pieces, personality politics and satire. Buttons proclaimed him "Commoner" and "The Nation's Commoner." Others lampooned the Republicans as the party of "The Empty Dinner Pail," and buttons and postcards (fig. 150) insisted "The Bottom Out of the 'Full Dinner Pail'/Vote for Bryan." A postcard (fig.151) depicted "The Candidates at Exercise," Bryan "The Commoner" pitching hay, and Taft "The Plutocrat" playing golf with "29 Million Dollar John" D. Rockefeller. Items poking fun at Taft's monumental girth included "Nobody Loves a Fat Man" caricature buttons and postcards insisting "No Extra Large Chairs Needed at the White House" and "330 Pounds—Not Electoral Votes."

Taft items tended to focus less upon Taft himself than upon either his opponent or his predecessor. Although a "*Big* Man for a *Big* Party to Elect Him" linen handkerchief tried to make a virtue of Taft's rotundity, the main Republican weapon against such Democratic satire was a large number of satiric pieces of their own that lampooned Bryan as a perpetual loser, a windbag, and something of a crackpot. A button read "Vote for Taft This Time—You Can Vote for Bryan Any Time," and a postcard read "If Not Elected First Time, Run, Run Again." A superb postcard caricaturing Bryan as a cracked bust asked, "How much longer will it hold together?" and another (fig. 152) proclaimed him "The Nebraska Cuckoo Clock—Will Run Every Four Years if Properly Wound." Several postcards, including one variety featuring Bryan facing a battery of Taft and Roosevelt, used the baseball metaphor "3 Strikes and Out" or "The Third Strike for Bryan, Then Down and Out" to demean the Nebraskan's chances. Another postcard warned, "Look Out for a Windstorm, Bryan's Nominated," and yet another (fig. 152) urged "Don't Let Him Monkey with the Buzz Saw" of prosperity.

Many Taft items exploited the nominee as Theodore Roosevelt's chosen heir. Buttons spelled out Taft "*T*-ake *A*-dvice *F*-rom *T*-eddy" and others portrayed the two men shaking hands under the wordplay "U-N-I-TED." The big stick symbol of Roosevelt foreign policy was appropriated on Taft postcards (fig. 152) and "The Big Stick/Taft" ribbons with little baseball bats attached. Taft badges featured Rough Rider hat attachments, aluminum teddy bear bookmarks appeared with Taft celluloid inserts, an "Our Presidents Past, Present, Future" postcard portrayed Taft with McKinley and Roosevelt, and another Taft postcard featuring a carpenter's square proclaimed "A Square Deal for All."

Some effort was made to develop an identity for Taft himself. Postcards and ceramic plates featured absurdly grinning caricatures of Taft and running-mate James Sherman as "Smilin' Bill and Sunny Jim." Caricature

Figs. 149, 150, and 151. On these 1908 campaigns postcards, Bryan and corn are saluted as "America's Great Essentials," the 1900 Republican full dinner pail symbol is exploited by the Democrats, and Bryan pitches hay in the tradition of Lincoln splitting rails while Taft enjoys a game of golf with plutocrat John D. Rockefeller.

Fig. 152. On these 1908 postcards Taft is portrayed as the heir to Theodore Roosevelt's "big stick" foreign policy, while Bryan is caricatured tampering with the buzz saw of prosperity and as the "Nebraska Cuckoo Clock" that will "Run Every Four Years if Properly Wound."

buttons read "Hello Bill" and "Taft, Well I Should." Somehow (although a whale or a hippopotamus might have been more appropriate), Taft acquired an identity as "Billy Possum," and possum clothing buttons, fobs, and post-cards and a "Possum Klub" button promoted his candidacy. Remarkably few Taft items provided any indication of what a Taft presidency might mean for the nation. A ribbon pledged "Peace, Progress and Prosperity," and a postcard "Glory and Prosperity for Our Country." Several picture buttons announced, "I Am for Playgrounds," and another promised, "Taft Does Things/He'll Do in 1908." A coattail button picturing Taft and two South Dakota Republican candidates proclaimed them the "Progressive Trio."

Contests for both major party nominations produced at least two dozen buttons for such unsuccessful candidates as Democrats John A. Johnson, Judson Harmon, Joseph W. Folk, and William Randolph Hearst, and Re-publicans Joseph G. Cannon, Philander Knox, and Joseph B. Foraker. Among the campaign items produced for minor party candidates were but-tons promoting Populist Thomas E. Watson, Socialist-Laborite August Gilhaus, and Prohibitionist Eugene W. Chafin; some buttons and a "Work-ing Men—Vote Your Ticket/Enough for All—All the Time" poster for Socialist Eugene Debs; and a few buttons promoting Independence party nominees Thomas L. Hisgen and John Temple Graves. Again in 1908, these dynamic, colorful movements inspired few (and essentially dull) cam-paign objects.

Four years later, however, an unsuccessful bid for a major party nomina-tion that developed into the most impressive third-party candidacy in Amer-ican political history was largely responsible for endowing the material culture of the 1912 presidential election with a measure of creativity and imagination. Theodore Roosevelt's "Bull Moose" Progressive campaign, along with the major party bids of Taft and Democrat Woodrow Wilson and a surprisingly strong showing by Socialist Eugene Debs, produced the first truly exciting presidential race since 1896. Despite this large field and widespread public interest, 1912 was a rather lean year for material culture. Fewer buttons, half as many fobs, and much smaller numbers of ribbons, postcard, glass and ceramic pieces, and other types of campaign items were produced for 1912 than had been created for the essentially two-way 1908 contest.[16] In 1912, the practice of using material objects as partisan weapons began to exhibit signs of becoming a declining fad.

With another ride on the Roosevelt coattails an obvious impossibility, and with his soured presidency ruling out satire toward his opponents and such 1908 banality as "Billy Possum" and "Smilin' Bill," 1912 Taft items made no attempt to repeat the thematics or personality politics of his 1908 race, nor with few exceptions did they try to develop a new focus. Buttons proclaiming Taft "The sAFesT," and a mirror urging "It's Up to the Man on the Other Side to Put This Tried & Safe Man at the Head of the Govern-ment" promoted Taft's status as the lone conservative in the field, and buttons reading "Good Republicans Don't Bolt a Party Ticket" and "Unconditional Republican Club" utilized the "my-party-right-or-wrong" argument to minimize defections to the popular Roosevelt. Other Taft objects avoided thematics altogether.

Woodrow Wilson items in 1912 were even more vague, but for a very different reason. With the Republicans hopelessly divided, Wilson was virtually sure to win if his campaign could avoid major mistakes. Much like the campaign that inspired them, Wilson items avoided issues almost altogether in favor of such slogans as "Win with Wilson," "Man of the Hour," and "Pride of New Jersey." A button proclaimed him "For the White House Bound, with a Platform Safe and Sound," and another button and a postcard employed rowboat motifs for "Wood-Row" wordplays on his name.

In contrast, the material response to the 1912 Roosevelt campaign was much more imaginative. It also developed over a much longer time span. The man characterized by his daughter as having to be "the bride at every wedding and the corpse at every funeral" did not lose his celebrity status when he left the White House for an African safari in 1909, where his new persona as great white hunter "Bwana Tumbo" only added to his popularity. His 1910 return inspired buttons (fig. 153) featuring such greetings as "Welcome," "Welcome from Elba," "Welcome Teddy," and "Ted—He Came Back," and other buttons and several postcards (figs. 154, 155) depicting his homecoming being celebrated joyously by Uncle Sam, the GOP elephant, and President Taft. Within weeks, as progressives outraged by Taft policies enticed Roosevelt back into the presidential picture, it became apparent that Taft was dancing gleefully only on postcards and that these "welcome" items were in fact the first 1912 campaign objects. From them, through items created for the primaries he won and the Republican convention contest he lost, to those promoting his subsequent Bull Moose candidacy in the general election, Roosevelt inspired many campaign items reflecting in part his extraordinary charisma.

Despite the intensely ideological tenor of the Roosevelt "Stand at Armageddon," only a "Social and Industrial Justice" ribbon and "Progressive/Thou Shalt not Steal" buttons really reflected this characteristic. Other Roosevelt items utilized a number of symbols old and new to exploit the politics of personality. Many pins, postcards, and buttons celebrating his declaration of candidacy bore the slogan "My Hat Is in the Ring" (during the primaries and Republican convention) or "My Hat Is *STILL* in the Ring" (during the general election). Invariably, the hat was the familiar Rough Rider variety. "3rd Term for Teddy" lapel pins featured the Roosevelt big stick, as did a bandanna (fig. 156) also utilizing the teddy bear motif and Roosevelt's distinctive glasses and teeth. Buttons proclaimed "A Square Deal All Around/1912." The famous teeth, spectacles, and favorite expression "Dee-Lighted" were used to create some excellent caricature buttons and postcards (fig. 157). The ubiquitous symbol of his Progressive candi-

Figs. 153, 154, and 155. Inspired by Roosevelt's 1910 return from a highly publicized grand tour of Africa and Europe, such items as these "Welcome" buttons and caricature postcards became, in reality, the first campaign items for the raucous 1912 race between Roosevelt, Taft, and Wilson.

dacy, born with his declaration, "I feel fit as a bull moose," was featured on banners (fig. 158), postcards (fig. 159), bandannas, ribbons, and a host of buttons and other lapel devices.

Despite a campaign that attracted an impressive nine hundred thousand votes, the Socialist effort on behalf of Eugene Debs inspired a few buttons and pennants, none of them thematic in nature. A few buttons were also created for Prohibition candidate Eugene Chafin. Apart from the many primary and convention items promoting Roosevelt, the only campaign objects engendered by unsuccessful candidates for the Republican nomination were some buttons produced from Albert B. Cummins. Much more

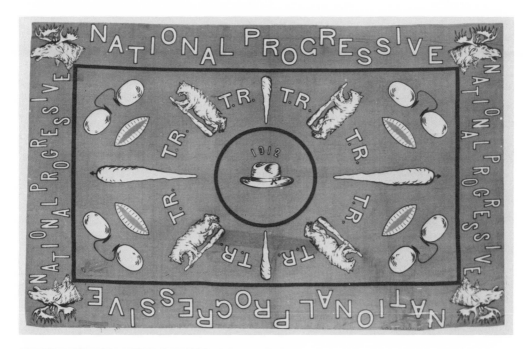

Figs. 156 and 157. Excellent examples of the use of symbolism and personality politics on 1912 Roosevelt campaign material are this "National Progressive" red bandanna, with the famous T. R. big stick, teddy bear, Rough Rider hat, spectacles, and toothy grin, and this "Delighted" postcard. (Fig. 156, Edmund B. Sullivan)

plentiful were items promoting such Democratic hopefuls as Oscar W. Underwood, John W. Kern, William J. Gaynor, and House Speaker Champ Clark. The Underwood and Kern delegations produced buttons, the Gaynor forces a "He Can Win" ribbon badge, and the Clark contingent more than a dozen buttons and fobs, including some "Vote for the Champ" buttons and several excellent "They Gotta Quit Kickin' My Dawg Aroun'" fobs and buttons.

The 1916 contest between Wilson and Republican Charles Evans Hughes inspired a significantly smaller number of campaign objects than the 1912 election, despite a race so close that its outcome was not decided until California's thirteen electoral votes fell into the Wilson column by less than four thousand votes on the morning after the balloting. With the exception

Figs. 158 and 159. Exploiting the celebrated Bull Moose symbol of Roosevelt's 1912 Progressive party campaign were this Roosevelt–Hiram Johnson poster and this postcard. (Fig. 158, Edmund B. Sullivan)

of the celluloid button, created in at least three hundred varieties in 1916, material culture gave every indication of a dying phenomenon. A few ribbons, fobs, posters, and postcards, and even fewer types of other items appeared. On the whole, 1916 produced the poorest material response of any presidential campaign since 1880.[17]

The Hughes items were overwhelmingly nonthematic, a reflection of the belief that a reunited Republican party could not be defeated if its Old Guard conservative and Roosevelt progressive factions held together. The few buttons (fig. 160) and other items that developed any themes at all tended to promote Republican unity and to foster the concept of Hughes as a patriot in a vague manner tailored to the public mood of indecision over the war raging in Europe. A button featuring the Republican elephant and Progressive bull moose urged "Republicans/Bull Moosers/Get Together." Others promoted Hughes's "Undiluted Americanism" and put him on re-cord "For Law and Liberty." Other buttons spelled his name with the *u* and *s* much larger than other letters. "It Fits Hughes" lapel pins featured Hughes wearing Uncle Sam's hat, and others insisted upon "Duty Without Fear." Other Hughes items bore such safe sentiments as "Security/Harmony/Jus-tice," "America First and Efficient," and "American Rights Respected and Protected/American Industry Promoted and Protected."

Buttons and other objects promoting Wilson's re-election reflected his need to stress repeatedly his progressive record and the tense world situation to defeat a strong candidate of a reunited majority Republican party. A button (portraying a dead elephant) proclaimed Wilson "Progressive," another read "Progressive Policies Become Law Under Wilson," and a pock-et knife urged "Justice and Progress Go Hand in Hand." Several button designs utilized a figure-8 motif or such slogans as "The Man of the Eight Hour Day," "8-Hour Wilson," "Champions of 8 Hour Law," and "I Am for Wilson and an 8 Hour Day" to exploit his popularity among workers for enactment of the eight-hour workday for railroad employees.

A much larger number of Wilson items (fig.161) reflect his campaign strategy of exploiting widespread fears over involvement in the European war and at the same time portraying him as a decisive national leader prepared to safeguard American interests in a crisis situation. Buttons read "War in Europe/Peace in America/ God Bless Wilson," "Peace & Prosper-ity," "Safety First," and "He Proved the Pen Mightier than the Sword," and a fob echoed "His Pen Mightier than the Sword." Alliterative paper stickers read "Woodrow Wilson's Wisdom Wins Without War" and buttons "Woodrow Wilson's Wisdom Wins" and Watchful Waiting Wins." The catchy and nicely ambivalent slogan "America First" was utilized on many buttons, some of them reading "They Have Kept the Faith/We'll Stand by Them/America First," "America First/Thank God for Wilson," and "America First/Liberty." Decidedly more hawkish was a button featuring artillery, a war eagle, and the slogan "An American for America/Preparedness," although calls for preparedness were more commonly tied to peace sentiments with such legends as "Peace with Honor/Preparedness/Prosperity," "Peace and Pre-paredness," and "Preparedness/Peace/Prosperity." Buttons urging "Stand by Wilson/The Man on the Job," "Stand by the President," and "For God and Our Country" implied that a capricious switch in leadership at such a perilous time was unthinkable.

With Wilson unchallenged for renomination, no Democratic rivals had reason to produce campaign items in 1916. Buttons promoting Socialist Allan L. Benson and Prohibitionist James Franklin Hanley were apparently the only minor party objects created. Buttons were issued for Republican hopefuls Samuel Walker McCall, Elihu Root, Frank Willis, and Laurence Sherman, and the hawkish dark-horse candidacy of John W. Weeks pro-

Figs. 160 and 161. With World War I raging in Europe and threatening to involve the United States in its first major foreign conflict in nearly a century, these 1916 campaign buttons promoting Hughes and Wilson reflected the themes of peace, preparedness, and patriotism.

duced two multicolor buttons and a convention badge urging "The Army and Navy Forever." The most intriguing 1916 Republican hopeful items, however, were inspired by speculation that Theodore Roosevelt would again seek the presidency, a possibility much more appealing to Republican interventionists than to his old Bull Moose comrades embarrassed by his zeal to use the big stick on Germany. Buttons and postcards featured the Roosevelt dictum "Fear God and Take Your Own Part," and another button urged "Preparedness 1916." The only echo of 1912 was a "Progressive/1916 & Victory" button. Even from the sidelines, as he had in every race since his 1900 vice-presidential bid, this irrepressible figure managed to hold the limelight on campaign objects.

NOTES

1. An outstanding contemporary account of the introduction of celluloid buttons into the American political process was written for *The Strand Magazine* (London) during the autumn of 1896 by American correspondent George Dollar and is reprinted in the *APIC Keynoter* 84 (Summer 1984): 20–22.

2. For a useful general survey of this material, see Bernard L. Greenhouse, *Political Postcards, 1900–1980: A Price Guide* (Syracuse, 1984).

3. Toby pitchers and mugs, drinking vessels shaped like human faces, date back to ancient times. The origin of the term *toby* remains something of a mystery. Some authorities attribute it to Shakespeare's Sir Toby Belch, while others argue that it comes from "Toby Fillpot," a seventeenth-century Yorkshire expression denoting a prodigious tippler. See Sullivan, *Collecting Political Americana*, 99.

4. See Paul W. Glad, *McKinley, Bryan, and the People* (Philadelphia, 1964); Stanley L. Jones, *The Presidential Election of 1896* (Madison, Wisc., 1964); Margaret Leech, *In the Days of McKinley* (New York, 1959), 66–96; Paolo E. Coletta, *William Jennings Bryan, I: Political Evangelist, 1860–1908* (Lincoln, Neb., 1964), 99–212; and R. Hal Williams, *Years of Decision: American Politics in the 1890s* (New York, 1978), 97–127.

5. See Fischer and Sullivan, *Political Ribbons and Ribbon Badges*, 269–74, 278–86, 288–95, 301–6, 310–12, 314–16; Hake, *Political Buttons, III*, 138–50, 152–59, 161–68, 172, 174–75, 241; Collins, *Threads of History*, 303–17; Theodore L. Hake, *Encyclopedia of Political Buttons: United States, 1896–1972* (New York, 1973), 14, 17–26, 28, 31–32, 38, 41–53, 254–55; Richard P. Bristow, *The Illustrated Political Button Book*, 4th ed. (Santa Cruz, Calif., 1973), 11–13, 17–32, 35, 37, 39–52; Sullivan, *Collecting Political Americana*, 8, 30–31, 57, 80–81, 93, 104, 107–9, 119–21, 126, 136, 148–49, 154, 171–72; and the illustrations accompanying Roger A. Fischer, "The Free Silver Crusades of William Jennings Bryan," *APIC Keynoter* 80 (Spring 1980): 4–15, and "Prosperity's Advance Agent: William McKinley and the Gold Standard," *APIC Keynoter* 84 (Summer 1984): 4–17. For an attempt to place this material within the context of the 1896 campaign, see Roger A. Fischer, "1896 Campaign Artifacts: A Study in Inferential Reconstruction," *Journal of American Culture* 3 (Winter 1980): 706–21; reprinted in *American Material Culture*, ed. Mayo, 112–27.

6. Although this appealing slogan was used extensively during McKinley's bid for the Republican nomination and remained in vogue to some extent throughout the campaign, it seems to have been used on only two or three campaign items. Especially surprising in light of the great number of McKinley pieces created, this represents one of the relatively few examples of commercial producers failing to utilize a clearly enunciated and quite promising campaign theme on their wares.

7. See Farran Zerbe, "Bryan Money: Tokens of the Presidential Campaigns of 1896 and 1900, Comparative and Satirical," *The Numismatist* 39 (July 1926): 313–76.

8. Jones, *Presidential Election of 1896*, 291–93.

9. See Hake, *Political Buttons, III*, 139–54, 156–59, 162, 165–66, 168–75; Bristow, *Illustrated Political Button Book* 13–27, 29–32, 35–48, 50–51; Hake, *Encyclopedia of Political Buttons*, 15–20, 24, 28–29, 32–35, 38–45, 49–52, 250–51, 254–55; Fischer and Sullivan, *Political Ribbons and Ribbon Badges*, 275–78, 286–89, 295–96, 302, 306–7, 313; Collins, *Threads of History*, 330–37; Sullivan, *Collecting Political Americana*, 35, 93, 172, 176; Greenhouse, *Political Postcards*, 3–5; and the illustrations accompanying Roger A. Fischer, "The McKinley Presidency, 1897–1901," *APIC Keynoter* 84 (Fall 1984): 4–17.

10. This splendid symbol, surely the most compelling since the 1860 Lincoln split rail, owes its origins apparently to the 1900 cartoon art of Grant Hamilton in *Judge*. See Stephen Hess and Milton Kaplan, *The Ungentlemanly Art: A History of American Political Cartoons* (New York, 1968), 110–11.

11. See Hake, *Encyclopedia of Political Buttons*, 55–69, 71–78, 250–51, 254–55; Hake, *Political Buttons, III*, 176–94, 195–203; Bristow, *Illustrated Political Button Book*, 53–67, 69–76; Fischer and Sullivan, *Political Ribbons and Ribbon Badges*, 317–22, 324–26, 328–30; Collins, *Threads of History*, 344–50; Greenhouse, *Political Postcards*, 6–10; and Sullivan, *Collecting Political Americana*, 34, 61, 96, 112, 136, 165. Especially valuable is the American Political Items Collectors' *Parker and Davis, 1904: An APIC Research Project*, 1971.

12. *Chicago Post*, Jan. 4, 1904. Although the San Juan Hill "Equality" button is illustrated in the *Post*, no known examples survive in major public or private collections.

13. Roosevelt to Silas McBee, Dec. 15, 1904; quoted in a letter from Marion G. Merrill to Herbert R. Collins, Feb. 18, 1970. I am also indebted to Ms. Merrill's research for the accounts of these fascinating buttons in the *Cincinnati Enquirer* and *Chicago Post*.

14. For an expanded account of these items and their role in the 1904 campaign, see Roger A. Fischer, "Teddy and 'Equality,'" *APIC Keynoter*, 81 (Summer, 1981): 10–13.

15. See Hake, *Political Buttons, III*, 157–60, 162–66, 169–74, 204–18, 241; Hake, *Encyclopedia of Political Buttons*, 36–39, 41–45, 49–50, 52–53, 80–90, 250–51, 254–55; Bristow, *Illustrated Political Button Book*, 36–48, 50–51, 77–86; Greenhouse, *Political Postcards*, 12–40; Fischer and Sullivan, *Political Ribbons and Badges*, 302, 308–9, 313, 331–32, 335, 337; Collins, *Threads of History*, 356–62; David Frent, "The World of Political Postcards," *APIC Keynoter*, 80 (Fall 1980): 14–17, and 80 (Winter 1980): 18–19; and Sullivan, *Collecting Political Americana*, 35, 61–63, 95–96, 107, 163, 165.

16. See Hake, *Encyclopedia of Poliltical Buttons*, 58–59, 62–64, 66–69, 83, 87, 90, 92–97, 250–51, 254–55; Hake, *Political Buttons*, III, 177–78, 180–83, 186, 189, 192–94, 204–5, 209, 211–14, 217–18, 219–31, 241; Bristow, *Illustrated Political Button Book*, 55–56, 59–60, 62–67, 77–78, 81–82, 84, 86, 89–97; Greenhouse, *Political Postcards*, 42–51; Fischer and Sullivan, *Political Ribbons and Ribbon Badges*, 317–18, 323, 326, 332, 334, 336, 338–342; Collins, *Threads of History*, 367–77; and Sullivan, *Collecting Political Americana*, 9, 41–42, 62, 95, 100, 126, 136, 165.

17. See Hake, *Political Buttons*, III, 219–21, 225–26, 228–31, 232–35; Bristow, *Illustrated Political Button Book*, 91–97, 99–102; Hake, *Encyclopedia of Political Buttons*, 93–97, 99–101, 250–51; Fischer and Sullivan, *Political Ribbons and Ribbon Badges*, 338–40, 342–44, 347; Greenhouse, *Political Postcards*, 53–54; Sullivan, *Collecting Political Americana*, 9; and Collins, *Threads of History*, 396.

6

Into the Age of Marconi and Ford 1920–48

The three decades from World War I through 1948 brought substantial changes in the life-styles of the American people and in the nature of campaigns to choose our national leaders. Although the sharp decline in voter turnout after World War I was primarily because of other factors,[1] there is little question that fewer and fewer Americans regarded membership in a political party, participation in its rituals and activities, and the outcome of presidential elections with quite the same degree of commitment and enthusiasm exhibited by earlier generations. To a great extent, this waning preoccupation with elective politics was a direct result of such new forms of competition for public attention as the radio, the development of motion pictures and spectator sports into billion-dollar industries, and the automobile. Although candidates became increasingly visible to the electorate through extensive travel and radio and newsreel coverage, the only American political figure from Warren Harding through Harry Truman to rival even remotely the celebrity-hero status of the likes of Babe Ruth, Rudolph Valentino, and "Lucky" Lindbergh was Franklin Delano Roosevelt, in part because of his mastery of radio communication.

As more voters began to behave like spectators and fewer like participants, and as grass-roots activities became less important elements in presidential campaigns, material culture inevitably suffered a decline in political significance, for buttons and banners and the like simply could not compete with fireside chats and Movietone News as persuaders of a passive electorate. This diminution in importance did not bring about a corresponding decline in the variety or volume of items manufactured for campaigns, although it did precipitate a definite trend toward the much less expensive (and usually tackier and less durable) sorts of objects used as giveaway items by presidential campaign committees and a drift away from the types of relatively expensive keepsake items purchased by individual partisans.

Decorative household objects of a presidential nature became real rarities after World War I, with two main exceptions: plates and other souvenir items manufactured for sale to the tourists who flocked to Washington and other national shrines, and a massive variety of bric-a-brac featuring Franklin Roosevelt, including mantle clocks, statuary, ceramic plates and miniatures, wall plaques, tiles, glasses, desk thermometers, mugs, and paper-weights. Neither the souvenir-stand items nor most of the Roosevelt memorabilia were overtly partisan in nature or campaign objects in any direct sense. Among the few examples of campaign-inspired bric-a-brac were a glass John W. Davis berry dish, matching Al Smith and Herbert Hoover tobies (fig. 162), and glass tumblers featuring Roosevelt, Alf Landon, and Wendell Willkie.

Other traditional types of political objects also became much less common in the new era. Some outstanding watch fobs and straight razors were made for the 1920 campaign, but very few thereafter, doomed as they were by the emergence of the wristwatch and the safety razor. The 1920–48 period was a rather lean one for political textiles in general, with ribbons, banners, bandannas, and handkerchiefs produced in very limited quantities. A notable exception, however, was the 1940 campaign, when cotton bandannas enjoyed a major revival, and a host of satin mini-banners for windows and desks was marketed. Some pocket lucky pieces made of brass were struck for the 1928 and 1932 races and appear to have been the main representatives of the once-proud tradition of political medallic art. With the exception of several anti–Roosevelt varieties printed in 1940, political postcards were rather uncommon after World War I

The postcard may well have been the only type of paper campaign item to experience such a decline during this period, for the races from 1920 through 1948 inspired and utilized an unprecedented variety and volume of political paper. Posters were produced in much greater numbers than ever before, especially smaller, thin paper varieties printed in extraordinary volume to turn millions of telephone poles along city streets and country roads into instant political billboards. Stamps, used as campaign devices in very limited quantities since the dawn of the twentieth century, began to appear in much greater number in 1928 and subsequent races (fig. 163). Stickers and window decals emerged during the 1920s as prime vehicles for partisan propaganda. The development of the practice of knocking on doors as a prominent grass-roots activity to get out the vote inspired a number of ingenious varieties of doorhangers, including John W. Davis teapots (see fig. 174) and Alf Landon sunflowers. Political matchbooks made their debut in 1928, soon after paper matches began to replace wooden ones.

The celluloid button retained its position as a popular campaign lapel device throughout the period and in 1940 experienced an all-time vogue, but its virtual monopoly was doomed after World War I by new technology and cost considerations, the very factors that had assured its ascendancy a

Fig. 162. These matching 1928 Al Smith and Herbert Hoover toby mugs were among the few really creative political ceramic objects marketed after World War I, a manifestation of diminishing interest in bric-a-brac of all sorts. (Edmund B. Sullivan)

generation earlier. Buttons and "tabs" stamped from lithographed sheets of tin (fig. 164), introduced experimentally during the 1916 race and adopted widely in subsequent campaigns, provided political organizations with giveaway lapel pieces much less expensive in large quantities than the celluloids. Ordered in enormous numbers from such manufacturers as Chicago's Green Duck Company, these "lithos" quickly evolved into the dominant type of lapel item distributed by national campaign committees to local headquarters, despite the rather severe thematic and aesthetic limitations imposed by the lithographic process. Vastly superior in design and color potential and less expensive to produce in limited quantities, celluloid buttons continued to dominate commercial vendor markets and those campaign situations where economy of scale was not a consideration.

With the addition of women to the franchise on a nation-wide basis in 1920, it would be logical to assume that material culture would follow magazine advertising and other campaign phenomena in reflecting this breakthrough, but such was not really the case. Indeed, when one takes into account the sharp decline in political ceramic and glass bric-a-brac and other decorative household items, fewer objects designed to appeal

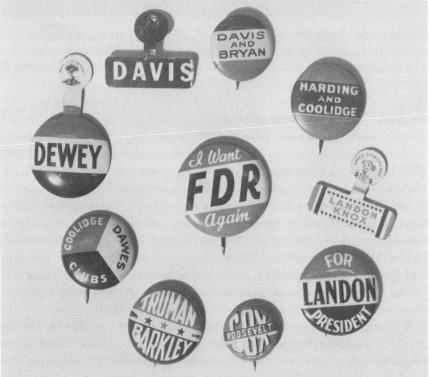

Figs. 163 and 164. Indicative of the trend toward inexpensive giveaway items in political campaigns after World War I were these political stamps and lithographed buttons and tabs.

exclusively or primarily to women appear to have been produced after suffrage than before. Items reflecting the reform were primarily Republican, including Warren G. Harding ribbon badges reading "Women's First Vote/ Vote the Straight Republican Ticket," and 1920, 1924, and 1928 celluloid mirrors requesting "the lady on the other side" to cast votes for Harding, Calvin Coolidge, and Herbert Hoover. Compacts featured Al Smith and Wendell Willkie. Other women's items produced during the period indicate that the old Victorian cult of domesticity was far from dead, at least in the minds of creators of campaign artifacts. Thimbles promoted most candidates from 1924 through 1940 and featured such slogans as "Hoover-Home-Happiness." Needle packs (fig. 185) were popular in 1928 and subsequent races, as were sewing kits.

The new American love affair with the automobile created a challenge to which the producers of campaign items responded with real creativity. In 1920, political decals (see figs. 168, 171) were used on car windows, but the first purely automotive political objects were the license plate attachments (fig. 165) introduced in 1924, the year that the Republican "Lincoln tour" motor caravan began motorized campaigning.[2] In subsequent races, license attachments were marketed in a number of styles, including thin strips for mounting on top of the license plate, larger rectangular ones used primarily on front bumpers in the states that mandated only a rear plate, circular and shield-shaped reflectorized models, and several imaginative figural varieties. License attachments played an important role in political material culture until the widespread adoption of the bumper sticker during the 1950s and remain relatively popular in southern states that have resisted the use of plates on front bumpers. Oilcloth covers for spare tires (fig. 166) enjoyed a minor vogue until after the 1932 campaign, when automobile manufacturers introduced models with spares inside the trunks. Bumper stickers did not evolve into a significant factor in political campaigns until 1956, although early nonadhesive prototypes were being used as early as the 1932 campaign. Most were much like their modern descendants in shape and size, although a 1940 variety proclaiming "A Carload of Willkie Votes" more closely resembled a paper street banner. The political billboard made its debut at least as early as 1940, when one variety depicted a little girl asking, "Daddy, what's a Democracy?" and receiving the explanation, "It's America with Willkie!"

These automotive items were not the only innovations during the period to attest to the impact of modernization on the political process. Among the objects promoting the 1920 candidacy of James Cox was an electric glass sign eight inches high and sixteen inches wide, apparently meant for tables in front of windows. In 1940, the Wendell Willkie campaign inspired a "Hoosier Favorite!/Willkie" miniature airport wind sock and a little put-together talking machine similar to nonpolitical varieties offered as cereal premiums. When assembled and its string was pulled, this gadget urged

Figs. 165 and 166. Among the many types of items pioneered between 1920 and 1948 to turn automobiles into moving political billboards were these license plate attachments and this oilcloth 1932 Hoover spare tire cover. (Edmund B. Sullivan)

support for Willkie and Iowa Governor George Allison Wilson with the message "Willkie and Wilson." Other innovations during the period included a set of Al Smith and Herbert Hoover chimney covers for stoves in 1928, political cigarette lighters in 1932, mechanical pencils in 1936, and "Please Don't Talk 3rd Term to Me/I'm for Willkie" paper earmuffs in 1940. One of the first known campaign edibles in American politics was a large Franklin Roosevelt figural lollipop.

The 1920 landslide victory of Republicans Warren Harding and Calvin Coolidge over Democrats James M. Cox and Franklin Delano Roosevelt inspired a rather limited material response, including fewer than two hundred button varieties, many posters, some pewter studs, enamel lapel pins, fobs, ribbons, and ribbon badges, and such other memorabilia as cigars, straight razors, stamps, postcards, beanies, pennants, celluloid bookmarks, paperweights, window decals, Cox–Roosevelt jigsaw puzzles, and Harding mechanical nose-thumbers.[3] Neither campaign invested huge sums in items, especially the poverty-stricken Cox–Roosevelt forces, who apparently limited their giveaway material to miniscule quantities of literature and three styles of tiny lithographed buttons. Neither the paucity of these items nor the fact that one variety of button read "Coxsure" pleased Roosevelt, who was painfully aware that his ticket had little cause to wax smug. As he prepared to embark upon a western tour in September, he begged the head of the Democratic National Committee's publicity bureau: "I am throwing myself on your mercy. It is imperative we have plenty of literature for this trip—a package at least of everything you have. We need thousands of buttons—not those damn 'Coxsure' buttons, but both the other two kinds. This is one of the best ways in the World to get them to individuals, and I wish you would give us a plentiful supply, as they cry for them everywhere we go."[4]

Aside from such giveaway material, most 1920 campaign objects were produced not for the national campaign organizations but for sale by retail vendors and, in some instances, for distribution by local political groups. Shortly after Roosevelt's nomination, he received a letter from the St. Louis Button Company, identifying itself as "one of the leading concerns in America specializing in the manufacture of campaign buttons," requesting of FDR "a picture of you, one which will reproduce to the best advantage for campaign button purposes." Roosevelt sent the photograph after receiving a reminder two weeks later in which the producer complained, "We have on hand orders for thousands of these buttons and cannot fill them unless we have your picture. Governor Cox has supplied us with his picture, also Senator Harding and Governor Coolidge, and we are badly in need of your picture to be used on buttons to show portraits of the candidates for President and Vice President on the Democratic ticket."[5] Made in two sizes with Cox and FDR accompanied by an eagle, rays, and Old Glory, these buttons were by far the jauntiest of all Cox–Roosevelt varieties (fig. 167) produced.

Fig. 167. Among the eight known varieties of Cox–Roosevelt jugate buttons produced in 1920 are the colorful St. Louis Button Company varieties at right, made
from a photograph begged personally from FDR, and the puzzling "Americanize
America" variety at lower left. (Ronald T. Marchese)

Reflecting a campaign that downplayed issues because victory was virtually assured, designers of Harding items avoided the difficult task of depicting "normalcy" through graphics and exploited party identification with
frequent use of the Republican elephant symbol. Cox items utilizing
wordplays on his name included some pewter studs featuring roosters and
the aforementioned "Coxsure" buttons. With the exception of a "Cox and
Cocktails" button protesting Prohibition and a "Prosperity/Protection"
Harding button, issue-oriented items promoting both tickets reflected the
simmering controversy over American entry into the League of Nations.
Harding buttons and cigar packs proclaimed "America First," and another
button insisted "Think of America First." Harding–Coolidge window decals
(fig. 168) read "America Always First/Back to Normal/Law & Order." Less

ambiguous in its rejection of Wilsonian internationalism was an "America First" Harding postcard (fig. 169) repeating his words "I would rather break the heart of the world than to break the heart of the people of these United States." A number of 1920 Democratic items reflect the party's basic quandary between a vigorous commitment to entry into the League and an opportunistic retreat into ambiguous rhetoric. A sticker (fig. 170) urged "Keep Faith With Our Sons/Bring America into the League of Nations," but a poster echoed the Republican refrain "America First," and a decal (fig. 171) bore the cliche for all seasons "Peace with Honor." Easily the most bizarre of all such 1920 items was a Cox–Roosevelt button (fig. 167) urging "Americanize America," a rather inappropriate slogan (whatever its intended meaning) for a party so heavily dependent upon the votes of millions of recent immigrants.

The 1920 primaries and Republican and Democratic conventions provided arenas for buttons and other objects promoting such hopeful candidates as General Leonard Wood, Hiram Johnson, William E. Borah, Vice-President Thomas Marshall, Wilson son-in-law William Gibbs McAdoo, Carter Glass, and "red scare" architect Attorney General A. Mitchell Palmer. Republican reactionary Miles Poindexter issued buttons demanding "Government by Law/No Red without the White and Blue." Buttons promoted Farmer-Labor candidate Parley Parker Christensen and Socialist Eugene Debs, who received a record 919,800 votes although he was confined to a cell in Atlanta Penitentiary for exercising his civil liberties protesting American involvement in World War I. Several 1920 Debs items flaunted his incarceration by depicting him in prison garb (fig. 172) with such captions as "Convict No. 2253 for President" and "For President Convict No. 9653."[6]

Calvin Coolidge's overwhelming 1924 victory over Democrat John W. Davis, Progressive Robert LaFollette, and several minor party candidates produced a slightly larger and much more imaginative assortment of campaign objects than had the 1920 election, including more than two hundred varieties of buttons, several posters and other paper items, the first political license attachments, and such miscellaneous memorabilia as fobs, mirrors, pennants, and thimbles. Again in 1924, despite the availability of more campaign funds, the Democrats gave very short shrift to material culture in their rather moribund effort to elect Davis and running-mate Charles W. Bryan, inspiring fewer varieties of objects in smaller quantities than any other major party campaign since Reconstruction. The Republican effort on behalf of Coolidge and Charles G. Dawes proved much more prolific, however, and the Progressive ticket of LaFollette and Burton K. Wheeler was promoted on pennants, fobs, brass lapel pins, license attachments, some paper items, and at least thirty varieties of buttons. The Communists, Prohibitionists, and American party also produced buttons, as did Democratic hopefuls Oscar Underwood, Albert C. Ritchie, and Alfred E. Smith and Republican contender James E. Watson.[7]

In terms of their thematics, 1924 campaign items fell essentially into two categories, those promoting the virtues of Coolidge and those (fig. 173) exploiting the scandals of predecessor Warren Harding. Among the latter was a Workers' party button demanding "Down with the Capitalist Teapot Dome/Forward to a Workers & Farmers Government." A "C'mon Bob Let's Go!" Progressive button offered the choice of LaFollette or a teapot, and a small brass teapot lapel pin bore the legend "LaFollette Did It," a reference to his role in the Senate's investigation of the Harding scandals. Davis buttons pledged "Back to Honesty with Davis" and "Honest Days with Davis" and a teapot doorhanger (fig. 174) urged a vote against "Special Privilege" on one side and "The Party Responsible for Tea-Pot Dome" on the other. Buttons featured teapots labeled "Doom" and a GOP elephant simmering in a "Teapot Dome" teapot. A "GOP/Your Waterloo" button superimposed a teapot against the Capitol dome, and another invited "Take a Kick at the Teapot." A teapot brass lapel pin reminded, "Don't Forget Teapot."

Items promoting Coolidge did so with a mixture of personality politics and appeals (fig. 175) to traditional Republican verities. The slogan "Keep Cool with Coolidge" or its variant "Keep Cool-idge" appeared on paper fans (fig. 176), buttons, pennants, license attachments, and stamps depicting electric table fans. Although this remote, dour man ("weaned on a pickle," it was joked) who loved sleep and abhorred activist leadership may have seemed a most unlikely subject for personality politics, such was clearly not the case. "Deeds—not Words" buttons highlighted his identity as "Silent Cal." His almost antediluvian conservatism was lauded on "Careful Cautious Calvin Coolidge" postcards, "Safe-Sane-Steady" posters, and "Let Well Enough Alone," "Safe with Cal," and "Safe and Sane" buttons. A "Firm as the Rock of Ages" button promoted him as a symbol of Puritan righteousness in an era of bathtub gin and flappers, as did a "Coolidge/On the Square" button picturing a little red schoolhouse. Others read "Coolidge and Courage," "Courage/Duty/Confidence," and "Courage/Confidence and Coolidge." Another button portrayed him (inside a ship's wheel) as "Our Pilot Calvin Coolidge." Buttons with such slogans as "Full Dinner Pail" and "Keep Square Deal" cast Coolidge as heir to the tradition of McKinley and Roosevelt. Postcards and license attachments featured the agenda "Less Taxes/Larger Service/Balanced Business." All things considered, the designers of campaign items in 1924 made Calvin Coolidge a much more interesting figure than did nature.

The 1928 contest between Republican Herbert Hoover and Democrat Al Smith engendered a larger and much more creative material response than any presidential race since 1912, primarily because Smith's nomination transformed the election into a national referendum on religion, geography, and the "noble experiment" of Prohibition as well as a struggle for the White House between two well known and rather interesting candidates in their own right. The contest inspired more than three hundred varieties of

Figs. 168 and 169. Reflecting the 1920 Harding campaign's attempt to appeal to isolationist voters without actually going on record against American entry into the League of Nations were this window decal and postcard. (Fig. 168, Edmund B. Sullivan)

PEACE WITH HONOR

OUR CHOICE

COX
FOR PRESIDENT

ROOSEVELT
FOR VICE PRESIDENT

Keep Faith With
our Sons
Bring America into
The League of Nations
Vote For
Cox and Roosevelt

Figs. 170 and 171. This strongly pro–League of Nations sticker and ambiguous "Peace with Honor" sticker faithfully mirror the two faces of a 1920 Democratic campaign unable to decide between forthright internationalism and opportunistic waffling. (Ronald T. Marchese)

Fig. 172. Flaunting the fact that presidential nominee Eugene Debs was serving time in Atlanta Penitentiary for sedition, these 1920 Socialist buttons were among the more unusual of all American political campaign items. (Robert A. Fratkin)

buttons, the most diverse and imaginative assortment of other types of lapel devices in many years, many license attachments, several styles of posters and other types of political paper, a larger array of campaign textiles than any race since 1912, a few ribbons, ribbon badges, and fobs, cigars, pencils, mirrors, and such intriguing miscellany as a matched set of toby mugs, oilcloth spare tire covers, chimney covers for iron stoves, thimbles, rings, little enamel "Hoo but Hoover" owls, and miniature figural Smith moonshine jugs and derby hats.[8] Not since Theodore Roosevelt's retirement from the campaign trail had material culture reflected so well the exuberant banality of American elective politics.

Some 1928 buttons, however, attest that the race had its ugly underside, the virulent Protestant backlash against the first Catholic nominated for the presidency by a major political party. Although the closest that items distributed by the Hoover campaign came to exploiting the religious issue openly was a "Hoover/100% American" button, pieces produced independently were much more explicit. In the South, where the issue was especially intense, Protestants who chose faith over party sported "A Democrat for Hoover," "Another Democrat for Hoover," "Anti-Smith," "A Christian in the White House," and "Principle Above Party" buttons. Motivated in part by the liquor issue and in part by religion, the Women's Christian Temperance Union distributed "WCTU/Vote for Hoover" buttons. The

Figs. 173 and 174. Among the many items seeking to exploit the misdeeds of Warren G. Harding's administration to take votes from his successor Calvin Coolidge in 1924 were these Democratic, Progressive, and Communist buttons and the ingenious figural cardboard doorhanger. (Fig. 173, Robert A. Fratkin)

Figs. 175 and 176. Among 1924 campaign items that sought to improve upon nature by endowing Calvin Coolidge with an aura of personality were these buttons promoting him as an apostle of Republican virtues as "Firm as the Rock of Ages," and this "Keep Cool-Idge" fan. (Robert A. Fratkin)

1928 item best reflecting the panic among fundamentalist Protestants was a button (fig. 177) featuring the Statue of Liberty and the legend "My Country 'Tis of Thee/100%/The Crisis Is Here!" To assure voters that Smith was not part of an international cabal to establish papal dominion over the United States, Democratic buttons, mirrors, and stickers featuring the Liberty Bell and the Statue of Liberty (fig. 178) promoted their standard-bearer as "American Liberity Smith."

Smith campaign items were not all so defensive, however. His Lower East Side background was flaunted by such pieces as a "From the Sidewalks of New York to the White House" license attachment and an "Up From the Street" button that echoed the title of his official campaign biography. He was proclaimed "America's Biggest Man for America's Biggest Job" on a cotton tapestry, "Honest-Able-Fearless" on a poster, and "The Guiding Star of Our Nation" and "A Man of Service" on buttons. Other buttons and posters presented him as the "Happy Warrior," the nickname bestowed upon him by Franklin Roosevelt's nominating speech. Smith's nickname, "Al," was highlighted on nearly one hundred different items, including buttons, lapel pins, license attachments, stamps, fobs, rings, cigars, celluloid hats, and handkerchiefs, some sporting such slogans as "I'm for Al," "All for Al," "Me for Al," "We Want Al," "Good Bye Cal, Hello Al," and "No Oil on Al."[9] Smith's ubiquitous trademark, the brown derby hat, was celebrated on license attachments, metal and plastic lapel pins, and buttons, including one that read "What's Under Your Hat? Al Smith for President." Miniature celluloid and cloth derby hats appeared. A miniature ceramic moonshine jug with the legend "Al Smith" was one of the few known 1928 Democratic campaign items to tie the candidate to the "wet" faction in the controversy over Prohibition.

Reflective of Hoover's much less flamboyant personality but his close association (as secretary of commerce under Harding and Coolidge) with eight years of Republican prosperity, 1928 Hoover campaign items stressed economics and not charisma. A sailcloth banner exulted "Four More Years of Prosperity! Why Change?" Buttons urged "Help Hoover Help Business," and stickers and stamps alike promised "Hoover for Continued Prosperity." Posters insisted "Hoover for Good Business," "Elect Hoover and Insure Prosperity," and "How About Our Jobs? Vote for Hoover and Keep Our American Factories Running." Alliterative thimbles proclaimed "Hoover/Home/Happiness," and buttons "Honest/Hoover/Humane." Window cards lauded Hoover for "Service–Achievement–Vision–Integrity," and buttons highlighted his engineering background with the logo of the Engineers' Corps. Several owl lapel pins and buttons bore such plays on Hoover's name as "Hoo but Hoover?," "Hoo Hoo Hoover," and "Who? Who? Hoover."

For the first time in memory, virtually every 1928 item that could be considered thematic in any sense was issued for one of the two major party nominees. Buttons promoted Republican hopefuls Frank Lowden and Vice-

Figs. 177 and 178. Reflecting the ugly backlash of bigotry provoked by the Democratic nomination of the Catholic Al Smith in 1928 were these Statue of Liberty campaign buttons.

President Charles Dawes, Democrats Joseph T. Robinson and James Reed, Socialist Norman Thomas, and Communist William Z. Foster, but none of these demanded ideological imperatives or attempted to exploit personality politics. With few exceptions, a similar sterility pervaded the campaign items promoting splinter party nominees and major party hopefuls in the next four presidential elections. From 1932 through 1944, buttons touted 1932 Democratic hopefuls John Nance Garner and Albert C. Ritchie, Republican contenders Arthur Vandenberg, Robert Taft, Frank Knox, Frank Gannet, Arthur Cappen, Styles Bridges, Harold Stassen, and John Bricker, Socialist Norman Thomas, 1936 Union party candidate William U. Lemke, and 1940 Prohibitionist nominee Roger Babson, but virtually none went beyond primary identification. This dearth of imaginative thematics over such an extended period is difficult to understand, because third-party movements and dark-horse bids for major party nominations have so often served as the vehicles for unconventional beliefs and personalities, and the material culture inspired by such campaigns has almost always reflected their distinctive natures. Preventing this tradition from dying altogether (on objects, as least) were the Communists, who issued "For a Free, Happy, Prosperous America" buttons in 1936 and "For Job Security, Civil Rights and Peace" ones in 1940, either to promote Earl Browder's two presidential bids or for general propaganda efforts. Not until 1948, however, would the tradition of thematic creativity truly revive with the campaign items of Dixiecrat Strom Thurmond, Progressive Henry Wallace, and Republican hopeful Douglas MacArthur.

The 1932 mismatch between Hoover and Democrat Franklin Delano Roosevelt inspired nearly as many different varieties of campaign items as 1928,[10] but the onset of the Great Depression was clearly reflected in the cost and purpose of objects used. Posters, stickers, stamps, and other types of political paper were printed in more varieties and greater quantities than ever before, while the more expensive items created for sale to individual partisans diminished dramatically, perhaps because most Democrats could not afford them and most Republicans felt no urge to celebrate. Fewer than two hundred button varieties, a few other types of lapel devices, many license attachments, some textile items, and such miscellany as neckties, pencils, napkin rings, and oilcloth spare tire covers were also put to use. Like so many other manifestations of depression culture, many inexpensive 1932 giveaway items (particularly Democratic ones) demonstrated through their creative, often exuberant exploitation of issues and personalities that material want and poverty of spirit do not necessarily go hand in hand.

With the Republicans beset with an economic collapse they could neither ignore nor disown (after taking credit for good times in 1924 and 1928), 1932 Hoover campaign items reflected his essential strategy of implying that Roosevelt was a dangerous radical while doggedly insisting that only Republican rule could bring back prosperity. Campaign stamps insisted "Vote for Hoover and Be Safe," license attachments advised "Safe and Sane with Hoover," buttons urged "Be Safe with Hoover" and "OK America!! Play Safe with Hoover," and brass lapel pins admonished "Be Safe/Keep Hoover." Stickers read "Vote for Hoover—Don't Change Now," a Hoover–Charles Curtis poster urged "Keep Them on the Job," and a button advised "Hold ·on to Hoover." A brass lapel pin read "Don't Swap Horses/Keep Hoover," a button insisted "Don't Swap Horses/Stand by Hoover," and a stamp and a card enlisted the oldest and greatest of Republican icons in attributing the "Don't Change Horses in the Middle of the Stream" sentiment to "A. Lincoln." Stickers urged "Speed Up Recovery/Re-elect Hoover," and buttons insisted "One Issue–One Platform–Recovery." "Hoover Will Pilot Us Back to Prosperity" pledged wooden napkin rings. Buttons, mirrors, postcards, and stickers (fig. 179) proclaiming "It's an Elephant's Job—No Time for 'Donkey Business'!" portrayed a Democratic donkey fleeing as a GOP elephant pushed a stalled truck labeled "US & Co." a singularly ill-advised use of corporate imagery three years after the business mystique became an early victim of the depression.

If 1932 Hoover items convey the distinct impression of a party whistling past a graveyard, those issued for the forces trying to bring about his replacement by Franklin D. Roosevelt clearly evoke the jaunty exuberance of a party scenting victory after three overwhelming defeats, a campaign that took as its anthem "Happy Days Are Here Again," and as its standard-bearer a man who spoke not of mere survival but of a "rendezvous with destiny." Perhaps never before or since has material culture come closer to capturing the intangible spirit of a presidential candidate and his campaign.

A manifestation of this exuberance was the large number of buttons (fig. 180) and other items featuring caricatures of the Democratic donkey as

Figs. 179 and 180. Offering conflicting views on which party was better able to lead America to economic recovery in 1932 were these "No Time for 'Donkey-Business'" Republican items and these Democratic buttons. (Ronald T. Marchese)

"Depression Buster" kicking away hard times (commonly personified by the Republican elephant) or wiping clean the slate of a GOP white elephant. Another button urged "Get Rid of the White Elephant, Turn Democratic," and another lampooned the Republican full dinner pail symbol, taunting "Grand Old Prosperity/Nothing in It." Donkeys cavorted on "Help Vote Out Depression" window stickers. Stamps predicted "Happy Days Will Come Again." Departures from this blithe demeanor included such hard-sell items as "Roosevelt or Ruin," "Roosevelt/Conditions Demand Him," and "Return Our Country to the People" buttons and "Give America Back to the People" campaign stamps. Other recovery-related objects were "Rise with Roosevelt" license attachments, and buttons pledging "Economic Security" and "Prosperity with Roosevelt."

Many other 1932 Roosevelt campaign items (fig. 181) echoed the Democratic call for an end to the "noble experiment." Arm bands insisted "Repeal & Roosevelt," stamps read "Repeal with Roosevelt," and an assortment of buttons and other FDR objects echoed the demand. Distinctive license attachments featured Roosevelt, running-mate John Nance Garner, and a foaming stein of beer. Other objects combined the plea for repeal with the recovery issue. Buttons and license attachments read "For Repeal and Prosperity," and stamps demanded "Repeal and Employment." A convention button promoting James Hamilton Lewis as Roosevelt's running-mate urged "Bring Back Beer/Bring Back Business." Pennant-shaped stickers featuring the "Kick Out Depression" button design exhorted "Put a—Kick in Your Beer With a Kick—Like This." Other stickers advising "Forget Party Lines/ Good Times Are Coming" linked the two issues with a "Prosperity Formula" suggesting that repeal would bring recovery through the creation of brewery jobs and taxes.

Roosevelt enjoyed an enormous asset (especially among Republicans and independent progressives) in his family name. Buttons and stamps announced "America Calls Another Roosevelt, Franklin D." As items had done during the campaigns of cousin Theodore, buttons, lapel pins, and a small ceramic plate made rebus wordplays of the Roosevelt name with floral designs. A stamp linked the programs of the two Roosevelts with the legend "A New Deal/A Square Deal." Somewhat surprisingly, this stamp was one of only three or four known 1932 Roosevelt campaign items to utilize the New Deal slogan. Another was a bronze "A New Day/A New Deal" lapel pin designed by Gutzon Borglum and sold for a dollar each by the Roosevelt organization "National Shareholders of America." Given out free were an estimated nine million "The Friends of Franklin Roosevelt" buttons by his similarly named main campaign group. No known 1932 items utilized the Roosevelt initials, FDR, which apparently did not come into common use until after he assumed the presidency. His mania for stamp collecting inspired a set of campaign stamps endorsing "A Stamp

Collector for President" by the American Philatelic Society, an unusual action for a group of this nature.

Despite the best efforts of Hoover and many of his campaign objects to portray Roosevelt as something of a radical, very few 1932 Democratic items exhibited defensive tendencies. With the exception of a truly ironic "Out of the Red with Roosevelt" button echoing FDR's call for a balanced federal budget in a San Francisco speech that turned the tables on Hoover by depicting him as a profligate spendthrift, it almost seemed as if the Democrats were less uneasy over the demagogy of their 1932 opponent than the religion of their 1928 standard-bearer. "Roosevelt/100% American" and "He Will Protect Our Flag" buttons assured voters that this Democrat's patriotism was above suspicion.

In 1936, the combination of a partially revived economy, widespread predictions of a very close contest between Roosevelt and Republican challenger Alf Landon, and the extraordinary polarization of the electorate into camps that idolized or abhorred the president with equal fervor inspired a material dimension not surpassed since the early years of the century. Nearly four hundred styles of buttons and tabs, fifty or more lapel pins and other jewelry items, record numbers of license attachments, and large assortments of posters, stickers, stamps, and other types of political paper were created for Roosevelt and Landon supporters, along with ribbons, pencils, pennants, neckties, and bandannas. A sign of reviving Democratic economic fortunes and Republican spirits were such comparatively expensive campaign mementos as Roosevelt serving trays and Landon tumblers, glass plates, and cast-iron elephants.[11]

Made in many more varieties than Roosevelt items, Landon objects fell with few exceptions into two categories, those celebrating his Kansas heritage and those castigating Roosevelt, directly or by implication, for endangering the economy through runaway deficit spending and the Constitution through bureaucratic proliferation. Considering the miniscule number of electoral votes cast by Kansas and the fact that everybody comes from somewhere, it is difficult to fathom why Landon's identity as a Kansan—expect perhaps as a symbol of the traditional agrarian values of the prairie—was deemed so significant, but never before or since has a candidate's home state loomed so large as a theme on his material culture. The ubiquitous symbol of the Landon campaign was the Kansas sunflower, featured on nearly half of all known button varieties (fig. 182), several jewelry items, tabs, stickers, and license attachments, and on celluloid bookmarks, ribbons, matchbooks, pennants, and posters. A large proportion of these items sport the sunflower's brown and yellow coloring, as did many other Landon objects. A figural license attachment featured the University of Kansas jayhawk. Not ignored, however, was a national symbol, the Republican elephant. After being downplayed almost to extinction on items made for the 1932 Hoover debacle, the elephant was featured in 1936 on license attachments, tabs, jewelry items, posters, and more

Fig. 181. Among the more creative 1932 Democratic campaign items promoting "Roosevelt and Repeal" were these unusual stickers linking beer and economic recovery and this striking license plate featuring FDR, running-mate John Nance Garner, and a foaming stein of beer. (Ronald T. Marchese)

than forty styles of buttons, including the standard brown and yellow lithographs backed with felt sunflowers distributed by the millions in Landon campaign headquarters throughout the nation, a sign of reviving Republican pride in party identity.

The other major theme on Landon items was the menace presented by Franklin Roosevelt. That he was ruining the economy and the American work ethic was argued by stickers that read "Farewell to Alms," "Last Chance to Vote Out the Spendthrifts," and "Willful Waste Makes Woeful Want." Another sticker, portraying a WPA worker leaning on his shovel, urged "Let's Vote Him a Regular Job." Posters and buttons demanded "Deeds not Deficits." "End This Extravagance" mirrors claimed that the New Deal was squandering $15,000 per minute, a figure raised to $16,894.59 on "It's Time to Wake Up" stickers (fig. 183). That a Landon victory would bring recovery through a restoration of the free-enterprise system was asserted by "Vote for Landon and Land a Job" and "Steady Work/More Jobs with

Fig. 182. Among the myriad 1936 Republican campaign items exploiting Alf Landon's identity as a Kansan were these sunflower buttons and lapel pins.

Landon and Knox" stickers, "Off the Rocks with Landon and Knox" buttons and license attachments, and "Liberty and a New Prosperity" enamel Liberty Bell lapel pins.

Other Landon items, echoing the rhetoric of Republican reactionaries that made this the most vicious presidential campaign of the twentieth century, depicted Roosevelt as a fiend and Landon as the last hope for preserving constitutional liberty. Stickers distributed by the National Republican Council (fig. 184) featured Roosevelt using a burning Constitution to light his cigarette and—with wife Eleanor flying the Soviet standard—riding a donkey over a cliff in search of Shangri-la. Another sticker portrayed him as "Frankenstein D. Roosevelt." "Americans Cannot Be Bought" insisted buttons. Other buttons and lapel pins featured Liberty Bells and such slogans as "Ring It Again with Landon" and "Landon and the Constitution." Buttons, glass plates, and license attachments beseeched "Save America," and other attachments summoned "The Spirit of '76 in '36" and demanded "Restore Americanism." Never before or since (with the possible exception of his successor Wendell Willkie in 1940) has a candidate so

Figs. 183 and 184. Such anti–Roosevelt paper items as the sticker at left and the National Republican Council stamps reflect a 1936 Republican campaign that ranks among the nastiest ever waged in the United States. (Ronald T. Marchese)

gentle and fundamentally decent as Alf Landon engendered material culture so hysterical and patently vicious.

A few 1936 Roosevelt items responded essentially in kind, although with more humor and much less venom. Stickers and buttons rhymed "Back on the Rocks with Landon and Knox." Buttons, one of them created for dissident Republicans, bore Landon sunflower designs and the legend "We Can't Eat Sunflowers/Lose with Landon." A button stating "We Don't Want Wall St. Again" was strongly indicative of a campaign directed less against Landon than Herbert Hoover.

For the most part, however, 1936 Democratic campaign objects simply ignored Landon and Republican propaganda, emphasizing instead a portrayal of Roosevelt as the great and humane national leader who had saved the republic from economic collapse. Stickers depicted his metamorphosis from "The People's Champion and Hope—1932" into "Their Proven Friend and Humane Leader—1936." Buttons, posters, and banners identified him as "A Gallant Leader," and other buttons boasted "He Saved a Nation" and "He Saved America." He was described on banners as "Acclaimed by All America," and on buttons as "Man of the Hour." License attachments proclaimed "FDR Is Good Enough for Me," and buttons bore such inscriptions as "Friend of the People," "His Heart Is with the People," "We Rose with Roosevelt," and "Sweeping the Depression Out." A needle book (fig. 185) portrayed scenes of "Happiness Restored" to executives, farmers, factory workers, and seamstresses by "Roosevelt's New Deal Prosperity." A lapel pin and a "Let Freedom Democracy Remain" button pictured him with Lincoln and Washington (the button had a motif reminiscent of Mount Rushmore), implying that Roosevelt had earned a place in the pantheon of immortal American statesmen.

Many 1936 Roosevelt items made reference to his New Deal program, including "The New Deal" brass fobs and buttons with such legends as "New Deal Democrat," "Vote the New Deal," "Extend the New Deal," "New Deal for Pennsylvania," "New Deal Is Youth's Deal," and "Have Faith in the New Deal for Prosperity." A rather large number of Democratic coattail buttons were issued in 1936 by lesser-office candidates eager to link their fortunes to Roosevelt's, a common phenomenon in each of his four presidential bids. Even more buttons were distributed as endorsement items by labor organizations. The endorsement, a departure from labor's traditional posture of neutrality, was initiated primarily by United Mine Workers president John L. Lewis and his new Labor's Non-Partisan League, the political arm of the Congress of Industrial Organizations. Among the labor endorsement buttons promoting Roosevelt in 1936 (fig. 186) were several LN-PL varieties, some issued by its New York affiliate the American Labor party, and ones distributed by such groups as the International Longshoremen's Association and the United Mine Workers. A rather interesting 1936 item was a "Roosevelt Allegiance/I'm not Taking a Walk" button rebuking 1928 nominee Al Smith for his threat to take a walk (and subsequent defection to Landon) unless Roosevelt repudiated deficit spending.

If 1936 represented something of a renaissance in political trinketry, the 1940 contest between Roosevelt and Republican challenger Wendell Willkie inspired a volume and variety of campaign objects without equal in American history. An estimated fifty-four million buttons were ordered by the two campaigns, thirty-three million by the Republicans and twenty-one million by the Democrats. When buttons made for sale by commercial vendors are taken into account, the Willkie buttons that claimed "100 Million Buttons Can't Be Wrong" may not have been a gross exaggeration. A total of more than two thousand styles of buttons promoted or insulted the candidates in 1940, if minor variations in the immensely popular slogan buttons are included. The year 1940 was also an extraordinary one for campaign jewelry and for such paper items as stamps (at least fifty Willkie varieties alone), posters, postcards, and stickers. Political textiles made a major temporary comeback, with dozens of different mini-banners and bandannas printed. Many license attachments appeared, as did some political paper bumper strips. Other 1940 campaign memorabilia included cigars, paperweights, ribbons, compacts, pennants, aluminum bookmarks, pocket

Figs. 185 and 186. Indicative of the 1936 Democratic campaign's emphasis on the New Deal's economic record is this "Prosperity" needle book, while the whole-hearted gratitude of American trade unions for improved employment opportunities and the 1935 Wagner Act is reflected in the FDR endorsement buttons. (Ronald T. Marchese)

knives, thimbles, tumblers, needle books, coasters, wooden and mechanical pencils, cloth hats, and the aforementioned Willkie miniature wind sock and talking machine and the "Please Don't Talk 3rd Term" pair of paper earmuffs.[12] In virtually every category of object, Willkie items outnumbered Roosevelt pieces by a very substantial margin, both in variety and in total volume. Together, both factions transformed material culture into a rather considerable cottage industry.

Precisely why this came to pass in 1940 cannot be determined, although several factors probably combined to create a climate conducive to campaign items on such a scale. There is no question that genuine Republican outrage over the Roosevelt bid for a third term (and the presumption that he was at long last very vulnerable because of it) added measurably to their partisan enthusiasm, or that Wendell Willkie was an appealing figure in his own right. Roosevelt continued to polarize Americans to an almost unprecedented degree between admirers and those who hissed "that man" rather than speak his name. Both parties mounted rather lively campaigns, and expectations of a close contest were widespread. A reviving economy meant that campaign committees and individual partisans, Republican and Democratic alike, had more money to spend for objects of this sort.

Unlike 1936, when Republican campaign items largely limited promotion of Landon to celebration of his identity as a Kansan, many Willkie items bear witness to a more imaginative effort to market the candidate in his own right. License attachments read "*Wisdom Leadership Willkie*," pencils declared him "The People's Choice," a button proclaimed him "America's Hope," and a coaster, a banner, and several buttons presented him as "The Hope of Our Country." A stamp exhorted "*Forward with Willkie in the Footsteps of Lincoln*," and a button stated "Each Time America Needs Him God Sends a Man." Many Willkie items used key designs (fig. 187) to create rebus wordplays, including buttons with such slogans as "Let *Willkie* Unlock Opportunity," "The Key to All Your Troubles," "Key to Prosperity," and "Republican Key to Prosperity Opens the Door to Better Times." At least two dozen stamps, several buttons, some posters and handkerchiefs, a license attachment, and a shaving mug featured the rallying cry "We Want Willkie." Other handkerchiefs, stamps, buttons, and banners bore the slogan "Win with Willkie," as did a pennant and a pencil. Shocked by the defection of large numbers of black voters to Roosevelt four years earlier, many Willkie items were issued in an attempt to win them back by exploiting his endorsement by heavyweight boxing champion Joe Louis. Portraying Willkie as the key to economic recovery were "A Living for All," "Let's Go to Work," and "Buying Power/We Want Willkie" stamps and a "We Want Willkie and Prosperity" license attachment, as well as the "key to prosperity" rebus items.

Again in 1940, however, the major theme exploited on Republican campaign items was the menace posed by Roosevelt. At the heart of this effort was the outcry against the third term. Buttons (fig. 188), stamps, postcards, window stickers, and licenses bore such legends as "No Third Term," "No Third Termites," "Exterminate Third Termites," "8 Years Is Plenty," "Two Good Terms Deserve a Rest," "Two Good Terms Deserve a Parole," "No Third Term/Keep America Free," "No—A 1000 Times No," and simply "No!" Many buttons adopted such baseball terminology as "Force Franklin Out at Third," "Out Stealing Third," and "Strike Three F. D./You're Out." A sexual analogy was made by items insisting "No Man Is Good Three Times," "Two Times Is Enough for Any Man," and "Confucius Say . . . Man Who Stand Up Twice, No Good Third Time." License attachments depicted George Washington declaring "No Third Term for Me," and buttons read "I'm Against the Third Term—Washington Wouldn't/Grant Couldn't/ Roosevelt Shouldn't." Ironically prophetic were buttons urging "Let's Stop the 4th Term Now," "F. D. R. How About a 4th Term?," "No 3rd, 4th or 5th Term," and "He Will Be Harder to Beat the Fourth Time than the Third/Do Your Duty Now!"

Closely linked were a host of items portraying Roosevelt as royalty (fig. 189) or as a totalitarian dictator along the lines of a Hitler, Stalin, or Mussolini. Buttons, postcards, and other items bore such slogans as "No Crown for Franklin," "No Royal Family," "No Franklin the First," "Roosevelt for King," "No Roosevelt Dynasty," "We Want Roosevelt to Abdicate," "No Crown Prince Jimmy," and "De-Thronement Day Nov. 5th." Much more vicious were paper items that drew the analogy "Think/ Hitler Nominated Hitler/Mussolini Nominated Mussolini/Stalin Nominated Stalin/Roosevelt Nominated Roosevelt/Do You Want a Dictator?" and buttons proclaiming "No Third Internationale/Third Reich/Third Term." "Don't Let Freedom Vanish" and "Safeguard American Tradition" urged Willkie stamps, while matchbooks implored "Save Constitutional Government" and "Preserve Your Freedom/Be Thankful You Can Still Do It." Buttons exhorted "Vote for Willkie if You Want to Vote Again," "Elect Willkie—Preserve Your Bill of Rights," "Willkie Now or the Roosevelts Forever," "Keep America Free to Laugh at the Great Dictator," "Dictators Don't Debate," "Caution/We Need Willkie not Dictatorship," and "No Dictator Later."

Other Willkie items attacked Roosevelt's record. Buttons (fig. 190) lampooned the New Deal as a "Raw Deal" and a "Misdeal" and the WPA as "Worst Public Aministration." A button bore the endorsement of a moronic "I. M. A. Simp," apparently a forebear of *Mad Magazine's* Alfred E. Neumann. Another used the title of Hollywood epic *Gone with the Wind* to caption a drawing of an elephant emitting a donkey from its anus. Other buttons dubbed the president "Franklin Deficit Roosevelt" and "A Costly Lesson" and parodied his initials into "Financial Debauchery Run-Riot." Others complained "60 Billion Bucks/Whee!" and "All I Have Left Is a Vote for Willkie." Stamps portrayed "New Deal Spending $23,000,000 a Day"

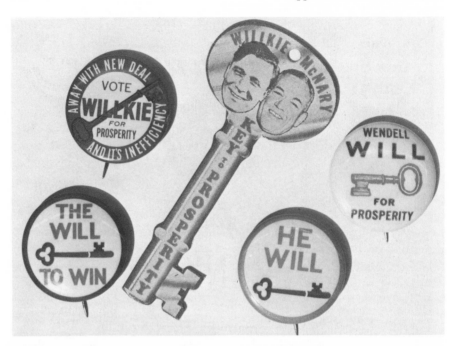

Figs. 187, 188, 189, and 190. Among the extraordinary array of buttons and other items available to Wendell Willkie supporters in 1940 were these imaginative key wordplay lapel devices and a huge number of stickers and vendor buttons castigating FDR's third-term pretensions, royalist tendencies, and New Deal programs. (Fig. 187, Edmund B. Sullivan; Figs. 188, 189, and 190, Ronald T. Marchese)

for an oil gusher, and "New Deal Finance" as balls for juggling. "New Deal Consolation/9,000,000 Unemployed" taunted a button. One attacked Roosevelt running-mate Henry Wallace for his role in implementing pork quotas under the Agricultural Adjustment Act with the rhyme "6,000,000 Piglets Squeal 'Hank Wallace's Raw Deal.'"

Many Willkie items attacked Roosevelt's foreign policy, simultaneously depicting him as a scheming war-monger and an inept weakling. Buttons warned menacingly, "Draft Roosevelt and He'll Draft *You*," used the Roosevelt and Wallace initials to spell "WAR," lampooned the Roosevelt accent with the gibe "I Hate Wah/Let's not Be Suckers Again," and insisted, "You Can't Pull a Wilson on Us," apparently hinting that Democratic presidents tended to draw the nation into war after being elected as peace candidates. Such items apparently surfaced rather late in the campaign, after Willkie began to hammer effectively at Roosevelt's alleged interventionist tendencies. Other Willkie items, however, tried to present Roosevelt as too weak to safeguard the nation's security. A poster read "For Unpreparedness France Dismissed Daladier/England Replaced Chamberlain/Why Should America Keep Roosevelt?" Another poster insisted "This Preparedness Business Is a Job for a Business Man," and another read "Willkie Means Jobs/Jobs Mean Preparedness/Preparedness Means Peace." A series of military motif stamps urged "Defense/We Want Willkie." Another stamp and a poster read "Preparedness/Prosperity/Peace," and buttons bore such maxims as "Defense/Common Sense" and "Defense/Unity/Prosperity."

Virtually no aspect of Roosevelt's public or private life was immune from attack. "I Hate Wah" and "Mah Friends, Goodbye" buttons lampooned his accent, and "Roosevelt Hide at Hyde" and "Dr. Jekyll of Hyde Park" buttons his residence. "Flash! Deeds Made America, Not Fireside Chats" buttons, and "No More Fireside Chats" postcards and buttons mocked his radio talks. Even son Elliott and wife Eleanor became targets for Republican put-down objects. Elliott's induction into the Army Air Corps Reserve in September 1940, with the rank of captain, inspired charges of favoritism and buttons with such taunting slogans as "I Wanna Be a Captain Too," "Papa:—I Want to Be a Captain," "Papa I Don't Want to Resign," "I Just Want to Be a Lieutenant," "I'll Settle for a Sergeant," "Wendell Is *Our* Captain," and "I Don't Want Elliott for My Captain." Eleanor Roosevelt, long a favorite target of the Republican right, became a butt of humor on 1940 buttons and other items (fig. 191) second only to her husband. Buttons satirized her syndicated newspaper column, "My Day." A "Project #UMP-000" button mocked her celebrated activism with a caricature of an outhouse. A button that read "Roosevelt Is Buying the Aquacade to Keep Eleanor Ho¹me" utilized Billy Rose's aquatic revue and its star to ridicule Mrs. Roosevelt's penchant for travel.

Unlike 1936, when Roosevelt material had all but ignored Alf Landon and Republican campaign propaganda, many buttons worn by FDR parti-

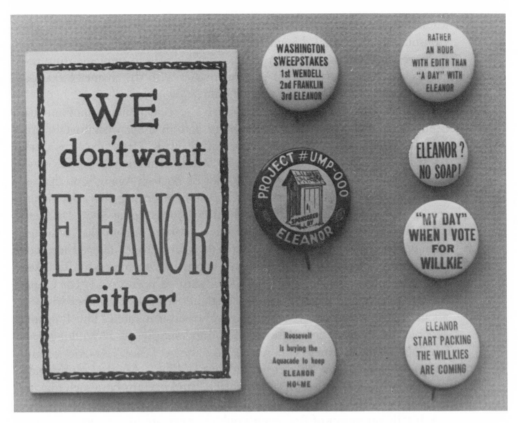

Fig. 191. A few of the many 1940 campaign items lampooning first lady Eleanor Roosevelt, a favorite target for Republican conservatives because of her uncommon visibility and her humanitarian activism. (Ronald T. Marchese)

sans in 1940 (obtained in most instances from commercial vendors) were somewhat defensive in tone. Many made the argument (fig. 192) "Better a Third Termer than a Third Rater." Portraying Willkie as the champion of the rich were vendor buttons that read "We Millionaires Want Willkie" and "Willkie for the Millionaires/Roosevelt for the Millions." His background as a utilities executive was scorned by buttons advising "Willkie for President of Commonwealth and Southern" and "Keep Roosevelt in Whitehouse/Willkie in Powerhouse." His campaign's enthusiasm for buttons inspired some that quipped "All You Can Get From Willkie Is Buttons." Other anti-Willkie buttons insisted "Watch Willkie Wilt" and "Repeat with Roosevelt or Repent with Willkie." A handmade button featured a horse's posterior with the verse "A Horses [sic] Tail Is Nice and Silky/Lift His Tail and You Will See Willke [sic]." Maybe the most effective of all 1940 Roosevelt slogan buttons were some that read "A Pauper for Roosevelt," inspired by a Philadelphia Willkie supporter's cruel and monumentally stupid remark that Roosevelt, a master campaigner, exploited to great advantage.[13]

Many 1940 Democratic buttons and other objects confronted the third-term issue directly. Headquarters give-away buttons proclaimed "We Want FDR Again" and "I Want Roosevelt Again." Posters, buttons, banners, and fobs carried the main campaign slogan "Carry on with Roosevelt," and buttons and bandannas urged "Carry on FDR." Other buttons read "Just Roosevelt" and "On with Roosevelt." One issued by the International Ladies' Garment Workers Union pleaded "Don't Change the Pilot," and a banner proclaimed "Not How Long, but How Well!/God Bless America with Roosevelt." Buttons advised "No Substitute for Experience." Other buttons bore such slogans as "Third Term Taboo/23 Skidoo," "Two Good Terms Deserve Another," "3/FDR," "3 Is a Lucky Number."

Many 1940 Democratic items echoed the 1936 effort to portray Roosevelt as a great and humane national leader. Matchbooks, stickers, and buttons read "Roosevelt and Humanity," ribbons featured the motto "For Freedom and Humanity," buttons proclaimed him "Friendly/Dependable/Resourceful," and license attachments lauded "Roosevelt the Great Humanitarian." Among the many satin mini-banners promoting Roosevelt were varieties with such accolades as "Our Gallant Leader," "Equality/Liberty/Justice," "America's Choice for Freedom-Humanity-Democracy," and "To Keep the Nation Firm Give Him Another Term." A poster printed for New York's American Labor party was one of very few 1940 Roosevelt items to echo the New Deal's economic dimension, doing so by contrasting "Hoover 1932" scenes of bread lines, bank runs, and the homeless with "New Deal 1940" scenes of higher wages, decent housing, and Social Security. This was just one of many labor items endorsing Roosevelt, despite John L. Lewis's ill-fated defection and the resulting neutrality of his Labor's Non-Partisan League. Among the buttons (fig. 193) issued by pro–Roosevelt labor organizations in 1940 were ones by the dissident New Jersey chapter of the LN-PL, American Labor party, Teamsters, ILGWU, Communication Workers of America, Millinery Workers, Brewery Workers, and the Pittsburgh Central Labor Union. Many other labor buttons with such slogans as "Labor's Choice," "Labor's Friend," "Roosevelt for Labor," "Labor for Roosevelt," and "Labor Wants Roosevelt" appeared, some of them distributed by the Democratic campaign to workers in neutral CIO unions.

With metals and plastics in critically short supply on the home front, the wartime 1944 contest between Roosevelt and Republican Thomas E. Dewey was a singularly poor one for material culture. No more than one hundred varieties of buttons and lapel devices of other types appeared, along with a few posters, pennants, mini-banners, ribbons, and stickers.[14] The shortage of items was especially pronounced on the Republican side, perhaps because 1940 taught them that trinkets alone do not ordain victory. Among the few thematic Dewey items were "Dewey the Racket Buster/New

Figs. 192 and 193. Produced in huge quantities for supporters of Roosevelt's third-term bid in 1940 were anti–Willkie vendor buttons like these and union endorsement buttons like this assortment. (Ronald T. Marchese)

Deal Buster" buttons exploiting his fame as a crime-fighting district attorney and such economic pieces as "Back to Work Quicker with Dewey and Bricker" shield decals, "Dewey and Bricker for Prosperity" buttons, and "Peace and Jobs Quicker with Dewey and Bricker" cardboard doorhangers. The fourth-term issue inspired surprisingly few items, among them a "No Fourth Term" button and a postcard featuring a baby with a bewildered look and the caption "A Fourth Term? Well, Goddam!" Another satiric anti–Roosevelt item produced in 1944 was a "Clear Everything with *Sidney!*" button, inspired by a Roosevelt suggestion that a Democratic vice-presidential possibility be approve by CIO chieftain Sidney Hillman. The only Republican effort to capitalize on wartime sentiment seems to have been a "Mothers/Sisters/Wives/Sweethearts" button.

Roosevelt items, however, milked the patriotic fervor for all it was worth. Buttons (fig. 194) bore such sentiments as "Support Your Commander in Chief," "Go 4*th* to Win the War," "I Am an American," "Save America," "For Freedom/44," "All Out for Durable Victory," and "We Are Going to Win This War and Win the Peace That Follows." Buttons and stickers declared "Four Freedoms/Re-Elect Roosevelt." Other buttons featured the "V" symbol for victory, as did several mini-banners and posters. A few 1944 Roosevelt buttons and tabs sought to counteract resistance to a fourth term with such slogans as "Three Good Terms Deserve Another," "I'll Take Roosevelt Again," and "Roosevelt More than Ever," and "Go 4*th* to Win the War." The only thematic echo of the New Deal was a "He Saved Our Home" button. Among the Roosevelt endorsement items issued by labor organizations were buttons distributed by the Teamsters, Millinery Workers, ILGWU, and New York's Liberal Labor Committee and "He Is Worth My Buck" buttons and "A Dollar You Won't Miss to Elect a Man You Can't Afford to Lose" posters by the CIO's new Political Action Committee. Roosevelt's celebrated speech to the Teamsters in Washington in September, when he provoked gales of laughter with his plaintive lament, "And now they are attacking my little dog Fala," inspired handmade lapel badges (fig. 195) punning "Fala Me to the Polls."

Although the 1948 election was widely perceived from the outset as a Dewey landslide over a hapless Harry Truman, the end of wartime shortages, contests for both major party nominations, and the ideological candidacies of Progressive Henry Wallace and States' Rights champion Strom Thurmond helped create a real revival in the use of campaign objects. More than three hundred buttons, a wealth of political paper items, several ribbons, pennants, and license attachments, and such souvenir items as bandannas, neckties, pencils, pens, and paper and cloth GI caps saluted the various 1948 presidential candidates.[15]

After something of a hiatus in 1944, Republican campaign items in 1948 returned to character assassination with a vengeance. No effort whatever was made to promote Dewey or any of the Republican platform imperatives.

Figs. 194 and 195. These 1944 Democratic campaign buttons exploited Roosevelt's role as commander-in-chief of a nation at war, while the imaginative handmade badge at left paid tribute to FDR's pet Scottish Terrier, Fala. (Ronald T. Marchese)

As one button insisted, "The Issue Is Truman's Record/Nothing Else!" Other ones bore such legends as "Harry Is Sorry," "Help Hustle Harry Home," "Save What's Left!," "Had Enough?," "Start Packing Harry/The Deweys Are Coming," "I Want a True-Man/Not Harry," and "Back to Independence." A button inspired by Truman's rebuilding of the White House portico read "Truman Was Screwy to Build a Porch for Dewey." Another button read "Washington Could not Tell a Lie/Roosevelt Could not Tell the Truth/Truman Does not Know the Difference." If their buttons are any indication, Republicans appear to have been enormously impressed by their discovery that the donkey and mule symbols of the Democratic party and Truman's Missouri shared a synonym that is also a slang expression for the human posterior. Buttons featured caricatures of jackasses to help form such slogans as "I'll Bet my———on Dewey," "Don't Be an———Vote for Dewey," and "Keep Your———Off the Grass/It's Dewey." Another variety combined a Capitol dome, several donkey heads, and the legend "Too Many Jacks from Missouri." Ignoring their candidate and their blueprint for a better America, these caustic, smug, and often smarmy 1948 Republican buttons provide cogent insights into a campaign that defied all odds to "snatch defeat from the jaws of victory."

Short on both funds and groups wanting to link themselves to a certain loser, the Truman campaign inspired fewer objects by far than Dewey's. Although Truman's whistle-stop tirades against the "do-nothing" Republican Congress made it the more negative of the two campaigns, the only items to reflect this tenor were buttons that read "Phooey on Dewey," "We Did It to Dewey Before and Will Do It Again," and "The Won't Do Congress—Won't Do!" Few Truman items attempted to play personality politics, among them little plastic whistles inspired by the whistlestop campaign tours and plastic donkey "I'm so Wild About Harry" lapel pins. Truman's standing as a world leader during the tense cold war era was highlighted by "Secure the Peace" posters (fig. 196) and "Our Goal Must Be—Not Peace in Our Time—but Peace for All Time" stickers and especially effective "Nobody Wants War/Harry S. Truman Knows Why" posters portraying Truman in his World War I captain's uniform.

The dominant theme on Truman items, however, was the continuation of the economic achievements and liberal initiatives of the New Deal. A poster featuring Herbert Hoover and apples warned "Don't Monkey with the Donkey in '48 or Sell Hoover Apples in '49." Other posters read "Homes for All" and "Count Your Many Blessings." Buttons and tabs distributed by the Political Action Committee of the CIO read "Jobs for 60 Million" and "60 Million Jobs," and another button asked "60 Million People Working/Why Change?" Ballpoint pens, mechanical pencils, and cigarette lighters proclaimed Truman "Friend of the People" and "Foe of Privilege." Two varieties of buttons distributed extensively by Truman's national campaign committee updated the old Roosevelt slogan to read "For-

Fig. 196. With its dignified presidential portrait and message reminding voters of Harry Truman's stature as a postwar world leader, this 1948 Democratic campaign poster provides an excellent example of capitalizing upon incumbency.

Fig. 197. A few of many Douglas MacArthur buttons issued during World War II and during the 1948 presidential primaries, when his fame as liberator of the Philippines and conqueror of Japan produced embarrassingly few votes for the Republican presidential nomination. (Edmund B. Sullivan)

ward with President Truman/No Retreat," and a banner exulted "Truman Is True to His Trust." An "Eddie's Friend Truman in '48" button, apparently an effort to enhance Truman's popularity among Jewish voters, exploited his longtime friendship and former business partnership with Eddie Jacobson, a Jew. Attempts to reap dividends from his recent civil rights initiatives included buttons with such legends as "Truman and Civil Rights," "Truman Fights for Human Rights," and "States Rights or Human Rights?"

The year 1948 was a vintage year for third-party items and for objects promoting major party hopeful candidates. Buttons were produced for Democrats Richard Russell and Paul McNutt and unwilling "Dump Truman" draftees Justice William O. Douglas and General Dwight D. Eisenhower. Buttons promoted unsuccessful Republican contenders Harold Stassen and

NOW IS THE TIME TO FIGHT!

FIGHT The Invasion of States Rights Proposed by Truman, Dewey and Wallace.

FIGHT The Vicious F.E.P.C. Which Will Create a Police-State In Free America.

FIGHT The Centralization of Government in Washington.

FIGHT For Local Self-Government.

Support The Presidential Electors Nominated By The Regular Democratic Party of South Carolina

PLEDGED TO SUPPORT

THURMOND - WRIGHT

Presidential Electors of The Democratic Party of South Carolina

EUGENE S. BLEASE
CHARLTON DuRANT
IRVING M. FISHBURNE
J. K. MAYFIELD
LEON W. HARRIS
HARRY M. ARTHUR
E. CLYBURN WILSON
THOMAS R. MILLER

HONORABLE J. STROM THURMOND
Governor of South Carolina
Democratic Party of South Carolina
Candidate for President of
the United States

HONORABLE FIELDING L. WRIGHT
Governor of Mississippi
Democratic Party of South Carolina
Candidate for Vice-President of
the United States

Your efforts and your energy are needed NOW to preserve a free America - - your rights to local self government - - your rights to individual liberty. Join the fight to defeat the FEPC and the abolition of segregation - - - and to protect States Rights

ACT NOW---TOMORROW MAY BE TOO LATE

Fig. 198. This strident poster faithfully echoed the reactionary nature of the 1948 "Dixiecrat" campaign waged by the South Carolina Governor J. Strom Thurmond and Mississippi Governor Fielding Wright that won them thirty-nine Deep South electoral votes.

Fig. 199. Featuring the familiar silhouette shadow of Franklin D. Roosevelt, this creative 1948 Henry Wallace campaign button was designed to appeal to New Deal loyalists who revered the memory of FDR above the reality of Harry Truman.

Ed Martin, and several Earl Warren buttons appeared, including one that enthusiastically stated "Bases Loaded/Warren Is Scorin'." The Douglas MacArthur boomlet produced at least thirty items (fig. 197), including buttons annointing him "America's Hero" and "The Man of the Hour," and others with such doomsday mottos as "Do or Die" and "Save America with MacArthur." The Socialist, Greenback, and Vegetarian tickets inspired buttons. Segregationist "Dixiecrats" Strom Thurmond and Fielding Wright, running under the States' Rights banner, were promoted on "For a Free People Under Constitutional Government" tabs, "States Rights/The Constitution" and "Jeffersonian Democrat" buttons, Statue of Liberty posters urging "Get in the Fight for States' Rights," and other posters (fig. 198) warning "*Now* Is the Time to Fight!" a host of evils, including FEPC efforts to "Create a Police-State in Free America." The Progressive ticket of Henry Wallace and Glen Taylor inspired tabs, pennants, bandannas, "Race Equality/Job Security" stamps, "Peace/Low Prices/Jobs/Housing/Civil Rights/Repeal Taft–Hartley" cards, and at least thirty varieties of buttons, including ones demanding "Wallace/One World," "Repeal Taft–Hartley," and "Repeal the Draft." Another Wallace button (fig. 199) featured as his shadow the familiar FDR silhouette, a clever design implying that Wallace and not Truman was the legitimate heir to the Roosevelt tradition of reform.

NOTES

1. After declining gradually from an average turnout of nearly 80 percent in presidential elections from 1876 through 1896 to an average of approximately 65 percent from 1900 through 1916, voter turnout plummeted to less than 45 percent in 1920 and 1924 before beginning a gradual rise in 1928. The primary cause for this dramatic percentile drop was almost certainly the addition of women to the electorate in 1920, many of whom apparently adjusted rather slowly to political participation.

2. On September 10, 1924, an automobile caravan left the Coolidge home in Plymouth, Vermont, for a trip of nearly five thousand miles along the Lincoln Highway to California, an endeavor that eventually involved thousands of cars in local demonstrations. Authorities believe this to have been the first organized use of the automobile in a presidential campaign, and it set a precedent for campaigns to follow. For an informative account of the role of the Roosevelt Motor Club in FDR's 1932 campaign, see John Vargo, "Roosevelt on the Road in '32," *The Political Collector* 5 (Dec. 1975): 1.

3. See Theodore L. Hake, *Political Buttons: Book II, 1920–1976* (York, Pa., 1977), 10–16; Bristow, *Illustrated Political Button Book*, 103–11; Hake, *Encyclopedia of Political Buttons*, 103–6, 108–9, 250, 253; Fischer and Sullivan, *Political Ribbons and Ribbon Badges*, 352–56, 384; Greenhouse, *Political Postcards*, 55, 58–61; John Vargo, "FDR: The Material Legacy," *Apic Keynoter* 83 (Spring - Summer 1983): 6–9; and Sullivan, *Collecting Political Americana*, 9.

4. Franklin D. Roosevelt to Roy Godsey, Sept. 22, 1920, quoted in Vargo, "FDR: The Material Legacy," 8.

5. St. Louis Button Company to Franklin D. Roosevelt, July 19, 31, 1920, quoted in Vargo, "FDR: The Material Legacy," 8–9. If this firm did indeed fill its orders for "thousands of these buttons," the subsequent fate of such buttons presents something of a mystery, for these and the other known varieties of Cox–Roosevelt jugate picture buttons (fig. 167) are all extraordinarily scarce and highly prized by curators and collectors.

6. Sentenced to ten years in prison for sedition under the draconian Espionage Act of 1917, Debs entered the West Virginia State Penitentiary in April 1919, where he was assigned number 2253. Two months later he was transferred to the federal facility in Atlanta and given number 9653.

7. See Hake, *Political Buttons, II*, 17–23, 233; Bristow, *Illustrated Political Button Book*, 113–22; Hake, *Encyclopedia of Political Buttons*, 111–14, 116–17, 249, 251, 255–56; Dick Bristow, *Third Party and Hopeful Campaign Items, 1896–1968* (Santa Cruz, Calif., 1972), 23, 27, 31, 40–42; Fischer and Sullivan, *Political Ribbons and Ribbon Badges*, 356–57, 385; Greenhouse, *Political Postcards*, 56, 62–63; Sullivan, *Collecting Political Americana*, 10, 111, 164; and Collins, *Threads of History*, 407. Especially valuable is The American Political Items Collectors' *The Political Campaign Items of John W. Davis: An APIC Research Project*, 1970.

8. See Hake, *Political Buttons, II*, 24–39; Bristow, *Illustrated Political Button Book*, 123–38; Hake, *Encyclopedia of Political Buttons*, 119–25, 127–31, 250–51; Sullivan, *Collecting Political Americana*, 10, 101, 127, 136, 164; Collins, *Threads of History*, 412–17; Fischer and Sullivan, *Political Ribbons and Ribbon Badges*, 357–58; and Greenhouse, *Political Postcards*, 57, 64.

9. "No Oil on Al" buttons may have been used either in 1924 (to support either Smith's bid for the Democratic presidential nomination or subsequent New York gubernatorial re-election effort) or in 1928, or possibly both. Teapot Dome was a major issue in 1924, and at the marathon Madison Square Garden Democratic convention that year an attack on Smith by William Jennings Bryan (implying that he was a pawn of Wall Street) brought a chant of "No Oil on Al" from Smith supporters in the galleries. Teapot Dome was revived as a campaign issue, however, during Smith's 1928 bid for the presidency when the renewal of Sinclair Oil Com-

pany leases on federal land at Salt Creek provoked new publicity in October 1928. The key figure in this controversy was Hubert Work, Coolidge's secretary of the interior, who negotiated the lease renewal and then resigned to become chairman of the Republican National Committee.

10. See Hake, *Encyclopedia of Political Buttons*, 119–25, 133–41, 143–46, 250–51; 253; Bristow, *Illustrated Political Button Book*, 129–42, 144–53; Hake, *Political Buttons, II*, 24–31, 40–41, 43–44, 46–48, 50, 53–54; Collins, *Threads of History*, 420–23; Bristow, *Third Party and Hopeful Items*, 24–41–42, 44; Fischer and Sullivan *Political Ribbons and Ribbon Badges*, 359, 362–63; Greenhouse, *Political Postcards*, 65, 69; and Sullivan, *Collecting Political Americana*, 164. Especially valuable on 1932 Roosevelt material and on FDR campaign items in general is Vargo, "FDR: The Material Legacy," 4–43, and accompanying illustrations from Joseph M. Jacobs's incomparable collection of Rooseveltiana.

11. Most useful for 1936 Roosevelt material is Vargo, "FDR: The Material Legacy," 25–30, and accompanying illustrations *passim*, 4–83. See also Bristow, *Illustrated Political Button Book*, 139–52, 155–61; Hake, *Encyclopedia of Political Buttons*, 133–41, 143–44, 146, 148–53, 250–51, 253; and *Political Buttons, II*, 40–41, 44–63, 237; Bristow, *Third Party and Hopeful Items*, 23, 31–32, 42–43; Collins, *Threads of History*, 428–32; Fischer and Sullivan, *Political Ribbons and Ribbon Badges*, 359–64, 366–67, 385; Greenhouse, *Political Postcards*, 66, 70–71; and Sullivan, *Collecting Political Americana*, 11, 127, 164, 167.

12. The most valuable guides to the copious quantity of 1940 campaign material are Vargo, "FDR: The Material Legacy," 30–35, and accompanying illustrations, 4–83, and Edward M. Stahl, *We Want Willkie: A Pictorial Guide to the Campaign Memorabilia of Wendell L. Willkie* (Trenton, N.J.: 1972). See also Hake, *Political Buttons, II*, 40, 43–54, 64–79; Bristow, *Illustrated Political Button Book*, 139–54, 163–76; Hake, *Encyclopedia of Political Buttons* 133–46, 155–64, 250–51, 253, 255; Collins, *Threads of History*, 444–58; Fischer and Sullivan, *Political Ribbons and Ribbon Badges*, 359, 361–64, 367–68, 386; Bristow, *Third Party and Hopeful Items*, 23, 31, 43–44; Greenhouse, *Political Postcards*, 67, 72–74; and Sullivan, *Collecting Political Americana*, 11, 62.

13. Late in October, Robert McCracken, a Philadelphia lawyer and Willkie activist, made a speech in which he asserted that Roosevelt's only supporters were "the Roosevelt family and paupers—those who earn less than $1200 a year and aren't worth that." Arthur Krock made reference to the slur in his *New York Times* column on November 1, and Roosevelt, speaking in New York that day, went for the Republican jugular. His voice quaking with emotion, Roosevelt answered McCracken that "these Americans whom this man calls 'paupers'" were "only the common men and women who have helped build this country, who have made it great, and who would defend it with their lives if the need arose. . . . *There* speaks the true sentiment of the Republican leadership." Several styles of "A Pauper for Roosevelt" buttons appeared during the closing days of the campaign.

14. See Vargo, "FDR: The Material Legacy, 33–37; Hake, *Encyclopedia of Political Buttons*, 133, 136, 138, 140–41, 143, 145–46, 166, 168–72, 250, 253; Bristow, *Illustrated Political Button Book*, 140, 142–45, 147, 149, 152–54, 177–82; Hake, *Political Buttons, II*, 45–46, 49, 51, 54, 80, 83, 86–88; Fischer and Sullivan, *Political Ribbons and Ribbon Badges*, 362, 364, 369; Greenhouse, *Political Postcards*, 68, 75–76; Bristow, *Third Party and Hopeful Items*, 31, 44.

15. See Hake, *Political Buttons*, II, 80–82, 84–94, 234, 237; Bristow, *Illustrated Political Button Book*, 177–86; Hake, *Encyclopedia of Political Buttons*, 166–72, 174–77, 249–50, 252–55; Collins, *Threads of History*, 474, 478–83; Fischer and Sullivan, *Political Ribbons and Ribbon Badges*, 369–71, 386; Bristow, *Third Party and Hopeful Items*, 27–29, 31–32, 42–46; Greenhouse, *Political Postcards*, 77, 80–82; and Sullivan, *Collecting Political Americana*, 164, 169.

7

Twilight of a Tradition?
1952–72

In recent presidential races, the whole concept of material culture has begun to present something of a paradox, for these contests have inspired objects unsurpassed in creativity and variety by those of any other period, while at the same time campaign items have diminished steadily in importance as functional facets of mainstream elective politics. This development has resulted, I think, from fundamental changes in the nature of modern campaigns and in public attitudes toward politics. Presidential campaigns have evolved inexorably into meticulously staged media events, with much less emphasis on participatory activities at the local level. While this transformation began with the emergence of the slick news-weeklies, Movietone News, and radio as important influences on American public opinion during the first half of the twentieth century, the odyssey of material culture from the political mainstream to the political periphery became unmistakeably apparent during the campaigns from 1952 through 1972, a period that coincided precisely with the emergence of television as the dominant force in modern national politics—from the first televised national conventions in 1952 through the 1968 and 1972 television extravaganzas waged on behalf of Richard Nixon.[1]

During the same period, a revolution in American journalism, along with such other phenomena as civics classes in the schools, an expanding middle class, and the availability of more leisure time, helped create a somewhat more informed and decidedly more cynical electorate. After World War II, increasing numbers of Americans began to identify themselves as political independents, and most of those who retained partisan loyalties surely did not do so with the old "my party right or wrong" devotion. Modern presidents and candidates for the office, despite the pervasive popularity of Dwight Eisenhower (and more recently Ronald Reagan) and the posthumous veneration of John Kennedy, have not been recipients of the sort of hero worship almost routinely accorded such figures in simpler times. In recent years, a spirit of introspective detachment has grown so pervasive that even intensely committed partisans have grown much less likely to flaunt their beliefs with buttons and other devices promoting their candidates or causes.

Since its genesis in the days of Andrew Jackson, the material tradition in American politics has depended upon grass-roots campaign activities and upon vast numbers of rank-and-file supporters with enough enthusiasm to covet objects promoting a candidate and enough flamboyance to promote that commitment proudly on their lapels or elsewhere. The decline of both of these phenomena has led to an inevitable diminution of the role played by campaign items among the general electorate. In recent presidential campaigns, the trend has been toward fewer types of giveaway items destined for distribution to the public and a much greater variety of objects created for a rather small corps of political activists and for such special events as party conventions and caucuses. In 1976, Jimmy Carter's media director, Gerald Rafshoon, decided to forgo giveaway campaign buttons altogether until a chorus of complaints from local Carter–Mondale headquarters caused him to reconsider, simply because "it wasn't worth it to have the complaints." He finally ordered two hundred thousand inexpensive lithographed tin buttons, roughly one for every volunteer, explaining, "Who wears buttons? It's the people who work in the headquarters operations. If you send them enough for themselves, they'll have them and that's that. This is to placate campaign workers."[2] Rafshoon's quandary was illustrative of the extent to which material culture had by 1976 ceased to be oriented toward persuasion of the masses and directed instead to serving the needs or pleasures of activists already committed to a candidate or ideological imperative.

Another factor in the decline of campaign buttons as a headquarters giveaway item to the general public during the 1960s and 1970s was the popularity of polyester double-knit fabrics for men's and women's clothing. Unlike woolens, cotton goods, and many earlier synthetics, the new double-knits proved notoriously vulnerable to damage from pinbacks. In response, producers turned out fewer straight pinbacks and more buttons with safety pin and lockpin fasteners to avoid exposed points to snag clothing, but along with the new mood of political introspection and detachment, fears of unraveling in public undoubtedly did much to dampen enthusiasm for buttons altogether. After enjoying widespread popularity during the Eisenhower–Adlai Stevenson contests in 1952 and 1956 and the 1964 Lyndon Johnson–Barry Goldwater race, lapel tabs and political jewelry items also began to diminish markedly as campaign devices in 1968 and 1972. The disposable lapel sticker (fig. 200) made its debut in 1968 as an inexpensive button substitute ("If I Had a Button It Would Say Humphrey–Muskie" read one style) compatible with the new double-knits. Although several iron-on and adhesive fabric varieties were produced in 1968 and 1972, paper stickers peeled from waxed sheets or rolls soon proved far superior in cost-effectiveness and simplicity.

A much more important innovation in political material culture during this period was the emergence of the bumper sticker as a major presence in modern presidential campaigns. Although early automobile stickers undoubtedly served in many instances as bumper decorations, the modern bumper sticker did not come into its own as a campaign device until 1956, when more than fifty different varieties turned countless bumpers into miniature billboards promoting Eisenhower or Stevenson. Inexpensive but very durable, perfectly suited to an electorate on wheels, and highly visible yet conducive to the preservation of a modicum of personal anonymity, the bumper sticker quickly developed into perhaps the most significant single avenue of personal political expression. Its major shortcoming, extreme difficulty of removal once a campaign had run its course, was alleviated by a conversion from paper to new vinyl varieties during the 1970s. Window stickers and decals and metal license attachments have been doomed to extinction as a result, although political license plates have survived as ornaments on front bumpers in single-plate states. Cloth antenna flags, as well as some rather cumbersome plastic antenna devices (fig. 201) produced in 1960 and 1964, were unable to complete with bumper stickers.

While bumper stickers evolved into campaign headquarters staples, other types of material once found there in great abundance began to disappear from headquarters shelves. A vogue in poster art during the 1960s and early 1970s inspired many decorative and creative political boutique wall posters, but ordinary window posters declined steadily in popularity, and local antilitter laws virtually doomed to extinction the small paper types that once found homes on telephone and power poles. Although the Goldwater and Nixon forces used imaginative Halloween jack-o-lantern doorhangers in 1964 and 1968, a dramatic decline in door-to-door presidential canvassing made relative rarities of doorhangers and sample ballots. Political matchbooks, cigars, and other smoking paraphernalia became less and less commonly used to promote candidates, especially north of the Ohio and east of the Mississippi, because attacks on the habit began to proliferate during the 1960s. Wooden pencils and plastic ballpoint pens are still found occasionally in campaign headquarters. Political postcards, more popular than ever in races for local offices, declined in importance as vehicles for promoting presidential candidates.

Largely limited to distribution and wear at such events as major rallies and party caucuses and conventions, where detachment and introspection have never prevailed, celluloid buttons became increasingly larger and more flamboyant in color and graphic design. Once rather rare, large buttons three and four inches in diameter (and enormous six-and nine-inch vari-

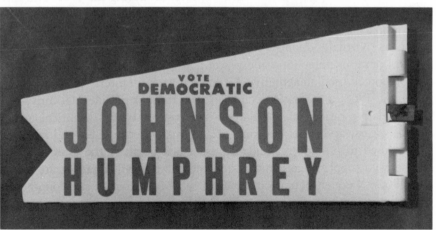

Figs. 200 and 201. Introduced during the 1968 and 1972 campaigns as substitutes for buttons were paper and fabric stickers like the ones pictured, while plastic antenna flags like the Johnson–Humphrey variety were doomed as campaign devices by bumper stickers. (Kenneth J. Moran)

eties) had become quite common by 1964, their bulk and vulgarity out-weighed by their sheer exuberance and great visibility (especially to television audiences). After a half-century of decline in aesthetic qualities, with buttons characterized essentially by dull designs and drab or ritual red, white, and blue coloring, the 1964, 1968, and 1972 campaigns inspired many varieties featuring imaginative graphics and festive color combinations. Many outstanding styles were created to sell in campaign boutiques, including a set of large "goggle-eye" buttons (fig. 202), which sported glued-on eyes of the sort used on toy stuffed animals, were sold in 1968 at Hubert Humphrey's Washington boutique, The Pharmacy. "Flasher" buttons (fig. 203) that refract light to portray alternating designs made their debut during the 1952 campaign and proved quite popular, although enthusiasm for them began to wane somewhat in 1968 and 1972.

If such traditionally utilitarian types of campaign objects as buttons and posters exhibited a renaissance in creativity and beauty as their functional role in the politics of persuasion was diminishing, the 1952–72 generation of political campaigning was a truly eclectic one for political items produced purely as novelties. Replacing the bandanna as the dominant type of political textile was the T-shirt (fig. 204), especially in vogue among the young and slender. Campaign hats in a multitude of styles—beanies, baseball caps, straw skimmers, and LBJ cowboy hats—became more popular than ever. Nylon stockings proclaiming "I Like Ike" and "I'm Madly for Adlai" did not establish a trend in feminine political dress. Garish plastic "Don't Be Static, Vote Democratic" and "I Like Ike" sunglasses appeared in 1956, and "The Eyes Have It for Humphrey" ones in 1968. Among the novelty consumables were bubblegum cigars, 1960 Nixon and John Kennedy ice cream bars, and 1964 "Johnson Juice" and "Gold Water" soft drinks (fig. 205). Campaign cosmetics included "I Like Ike" hand lotion packets, and deodorant soap promising Goldwater partisans "4-Year Protection." Kennedy was promoted on a sponge in 1960, Goldwater and Johnson dolls were marketed in 1964, plastic Nixon telephone dialers appeared in 1968, and a line of rather tacky vinyl posters (fig. 206), shopping bags, hats, and sashes promoted the 1968 Humphrey and Nixon campaigns. None of these items, apparently, tested Victor Hugo's dictum that "all the armies of the earth cannot stop an idea whose time has come," for they were not marketed in subsequent campaigns.

The 1952 and 1956 campaigns of Dwight Eisenhower and Adlai Stevenson inspired a rather substantial volume and variety of items, with Eisenhower pieces outnumbering Stevenson's by a much smaller margin than the two verdicts rendered by the voters. Included were nearly a thousand varieties of buttons, one hundred or more types of campaign jewelry, probably half that many lapel tabs, nearly three dozen different bandannas and handkerchiefs, many posters, matchbooks, and stickers, a few doorhangers, license attachments, banners, flashers, and ribbons, and

Figs. 202 and 203. Among the more successful types of novelty buttons produced during the presidential campaigns of the 1950s and 1960s were these Humphrey "goggle-eye" boutique varieties and the Eisenhower and Stevenson refracting "flashers" (Fig. 202, Kenneth J. Moran; Fig. 203, Robert A. Fratkin)

more than fifty known types of 1956 bumper stickers. Among the more esoteric items were nylon stockings, umbrellas, hand lotion, telephone dialers, garters, sunglasses, cloth and paper hats, neckties, bow ties, bolo ties, lighters, cigarettes, cigarette cases, real and bubblegum cigars, coasters, compacts, rulers, pens, pencils, key chains, cotton yard goods, pennants, and matching Ike and Mamie toby mugs.[3] The final presidential contests before television developed into the dominant medium for swaying

Figs. 204 and 205. Among the many innovations in material culture introduced during the 1964 campaign were T-shirts like the Goldwater varieties and Johnson Juice and Gold Water soft drinks. While the T-shirt has become the dominant type of modern political textile item, neither Johnson Juice nor Gold Water proved a threat to Coke, Pepsi, or 7-Up. (Fig. 204, Edmund B. Sullivan)

Fig. 206. Given out by the Democratic National Committee during the 1968 campaign was this aesthetically uninspiring vinyl poster, along with matching shopping bags, hats, and sashes. Similar varieties promoted the Nixon–Agnew ticket. (Kenneth J. Moran)

the electorate, 1952 and 1956 constituted a watershed period of political trinketry, the last great campaigns for many traditional types of items and years of genesis for many new forms.

Very few Eisenhower items were issued-oriented in 1952, and even fewer in 1956. A small number of 1952 pieces echoed the strident "twenty years of treason" undercurrent of a campaign that sought to depict the Roosevelt and Truman regimes as hotbeds of subversion and graft. A poster and three buttons read "Let's Clean House with Ike and Dick," a tab promised "They'll Clean House," and a poster urged "Send Ike and Dick to Washington/Clean Up the Mess!" The most demagogic of all 1952 Eisenhower items may well have been another poster (fig. 207) bearing such pleas as "Clean Up Truman's Mess" of the "cronies and grafters" and "Kick Out the Commies" who were allegedly "still betraying America." Stevenson was essentially ignored on items as well as in rhetoric in both Eisenhower campaigns, although the celebrated 1952 photograph of the Democratic nominee with a hole in one shoe inspired some "Don't Let This Happen to You! Vote for Ike" buttons (fig. 208), and stickers and speculation that Eisenhower's 1955 heart attack had left him too infirm for vigorous leadership prompted a 1956 button retorting "Better a Part-Time President than a Full-Time Phony." More subtle was a 1952 "Mothers for Mamie/Keep a Mother in the White House" button exploiting by implication Stevenson's status as a divorced man.

Much more common were objects portraying Eisenhower as a strong, trustworthy leader. Buttons proclaimed him "The Mighty Tower Eisenhower" and "Man of the Hour Eisenhower," and a card saluted him and running-mate Richard Nixon as "A Great Team for a Greater America." Buttons insisted "Eisenhower Will Guard My Future" and "Give Us Our Own Future/Vote for Ike," a 1952 poster urged "Vote for a Man You Can Trust," and 1956 matchbooks and buttons demanded "Keep America Strong with Ike." A flasher and several buttons promoted Eisenhower as the key to "Peace/Progress/Prosperity," plastic sunglasses and other buttons pledged "Peace and Prosperity," and 1956 paper stickers urged "For Peace and Prosperity Stick with Ike." A 1956 button read "Integrity/Knowledge/Experience," and other 1956 buttons lauded Eisenhower's economic achievements with such legends as "Ike Cut Taxes/Vote Republican" and "Ike's Workingman's Club/America's Record Employment/67 Members All Working/Memberships Increasing Daily." A "My Friend Ike" button featuring clasped white and black hands represented a 1952 Republican effort to recapture the allegiance of black voters. Given Eisenhower's enormous stature as the architect of our World War II victory over the Nazis, it is surprising that this theme was downplayed almost to the point of invisibility on his 1952 and 1956 campaign objects (a few five-star buttons and jewelry items and one or two buttons featuring him in uniform were the major exceptions), especially in light of the prominence of Korea as a 1952 issue.

VOTE THE WINNING TEAM IN NOVEMBER!

DWIGHT D. EISENHOWER   RICHARD M. NIXON

YOUR LAST CHANCE !!

END THE KOREAN SLAUGHTER
1000 killed and crippled every week —
our war production is the wounded and
dead. Is this what you want?

KICK OUT THE COMMIES
Truman's "Red herrings" and Steven-
son's "phantoms" are still betraying
America.

CLEAN UP TRUMAN'S MESS
Stevenson can't throw out the cronies
and grafters who are trying to put
him in.

STOP CRAZY SPENDING
$260,000,000,000 in debt—your $1.00
is worth 50¢—your income is phoney—
record taxes for everyone.

END OUR HIT-OR-MISS FOREIGN POLICY
Restore our National Self-respect. No
more Acheson—No more Appeasement
—No more Apologies.

Fig. 207. Distributed by Republican campaign headquarters, this demagogic 1952 Eisenhower–Nixon poster epitomized the element of character assassination and innuendo that Republicans blended so successfully with Eisenhower's charisma to produce a landslide victory. (Edmund B. Sullivan)

Perhaps his military identity was so well established that his 1952 advisors feared that further exploitation would only accentuate his political virginity.

Among the novelty items produced for the Eisenhower campaigns were 1952 "Time for a Change" buttons featuring babies in diapers and 1956 convention "We're Fore Ike" packages of golf tees, the only known Republican objects to call attention to Ike's celebrated preference for the fairways of Burning Tree Country Club over his desk in the Oval Office. The 1956 buttons given out by convention delegates who hoped to avert the dumping of Richard Nixon pleaded "Keep Dick on the Job," "Stick with Dick," and "Don't Change the Team in the Middle of the Stream." Paper stickers with clock designs rhymed "Now Is the Hour for Eisenhower," Republican Women's Federation buttons with female elephants pledged "Womanpower for Eisenhower," and other buttons read "Ike and Dick/Sure to Click."

The ultimate Eisenhower slogan, of course, was "I Like Ike," probably the most successful political jingle in American history, born during the 1948 "draft Eisenhower" boomlet (according to some accounts during halftime at a 1947 Texas high school football game, when the Abilene High School band spelled it out with flash cards and a marching formation) and introduced into material culture by such campaign item producers as Arthur Garfield Trimble and Emmanuel Ress. In 1952 and 1956, the legend "I Like Ike" adorned more than one hundred known varieties of buttons, as well as tabs, flashers, handkerchiefs, license attachments, matchbooks, bumper stickers, cloth patches, jewelry items, cigars (both tobacco and bubblegum), decals, cigarettes, sunglasses, banners, nylon stockings, neckties, bow ties, pennants, key chains, and hand lotion packets. Dozens of button varieties bore such foreign language translations as "Yo Quiero Ike," "J'Aime Ike," "Mi Piace Ike," and "Me Gusta Ike." Others featured the slogan in Morse Code, sign language for the deaf, and Braille. Spin-offs included "We Like Ike" rulers and buttons, "I Like Ike and Dick" buttons and bumper stickers, "I Like Nixon Too," "I Like Mamie," and "Ike Likes Me" buttons, and 1956 items with such adaptations as "I Still Like Ike," "I Like Ike Even Better," and "More than Ever I Like Ike." The popularity of the slogan was so pervasive that much of the material culture of Democratic campaigns from 1952 through 1964 was devoted to largely unsuccessful efforts to duplicate its magic.

Among these efforts were many 1952 and 1956 Stevenson objects—buttons, bumper stickers, flashers, jewelry, bandannas, ashtrays, neckties, nylon stockings, and real and bubblegum cigars among them—bearing such slogans as "I Say Adlai," "Madly for Adlai," "Gladly for Adlai," "We Need Adlai Badly," "All the Way with Adlai," "OK with Adlai," "I Like Adlai," "We Believe in Steve," even "Adlai and Estes Are the Bestes'." Much less contrived and more successful, for they exploited Stevenson's essential humanity and helped counteract his aloof image as something of an "egghead,"

Figs. 208 and 209. A celebrated photograph of Stevenson sitting cross-legged on a Flint, Michigan, platform in September 1952, with a large hole in the sole of one shoe inspired several popular 1952 campaign items, including this satiric Republican button and the assortment of Democratic items below. (Erroll J. Leslie)

were buttons, tabs, doorhangers, lapel pins, and tie tacs (fig. 209) featuring his famous holed shoe. Buttons with such tributes as "The Thinking Man's Candidate," "It Just Makes Sense," and "Integrity/Experience/Stability/ Maturity," and posters bearing his 1952 manifesto "Let's Talk Sense to the American People" sought to present Stevenson as a thoughtful man too decent to humbug the electorate.

A major theme expressed on 1952 and 1956 Democratic campaign items was an effort to portray both elections as referenda on the legacy of the New Deal and the Fair Deal. A 1952 Stevenson poster inspired by one printed in 1940 by the American Labor party contrasted bread lines, closed banks, and homeless people under "The Party of Hoover" with good wages and homes and Social Security under "The Party of Roosevelt." Another 1952 labor poster (fig. 210) warned "Don't Transfer to a Horsecar!" and promised "Full Civil Rights • Increased Aid For The Aged • High Wages, Steady Work" with Stevenson and running-mate John Sparkman. Other 1952 posters insisted "Continue Prosperity," "For All the People," and "We Must Look Forward to Great Tomorrows." Other 1952 buttons asked "Never Before Has Business Been Better nor More People Employed at Higher Wages/Why Change?" Ribbons, pennants, and buttons urged "And Don't Let Them Take It Away." In 1956, many items reflected a shift in emphasis from economics to social concerns. A poster portraying Stevenson with a small girl on his lap read "Pledged to Action on School Construction and Child Welfare." Other posters presented him and Estes Kefauver as "For All of You" and "The Ticket for You, Not Just the Few," and a button proclaimed them "The Team for You, Not Just the Few."

While Eisenhower items were on the whole somewhat more polite than the campaigns that inspired them, many Stevenson objects were uncharacteristically nasty. Limited in 1952 to such barbs at Eisenhower's military background as "No Brass Hat for President" tabs and "No General" and "Civilians for Stevenson" buttons, 1956 put-down items were both more numerous and more pointed. An "Under the Republicans You've Never Had It so Good" button appeared with "Never" and "So Good" crossed out to alter the message to "Under the Republicans You've Had It!" Another featured a monkey and the slogan "I Like Ike." Others read "No Like," "Nix–On Ike," and "Now Do You Like Ike?" Bumper stickers quipped "F.D.R.—The New Deal/Harry—The Fair Deal/Ike—The Ordeal." A number of "Joe Smith" items (fig. 211), inspired by votes cast for a fictitious character by anti–Nixon delegates to the Republican convention,[4] lampooned Nixon and by implication Eisenhower as well. Buttons warning "Fore! We'll All Be in the Same Hole Together!" satirized Eisenhower's penchant for golf, as did a Statue of Liberty stamp that read "I Would Like Ike to Retire to Play Golf in Peace." Another stamp, certainly one of the most tasteless campaign items ever printed, urged "Help Save Ike's Life/He Gave His Heart & Guts/Vote for Ike and You Help Take His Life." Given

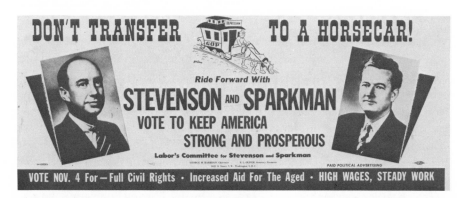

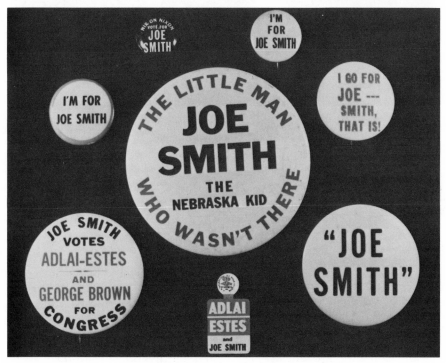

Figs. 210 and 211. Among the more sarcastic items issued by the Democrats during Stevenson's two campaigns against Eisenhower were this "Don't Transfer to a Horse-car!" Stevenson–John Sparkman poster and these 1956 "Joe Smith" buttons and tab lampooning Nixon's difficulties securing nomination for a second term as vice-president. (Erroll J. Leslie)

Eisenhower's broad popularity, greater wisdom was exhibited by such insipid items as buttons that read "I Like Ike but I am Going to Vote for Stevenson and "Join the Thoughtful Admirers of Eisenhower Who Now Support Stevenson," and bumper stickers with "I've Switched to Adlai" printed over "I Like Ike."

The 1952 and 1956 elections were much richer in primary and convention items issued by major party contenders than in splinter-party material.[5] The Socialists, Prohibitionists, and Progressive-American Labor party issued buttons in 1952, and the States' Rights party in 1956. More creative were several buttons, some with such legends as "Lower Taxes" and "Poor Henry," promoting one Henry B. Krajewski, who offered himself on the "Poor Man's party" tickets in 1952 and as the "America Third" candidate in 1956. Among the Democratic primary and convention items in 1952 were buttons promoting Claude Pepper, William O. Douglas, Richard Russell, and Brien McMahon, an Oscar R. Ewing "Swing to Ewing" button, and several Robert Kerr buttons, including a handsome log-cabin variety that sought to add a Lincolnesque touch to the image of the archconservative "senator from Oil." Supporters of Estes Kefauver and Averill Harriman issued large numbers of buttons and other items both in 1952 and 1956, including tabs and donkey caricature buttons featuring the famous Kefauver coonskin cap and buttons promoting Harriman with such slogans as "I Crave Aive," "Averill Will Fill the Bill," and (apparently issued early in 1952 before Truman's declaration of noncandidacy) "HARRI/TRU/MAN." Eisenhower had no real challengers in 1956, but the 1952 Republican primaries and convention yielded Earl Warren and Harold Stassen buttons and tabs and more than two dozen varieties of Robert Taft buttons, some of which read "Stop Graft/Elect Taft," "Vote Taft/Stop Graft," "I Like Bob Better," "I Like Ike but I Like Taft Better," and "Vote TAFT Not Yes Man Ike." One response from the Eisenhower camp was a "Remember 1912/Win with Ike or Lose with Taft" convention button.

The 1960 contest between John Kennedy and Richard Nixon inspired a slightly larger but infinitely less creative material dimension than the two Eisenhower–Stevenson races. More than five hundred known varieties of buttons, large numbers of bumper stickers, posters, matchbooks, and other types of political paper, many tabs and jewelry items, and some handkerchiefs, pennants, ribbons, banners, pencils, ballpoint pens, ashtrays, paperweights, clothing buttons, neckties, knives, plaques, potholders, skimmer hats, key cases, bubblegum cigars, eyeglass cloths, and even sponges and ice cream bars promoted the two adversaries.[6] Such a varied assortment of artifact types might well have inspired equally creative thematics, but such was not the case.

A large number of Kennedy buttons and other campaign objects indicated a strenuous but largely unsuccessful attempt to develop for him a cute and catchy slogan along the lines of "I Like Ike." Most often utilized were "Let's Back Jack," "I Back Jack," and "All the Way with JFK," but other efforts included "I'm Gone for John," "On the Right Track with Jack," "Give the Key to Kennedy," "Kennedy Is the Remedy," "Kennedy Is Best for Me," and "It Seems to Me It's Kennedy." Echoing Kennedy's stirring pledge to "get America moving again" were a host of campaign buttons, posters, bumper stickers, matchbooks, flashers, and other items exploiting the theme of leadership. Buttons, posters, bumper stickers, postcards, pennants, and matchbooks read "Leadership for the '60s," and other buttons bore such legends as "For the Leadership We Need," "New Leadership," "For Experienced Leadership," "For America's Future," and "Progress for All." Several flashers proclaimed Kennedy "The Man for the '60s," and matchbooks urged "Restore America" and "The Stronger Man for a Stronger Nation." Buttons, posters, and flyers read "A Time for Greatness." A few buttons, a matchbook, and a license plate utilized Kennedy's "New Frontier" slogan, including a rocket motif matchbook that read "The New Frontier/Firm Guidance for Tomorrow's World—Today." PT–109 lapel pins and tie bars (fig. 212) exploited Kennedy's renown as a World War II naval hero, and some rocking-chair jewelry items played up his celebrated fondness for his Boston rocker.

With the possible exception of the leadership and PT–109 items, one cannot escape the conclusion that Kennedy was very poorly served by his material culture. No headquarters pieces (and only two "Prosperity for All" vendor buttons) played up economic themes, despite the 1957–58 "Eisenhower recession." No effort was made to use objects to exploit the peace issue, despite Nixon's reputation as a rather truculent red-baiter, perhaps because Kennedy forces were too worried that doing so would only invite "soft on communism" allegations. A similar defensiveness on the religious question may have caused a virtual absence of items exploiting Kennedy's Irish heritage, unfortunate in an era when lace-curtain suburban Irish voters were increasingly abandoning the party of their fathers. One shamrock button was virtually the only hint of Kennedy's lineage in a campaign conspicuously lacking in green objects. No known items highlighted his religious affiliation in Catholic enclaves or made a case for toleration elsewhere. No items echoed the title or theme of Kennedy's Pulitzer Prize volume, *Profiles in Courage*, despite the compelling nature of its thesis and the intellectual credentials it gave to its author, an especially crucial consideration among Democratic liberals still devoted to Adlai Stevenson. That these individuals never completely surrendered their hearts to the Kennedy mystique was demonstrated by their "Stevenson Democrats for Kennedy" bumper stickers. Most surprising of all, only a "High Office Demands High Principle" button sought to exploit the moral or ethical dimension, where Nixon—so widely dismissed as "Tricky Dick"—was so enormously vulnerable. Few American presidential campaigns have inspired items characterized by so many missed opportunities.

A few 1960 Nixon buttons—featuring such legends as "My Pick Is Dick," "Click with Dick," "Nixon Now," "Nixon in November," even "I'm Afixin'

Fig. 212. Commemorating JFK's heroism in the South Pacific during World War II, PT–109 lapel pins like the sterling silver variety shown (given out sparingly to friends, dignitaries, and campaign workers) ranked among the most popular 1960 Kennedy campaign mementos.

to Vote for Nixon"—sought to duplicate the "I Like Ike" syndrome, but the most effective and widely utilized slogan on Nixon items was "Experience Counts," utilized on flashers, posters, matchbooks, paper hats, bumper stickers, and nearly two dozen different buttons to promote the premise that Nixon's eight years of being only the proverbial heartbeat away from the Oval Office gave him a great advantage over the youthful Kennedy. Variations on the theme included "Experienced Leader" posters, "Experienced!" tabs, and "No Substitute for Experience" buttons. Other buttons read "Peace/Experience/Prosperity." Objects stressing Nixon's leadership potential included a "World Leadership thru Nixon" silk banner and "Keep America Strong" posters. Among 1960 campaign items portraying Nixon as a man of sterling personal virtues (some of them extraordinarily ironic in light of subsequent developments) were "Integrity" Nixon–Eisenhower–Lincoln tokens and buttons proclaiming the candidate their "Man of Steel" and the White House "Not for Sale." A rather interesting button advised "Goldwater Says Don't Dodge/Vote Nixon and Lodge," perhaps inspired by Goldwater's Republican convention press conference that helped defuse a conservative threat to "sit it out" because of Nixon's platform concessions to Nelson Rockefeller. A button reading "Ike's for Dick and So Am I" was one of the surprisingly few 1960 efforts to exploit some of Eisenhower's massive popularity on behalf of his former understudy.[7]

A major challenge faced by creators of Nixon campaign objects was the projection of Nixon as a likeable human being. One approach taken was a major emphasis on his wife, Patricia. Many buttons did so with such legends as "Pat for First Lady," "We Want Pat Too," "Ask Me About Pat," and "I'm for Dick and Pat." Two types of headquarters giveaway pencils advised "Make a Note to Vote for Dick and Pat Nixon." Another humanizing tactic was the great prominence given Nixon's nickname, "Dick," on campaign items, although some uniquely tasteless varieties of buttons that read "They Can't Lick Our Dick"—at least one of them given out by the campaign itself—probably did little to project Nixon as a latter-day Lincoln.

Unlike Kennedy's material culture, which rather foolishly ignored Nixon's perceived shortcomings almost altogether, many 1960 Republican objects (a few of them official headquarters items, but most produced for commercial vendors or independent conservative groups) leveled scathing attacks on the opposition standard-bearers. Kennedy's youth was satirized on "Don't Send a Boy . . . " buttons and cardboard disks with a caricature of JFK as a child and the dialogue "'What Would You Like to Be, Son?'/ 'President, Dad'/'I Mean when You Grow Up.'" His family wealth and alleged aversion to fiscal restraint prompted buttons with such admonitions as "Remember It's Your Charge-a-Plate Jack Will Be Using" and "It's Not Jack's Money He'd Spend . . It's Yours" and bumper stickers echoing "It's not Jack's Jack He'd Spend, *It's Yours!*" Other bumper stickers lampooned Kennedy's naval heroics and ties to Hollywood's Frank Sinatra-Peter Lawford-Sammy Davis-Dean Martin "ratpack" with such barbs as "Remember the PT–109/Like Who Gets a Chance to Forget?" and "No Kennedy–Lawford–Sinatra." Buttons read "Nix–on Kennedy" and "Don't Be a 'Jack' Ass/Vote Republican." Much more inherently vicious were a number of items, issued by such right-wing groups as the Young Americans for Freedom, depicting Kennedy as a lackey of the Soviet Union. These included "Sorry Nik/I Like Dick" tabs, *"Don't* Change Front in the Face of the *Enemy"* buttons, and jugate flashers featuring Kennedy and Nikita Khrushchev pounding his shoe.

Several vendor buttons lampooned both Nixon and Kennedy, the most imaginative of which announced *"Prostitutes* . . . Vote for Nixon or Kennedy/We Don't Care Who Gets In!" Others insisted "Vote for Neither" and "I Don't Want Nixon or Kennedy." Leftist beliefs that both men were champions of the status quo inspired buttons complaining "Jack & Dick Are No Answer/We Demand Disarmament, Civil Rights and Jobs" and "Kennedy Is No Remedy/Nixon Won't Do Any Fixin/We Need a Labor Party." The year 1960 was singularly poor one for minor party items, except for a series of buttons reportedly produced for collectors, but it was much more fertile for primary and convention buttons supporting major party contenders. Buttons sported by Republican liberal and right-wing wishful thinkers promoted noncandidates Nelson Rockefeller and Barry Goldwater. The much more fiercely contested struggle for the Democratic nomination produced a few Stuart Symington buttons, several Lyndon Johnson items featuring his Stetson symbol to enhance his identity as a westerner (and downplay his image as a southerner), many "It's Humphrey in '60" buttons and posters (deliberately vague as to the office sought so that if Humphrey did poorly in the presidential primaries, his impoverished campaign could later use them to promote his re-election to the Senate),[8] and several buttons issued by the eleventh-hour movement to draft Adlai Stevenson for a third try. Some of the 1960 Stevenson buttons insisted "I'm Still Madly for Adlai," "2 Strikes Are Not Out," and We Can't Afford a Lesser Man."

The 1964 mismatch between Lyndon Johnson and Barry Goldwater engendered one of the most impressive harvests of campaign items of any

American presidential election, surely the most varied and creative since the 1940 Roosevelt–Willkie contest. Promoting Johnson or Goldwater were as many as one thousand different buttons, perhaps two hundred types of bumper stickers, an exceptional assortment of campaign jewelry, many posters, tabs, flashers, and matchbooks, some pennants, bandannas, license plates, and antenna flags, and such ephemera as bubblegum cigars, ashtrays, lighters, shot glasses, umbrellas, emery boards, tumblers, hats, clothing buttons, and ballpoint pens.[9] Political T-shirts (fig. 204) made their debut. LBJ and Goldwater dolls were marketed, as were Johnson Juice and Gold Water canned soft drinks and bars of Gold Water deodorant soap. Although most of the suspense involved only the ultimate dimensions of the Johnson landslide, 1964 provided an ideal environment for material culture. Goldwater would win fewer than two of every five votes cast, but to much of that minority he was literally a cult hero, no "dime-store New Dealer," but a champion of unabashed and unadulterated conservatism who polarized the electorate like no public figure since Franklin Roosevelt. Johnson was still a genuinely popular man in his own right. More than any other modern presidential race, 1964 developed into a national referendum on widely divergent political philosophies. One result was a material dimension exceptional in volume, variety, and thematic expression.

Many Goldwater items (fig. 213) defied conventional wisdom by openly flaunting his conservative disdain for moderate, mainstream politics-as-usual. Buttons, tabs, and flashers featured arrows pointing rightward, and a button asked "What's Wrong Being Right?" Bumper stickers warned "Goldwater or Socialism," posters insisted "Victory for America," and buttons issued by the John Birch Society demanded "Victory over Communism." Other buttons bore such maxims as "Vote Conservative in '64," "Goldwater for Freedom," "A Choice not an Echo," "A Choice for a Change," and "Choice not Chance." Cans of Gold Water promoted the soda as "The Right Drink for the Conservative Taste," and Gold Water soap wrappers read "The Soap for Conservative People/4-Year Protection." Liberty Bell badges proclaimed "Ring in Freedom with Goldwater for President." A number of items echoed Goldwater's controversial acceptance address dictum that "extremism in defense of liberty is no vice," including a button repeating the full quotation and others featuring such slogans as "I'm *Extremely* Fond of Barry," "I Am a Right-Wing Extremist," and "I'm an Extremist/I Love Liberty." Objects lampooning Democratic efforts to frighten the electorate by branding Goldwater a dangerous extremist included "Don't Be Spooked by the Goblins/Go Goldwater" Halloween jack-o-lantern doorhangers and mechanical plastic panic buttons (fig. 214) with pop-up "Goldwater-Miller" or "Vote for Goldwater" flags.

Even more numerous than items highlighting Goldwater's conservatism were those exploiting the politics of personality. The celebrated Goldwater horned-rim glasses inspired many varieties of distinctive buttons and jewelry items and some fold-out wall hangers. His prowess as a jet pilot was reflected

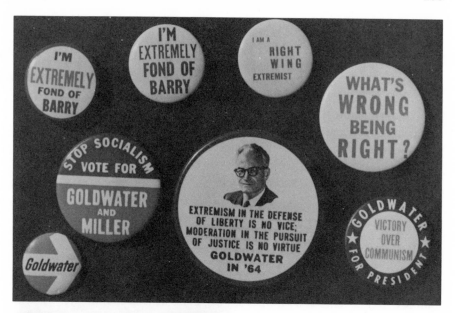

Figs. 213 and 214. This assortment of 1964 Republican campaign buttons represents a few of the many items openly flaunting the conservative extremism of party nominee Barry Goldwater, while the ingenious pop-up Goldwater plastic panic button was created to poke fun at Democratic attempts to frighten the electorate with Goldwater's alleged right-wing recklessness. (Kenneth J. Moran)

by buttons featuring jet airplane designs and a poster featuring Goldwater in a flight suit and the legend "We Need a Space Age Candidate." His name provided unique opportunities for creators of campaign material. Metallic gold coloring became a ubiquitous symbol of the crusade, doing much to liberate political material culture from an almost slavish reliance on red, white, and blue. Buttons read "IN GO$_L$D WE TRUST" and "Gold for Goldwater." Others featured glasses of golden water or bubbles with water laden with gold particles. Many items—bumper stickers, buttons, license plates, tie tacs, lapel pins, and bars of soap—promoted the Republican candidate as "AuH$_2$0," the chemical formula for gold water. His surname inspired buttons with such maxims as "It's Barry Pickin' Time" and a "bare-e" rebus design portraying a naked woman with her body arched in the shape of a lower case letter *e*. A rebus lapel pin utilized a strawberry, gold nugget, and water drop. Several Goldwater buttons (fig. 215) echoed his main campaign slogan: "In Your Heart You Know He's Right."

An unusually large number of anti–Johnson put-down items appeared in 1964, some of them official headquarters objects, but most of them produced for independent conservative groups or commercial vendors. Buttons lampooning the Johnson Great Society agenda as "A New Leech on Life," an "Abominable Snow Job," and a chance to "Serf Yourself" were distributed by the Young Americans for Freedom, as was a button featuring "The LBJ Cocktail—America on the Rocks." Other buttons quipped "LBJ Will Be Home on the Range when Goldwater Gets Done," "Half the Way with LBJ/The Tale of a Tall Texan," "Lyndon's Bridge Is Falling Down," "Get R.I.D. of L.B.J.," and "Let's Put an Honest Man in the White House." Bumper stickers bore such insults as "Big Lyndon Is Watching You." Fabric pin-on badges proclaimed "Tax Payers for Goldwater/Free Loaders for Johnson." Doorhangers resembling padlocks warned "LBJ Keep Out/It's My Money You're Spending." Buttons ridiculed Johnson's wife Lady Bird and her interest in beautification with such insults as "Keep America Beautiful— Hide Lady Bird" and "You're Absurd Bird." Johnson's rather contrived cutback on White House lighting to demonstrate his frugality inspired a superb "Turn Out Light Bulb Johnson" caricature button (fig. 216) and buttons and bumper stickers reading "Light Bulb Johnson/Turn Him Out in November." Scandals involving former Senate page and Johnson aide Bobby Baker inspired a host of buttons, and the rather tragic involvement of LBJ lieutenant Walter Jenkins in a homosexual incident at a Washington YMCA engendered a few buttons, including a large, garish vendor item proclaiming "All the Way with LBJ, but Don't Go Near the YMCA."[10] Probably the most tasteless 1964 anti–Johnson object, however, was a license plate marketed by a Doraville, Georgia, firm for sale at southern truck-stops and featuring an enormously pregnant black woman confessing "I Went All de Way wif LBJ."

The contest also produced an exceptional number of anti-Goldwater items, some of them hawked by commercial vendors and others made for Democratic and labor campaign groups. "In Your Guts You Know He's Nuts" buttons parodied the Goldwater slogan. Lampooning Goldwater chemistry were "AuH$_2$O—Fool's Gold" bumper stickers and buttons that read "$C_5H_4N_4O_3$ on AuH$_2$O," quite literally "uric acid on gold water." Bumper stickers reading "Goldwater for Poverty" and buttons predicting "Goldwater in '64/Hot Water in '65/Bread and Water in '66" satirized Goldwater's economic beliefs. His views on the modern general-welfare state prompted "Goldwater in 1864" buttons, and his perceived disregard for civil liberties inspired "Goldwater for Fuhrer" buttons. A button depicting an elephant's rump proclaimed

Figs. 215 and 216. Among the more imaginative buttons worn by Goldwater supporters in 1964 were these "In Your Heart, You Know He's Right" varieties and this trio of satiric celluloids lampooning LBJ's conservation of White House electricity. (Kenneth J. Moran)

"Barry Is the Living End." Bumper stickers derided him as "Bilgewater" and "Beri Beri" and insisted "Bury Goldwater." A button quipped "Mets Rooters! Edsel Owners! Back a *REAL* Loser—Goldwater." The most creative—and inherently unfair—of 1964 anti-Goldwater items were ones echoing a major tenet of the Johnson campaign, the portrayal of Goldwater as a latent warmonger enthralled with nuclear weaponry.[11] Bumper stickers warned "Barry G. and World War III" and "Help Goldwater Wipe Out Peace," and buttons read "Hari-Kari with Barry" and "Ban the Bomb and Barry." Buttons featured mushroom clouds and the slogans "Go with Goldwater" and "What—Me Worry?" Linking Goldwater to the title character in the nuclear farce *Dr. Strangelove* were some "Doctor Strangewater for President" and "No General Strangewater for America" buttons.

Many Johnson campaign items highlighted his identity as a Texan and a westerner, motivated perhaps by Johnson's almost compulsive fear that a southern image was a kiss of death in national politics. Buttons, tabs, and an enormous array of LBJ jewelry items (fig. 217) featured such symbols as the celebrated Johnson Stetson, cowboy boots, spurs, and Texas maps. Campaign bric-a-brac included cloth mini–Stetsons and figural Stetson ceramic ashtrays. The LBJ doll wore a Stetson. Buttons read "My Brand's LBJ" and "Keep a Firm Hand on the Reins LBJ." Shot glasses featuring cowboy boots announced "You Bet Your Boots We're for Johnson!"

The effort to develop for Johnson a jingle as successful as "I Like Ike" led to many campaign items featuring such slogans as "All the Way with LBJ," "USA Likes LBJ," and "LBJ for the USA," the latter featured on buttons, matchbooks, bumper stickers, flashers, posters, tie clasps, hats, clothing buttons, emery boards, and a whole line of headquarters material produced for the Johnson campaign by the Philadelphia Badge Company. One such piece, a small lithographed button portraying running-mate Hubert Humphrey as prominently (or more so) as it did LBJ, reportedly provoked Johnson's displeasure and was quickly replaced (fig. 218) by a variety featuring a somewhat diminished Humphrey. Several buttons—with such legends as "Strength and Moderation/The Spirit of the Nation," "It's not Luck that Rules the Nation/It's the Man," "Responsible Leadership," "For the Leadership We Want," and "The Choice Is Clear"—sought to contrast the candidates by presenting Johnson as a responsible and moderate national leader. Portraying him as heir to the Democratic tradition of social and economic justice were buttons reading "Support Johnson and Civil Rights," "Progress for All," "Prosperity for All," and "Peace, Prosperity and Progress." A New York Liberal party poster implored "Vote LBJ the Liberal Way/Defeat Goldwater and His Right Wing Extremists!" Especially effective were buttons (fig. 219) with the legend "Let Us Continue," Johnson's pledge to carry on the unfinished agenda of John Kennedy, the only real effort to capitalize on the extraordinary posthumous popularity of Kennedy on 1964 campaign items.

Figs. 217 and 218. The button, tab, and lapel pins represent only a few of the many 1964 Democratic campaign items promoting LBJ as a westerner and Texan. The standard Johnson–Humphrey headquarters giveaway button below is shown with an earlier prototype, modified after an LBJ outburst because he was not portrayed more prominently than his running-mate. (Kenneth J. Moran)

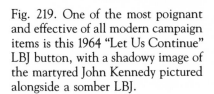

Fig. 219. One of the most poignant and effective of all modern campaign items is this 1964 "Let Us Continue" LBJ button, with a shadowy image of the martyred John Kennedy pictured alongside a somber LBJ.

Before his death, Kennedy inspired a number of early 1964 items in his own right. Buttons urged "Jack/Once More in '64" and "I Want Jack Back." Illinois Democrats produced a button supporting Kennedy and gubernatorial candidate Otto Kerner. A miniature California license plate read "JFK 464." Halfway prophetic at least was a "Back Jack/Bury Goldwater in 1964" button. That Kennedy was not as universally revered before his assassination as afterward was made manifest by buttons and bumper stickers issued by independent conservative groups, for example, "Kennedy for King/ Goldwater for President" and "Barry Will Flush the White House John."

George Wallace's segregationist crusade produced buttons and other campaign items used in the 1964 Maryland, Michigan, and Indiana Democratic primaries, and efforts to deny Goldwater the Republican nomination engendered a pennant and several buttons promoting Nelson Rockefeller and buttons for such possible contenders as Ambassador Henry Cabot Lodge, Minnesota congressman Walter Judd, Michigan governor George Romney, Maine senator Margaret Chase Smith, and perennial also-ran Harold Stassen. A belated coalition of Republican moderates in support of Pennsylvania governor William Scranton inspired a pennant and several buttons, including an "I'm Rantin' for Scranton" variety and a set of three with "Scranton" depicted in flamboyant script for liberal Republicans, ordinary lettering for party moderates, and almost microscopic letters for GOP conservatives. Among the 1964 minor party items were a Constitution party "Support the Constitution/Let a Lightburn in the White House" button playing up the name of nominee Joseph B. Lightburn (as well as chiding

Johnson for a darkened mansion), buttons for the Socialist Workers', National States' Rights, the Theocratic party tickets, and a button promoting Universal party nominee Kirby James Henley, perhaps a key to the nineteen popular votes he garnered.

The material culture produced for the 1968 presidential campaign[12] was quite unusual in at least one respect in that a distinct minority of the authentic[13] varieties of items issued were created for the general election campaigns of major party nominees Richard Nixon and Hubert Humphrey. With neither nomination decided until the delegates actually balloted, the 1968 primaries and party conventions were fertile theaters for campaign items, but the stretch run between Nixon and Humphrey was not. The well-funded Nixon campaign was able to distribute extraordinary quantities of a few standard giveaway items, minimizing the need for local Republican groups to create their own. With a sickly treasury and little enthusiasm among the Democratic and labor loyalists, the Humphrey effort left a limited material legacy. Neither Nixon nor Humphrey was a truly popular public figure. Democratic rallies were often better attended by antiwar hecklers than by supporters, and Republican events were often contrived affairs in television studios before meticulously screened audiences. Much more expressive than the Nixon and Humphrey campaign items were those inspired by the demagogic crusade of American Independent candidate George Wallace. The emergence of a militant "New Left" to engage in the politics of protest in 1968 meant that for the first time much of the most imaginative and thematic presidential material culture was being generated essentially from the outside. Campaign items from 1968, like the election itself, reflected a troubled and temporarily fragmented electorate.

Among the many Democratic primary items were a few Lyndon Johnson buttons issued before his withdrawal from the race and some tabs, flashers, posters, and nearly fifty types of buttons promoting Senator Robert Kennedy, including two "Kennedy for a Better America" flashers and an eerily prophetic "American Calls Another Kennedy" button featuring silhouette busts of RFK and his dead brother. Eugene McCarthy's bid for the nomination engendered tabs, posters, bandannas, flashers, stickers, and as many as one hundred varieties of buttons. Many of these featured a two-toned blue ribbon design used on buttons from his 1964 Senate race, perhaps because he had huge quantities left over and limited funds to buy new ones. Surprisingly few items echoed the themes of McCarthy's intensely ideological campaign, among them buttons that read "Save America Gene," "Integrity Is Alive and Well in McCarthy," "Peace," and "Peace/Equality." Reflecting McCarthyite bitterness over the "Bobby-come-lately" entry into the race were "Kennedy Is Sex, but McCarthy Is Love" buttons and tabs expropriating a popular Coca Cola slogan to proclaim McCarthy "The Real Thing." Other Democratic primary and convention items included buttons promoting favorite son governors Lester Maddox of Georgia and Roger Branigan of Indiana and some convention buttons supporting Senator George McGovern, a stand-in candidate for many Kennedy delegates.

Republican primary and convention items included buttons promoting General James Gavin, governors Winthrop Rockefeller and George Romney, and the tenacious Harold Stassen. Nelson Rockefeller's quest for the nomination produced many campaign items, several of them exploiting the theme that he was a winner (and by implication Nixon a congenital loser) with such legends as "Rocky Has Never Lost an Election," "Go with a Winner," "Rocky Can Win," and "Win with Rockefeller." Even more items promoted California governor Ronald Reagan, even though he delayed a formal announcement of candidacy until the convention was in progress. Surprising in light of the unabashedly conservative tenor of Reagan's pronouncements and the right-wing nature of his support was the virtual absence of items echoing conservative themes. An eleventh-hour coalition between Rockefeller and Reagan forces to deny the nomination to Nixon produced some "R & R" buttons, conveniently omitting details on which "R" would head the odd-couple ticket.

A successful stop Nixon effort might have led to much more imaginative items for the Republican general election campaign, for those promoting Nixon were probably the least creative in memory. Many read simply "Nixon" (or "Nixon–Agnew") or utilized a slanted "N" logo. The slogan "Nixon's the One" appeared on a host of objects, including buttons (in fifteen foreign-language translations as well as English), tabs, flashers, stickers, posters, matchbooks, bumper stickers, and bubblegum cigars. Unlike 1960, when references to Nixon as "Dick" were so common, only one 1968 button did so, and it was also the only known 1968 button to imitate 1960 thematics by featuring wife Patricia. No known Nixon headquarters items directly attacked Humphrey, although buttons reading "Dump the Hump" and "Don't get HUMPHed in '68/Vote Republican" were sold by vendors at party functions. Among the very few imaginative 1968 Nixon items were "Even the Great Pumpkin Is Voting Nixon–Agnew" jack-o-lantern doorhangers and a pair of A. G. Trimble buttons (fig. 220), one proclaiming the endorsement of Uncle Sam and the other ranking Nixon with Washington, Lincoln, and Theodore Roosevelt.

The dominant motif on 1968 Humphrey material was his initials "HHH," featured on tie tacs, cuff links, key fobs, necklaces, balloons, coasters bandannas, bubblegum cigars, bumper stickers, a bottle, and at least fifty different buttons. Much more creative were a number of items reflecting the old family drug store in Doland, South Dakota, many of them made for sale in his Washington boutique, The Pharmacy. An old-fashioned glass medicine bottle with rounded stopper pictured the boutique and prescribed "HHH for Good Government." Ballpoint pens advised "A Prescription for America/Humbert H. Humphrey for President." Buttons (fig. 221) offered

Figs. 220 and 221. Among the more imaginative 1968 campaign buttons were these
A. G. Trimble varieties casting Nixon in the tradition of Lincoln, Washington,
Teddy Roosevelt, and Uncle Sam and these Humphrey boutique buttons exploiting
his background as the son of a South Dakota druggist. (Kenneth J. Moran)

the Humphrey–Edmund Muskie ticket as a prescription "For a Better World" and announced "HHH Fills the Prescription." Wife Muriel was featured on a recipe card and on "We Love Muriel" and "Muriel for First Lady" buttons. Efforts to promote Humphrey as a crusading liberal, critical in winning the support of followers of the sulking Eugene McCarthy, included "1968 Action not 1868 Reaction" boutique buttons, "To Make the Needed Change" posters and buttons, and posters (fig. 222) insisting "Some Talk Change. Others Cause It." A button proclaimed "McCarthy Supporters for Humphrey Now." Others read "Progress & Unity," "For a New Day," "A Man for the People," "Public Service/Integrity/Dedication," and "Heart/Humanity/Hope." A poster insisted "Jobs/Humphrey Tells It Like It Is." Another sought to exploit the embarrassing campaign performance of Nixon running-mate Spiro Agnew by proclaiming Muskie "The Only Man Qualified to Be Vice President." Less subtle was a "Nixon + Spiro = Zero" boutique button. A Voting Is Beautiful/Be Beautiful—Vote Humphrey–Muskie" poster portraying a handsome young black couple used the black is beautiful theme, then at the peak of its vogue, to encourage a strong black turnout.

The neo–Confederate campaign of American Independent candidate George Wallace inspired some predictably truculent objects protesting the decline of states' rights, law and order, and neighborhood schools, although none (in deference to a need to win votes outside the South) overtly waved the banner of white supremacy. The basic 1968 Wallace slogan "Stand up for America" was featured on license plates, buttons, matchbooks, bumper stickers, decals, postcards, flashers, and posters. His opposition to federal encroachment into local affairs inspired "Against Big Gov't." matchbooks and "Restore States Rights" licenses, and his hostility to civil disobedience generated "Law & Order" buttons, "Stand Up for Law & Order" posters, and "For Local Police/Against Rioting" matchbooks. Other matchbooks read "Stand Up for America/Constitutional Government," "Defender of the Constitution/God Bless America," and "For Private Property/Against Aid to Reds." Bumper stickers insisted "Wallace—Yes!/Busing—No!" and "Johnson for King/Wallace for President." A license plate asked "Had Enough???," and a Confederate-flag variety read "Wallace Country." General Curtis LeMay, his running-mate, was virtually nonexistent on Wallace items, in part because his moronic remarks on nuclear weaponry made him a distinct political liability, but primarily because the American Independent party, despite its pretensions to the contrary, was in 1968 nothing more than a vehicle for George Corley Wallace. Other 1968 third-party items included buttons promoting the Socialist Labor, Communist, Prohibition, Peace and Freedom, Theocratic, Christian Constitution, and Universal party tickets and some Socialist Workers' buttons demanding "Bring the GI's Home" and "Black Control of the Black Community."

Fig. 222. Like many other items issued by the Humphrey campaign after the divisive 1968 Democratic convention, this handsome full-color poster sought to make Humphrey more acceptable to disgruntled Eugene McCarthy and Robert Kennedy supporters by casting him as a champion of progressive reform. (Kenneth J. Moran)

With dissent over Vietnam reaching its zenith, 1968 was a vintage election for protest items either issued by New Left groups or sold in bookstores and other shops on or near the major activist college campuses. Reflecting the peculiar "presentist" myopia of the antiwar movement, old hard-liner Nixon and the ultra-hawkish Wallace were much less frequently targets for such items than was the lifelong liberal Humphrey. Before he was driven from the race, Johnson had inspired a "Kill for Peace" bumper sticker and a host of buttons (fig. 223) with such inscriptions as "Dump LBJ in '68," "Drop LBJ on North Vietnam," "I'm a Nervous Nellie," and "Write in Lyndon Baines Johnson for Coroner." Ironic in light of the Democratic portrayal of Goldwater in 1964 were LBJ caricature "Strangelove Lives" buttons and "All the Way with LBJ" mushroom cloud varieties. Among the myriad New Left items attacking Humphrey (fig. 224) were buttons conveying such insults as "Humphrey Sucks," "Democracy Demands Stop Humphrey," "Dump the Hump," "The People vs. Humphrey," "Hawk/Hypocrite/H-Bomber," "Chicken Little Laid Hubert Humphrey," and "Why Trade the Ventriloquist for the Dummy?" Especially vicious in light of Humphrey's lifelong devotion to liberal causes were "Hitler Humphrey" bumper stickers and buttons with "HHH '68" portrayed in a swastika motif. In a similar vein, a bumper sticker depicted the x in Nixon as a swastika, and buttons and bumper stickers read "If You Liked Hitler, You'll Love Wallace" and "Wallace, Wallace Über Alles."

Despite his inauguration day pledge to "bring us together," Nixon's rather divisive style of leadership and our continuing military involvement in Southeast Asia set the stage for a presidential race in 1972 that generated an ample and uncommonly expressive material dimension.[14] Buttons bearing such legends as "Jobs/Justice/Peace/Liberation," "Don't Tread on Me," "An Alternative for '72," and "Student Power" promoted People's party nominees Benjamin Spock and Julius Hobson. The Socialist Workers' ticket of Linda Jenness and Andrew Pulley inspired buttons urging "Fight for Women's Liberation" and "Make Your First Vote Count," while "Peace, Jobs, Freedom" buttons advertised the candidacy of Communist Gus Hall. Libertarian John Hospers inspired a "Break Free" button, and the Universal, Socialist Labor, Prohibition, and Youth International ("Yippie") slates issued buttons. At least twenty varieties promoted American Independent nominee John Schmitz, including several evoking the legacy of George Wallace with such legends as "Stand Up for America" and "Keep on Sending the Message" and a "When You're Out of Schmitz, You're Out of Gear" variety punning a popular beer jingle.

The near certainty of Nixon's nomination for another term in 1972 limited campaign items promoting Republican alternatives to a few buttons featuring liberal California congressman Paul McCloskey and two "No Left Turn" varieties issued by supporters of conservative Ohio congressman John Ashbrook. A virtual free-for-all for the Democratic nomination, however,

Figs. 223 and 224. While producers of material culture protesting the Vietnam War virtually ignored conservative candidates Richard Nixon and George Wallace in 1968, the pro-war tendencies of Lyndon Johnson inspired many acid-tinged buttons like those shown, and his successor Hubert Humphrey was also satirized. (Kenneth J. Moran)

inspired an enormous number of buttons and other items promoting George McGovern's many challengers. Many buttons were made for supporters of prodigal son George Wallace, "Common Sense for a Change" buttons promoted Senator Henry "Scoop" Jackson, Eugene McCarthy buttons announced "Gene Lives" and "McCarthy More than Ever," a rebus heart-key tab was worn by New Hampshire supporters of Senator Vance Hartke, and "Catalyst for Change" and "Take the CHISHOLM Trail to 1600 Pennsylvania Ave." buttons promoted New York congresswoman Shirley Chisholm. Supporters of Indiana senator Birch Bayh issued buttons and tabs, and buttons lauded such worthies as Los Angeles mayor Sam Yorty, Iowa governor Harold Hughes, former North Carolina governor Terry Sanford, and Arkansas congressman Wilbur Mills. A John Lindsay, "Fight & Switch" button exploited his recent conversion to the Democratic party with a take-off on a popular cigarette commercial. Posters, buttons, and bumper stickers proclaimed Hubert Humphrey "The People's Democrat." His old running-mate Edmund Muskie inspired a handsome set of astrological buttons, an assortment of boutique items featuring a distinctive pine tree motif, and buttons with such slogans as "A New Beginning," "Believe Muskie," and "President Muskie! (Don't you feel better already?)."

During his uphill struggle for the Democratic nomination and in the general election campaign that followed, McGovern inspired a large number of unusually creative and expressive campaign items, in part because his impoverished national organization encouraged local groups to produce and sell their own fund-raiser pieces, and in part because this intensely ideological campaign, much like Goldwater's in 1964, provided a natural forum for thematic expression. Among the items promoting McGovern were some three hundred buttons, many bumper stickers, posters, T-shirts, jewelry items, and flashers, and such ephemera as tops, cloth patches, combs, key fobs, and license plates. A few buttons, tabs, and bumper stickers issued shortly after the Democratic convention featured original running-mate Thomas F. Eagleton, but the vast majority of McGovern–Eagleton items that appeared in 1972 were produced to sell to gullible collectors as instant rarities after Eagleton was dropped gracelessly from the ticket following revelations that he had undergone electric shock treatments. A characteristic of McGovern material culture (especially a truly attractive line of boutique items created for the campaign by Colorcraft Enterprises) was exceptional creativity in graphics, color, and thematic expression.

Several McGovern buttons reflected a calculated effort to turn the campaign's relative poverty into a political advantage by portraying it as a grass-roots movement financed by the dollars of millions of small contributors, in striking contrast to the enormous Nixon war-chest gleaned from the special interests. Twenty-five-dollar donors were given "McGovern Million Member Club" buttons, and membership cards and contributions of a dollar brought "Buck Nixon/(I Did!)" buttons. A grasshopper button read "Grassroots Democrat," another button announced "I Am a Grassroot," and a caricature variety declared "Skinny Cat for McGovern." A dozen or more different buttons proclaimed feminist support for "McG♀VERN." Even more McGovern items echoed his outspoken opposition to our on-going military presence in Vietnam. Many of these (fig. 225) featured dove designs and others read "Remember Oct. 9," the date in 1968 when candidate Richard Nixon insisted, "Those who have had a chance for four years and could not produce peace should not be given another chance." Buttons and posters carried the full text of Nixon's statement. Less subtle was a "Come Home & Stop Killing Little Babies" button issued by a midwestern chapter of the New Democratic Coalition. An "America the Beautiful/Let's Make It that Way" bumper sticker, and several handsome multicolor buttons featuring landscape designs echoed the campaign's environmentalist bent. Other McGovern items (fig. 226) utilized slogans ("Make America Happen Again," "Come Home America," "McGOVERN for our CHILDREN") and designs that reflected these commitments, but in a more abstract sense made a larger plea for a national renewal of faith in ourselves, our land, and our tradition of fair play and compassion.

Cloth patches and buttons proclaimed "I Love McGov," clever caricature buttons portrayed him as "Robin McGovern," and a number of "happy face" buttons exploited the current "have a happy day" vogue. "KMA" buttons recalled McGovern's "kiss my ass!" comment to a woman who had berated him for delaying her flight during the Illinois primary, a remark that helped allay impressions of him as a supercilious prig. No national McGovern items satirized Nixon, but buttons created for local groups and for vendors bore such insults as "Committee to Reject the President," "Nixon's Thru in '72," and the monumentally tasteless "Lick Dick in '72." Nixon's Vietnamization program inspired a "Re-Elect the Dike Bomber???" bumper sticker, his succession of ill-fated economic recovery plans led to a "Phase III/Dump Nixon" button, and allegations of his improper dealings with the International Telephone and Telegraph conglomerate engendered "Nixon Has Had ITT!" buttons. A "Nixon Is Doing the Job of 3 Men" vendor button featured caricatures of three of the Marx brothers. Lithographed "Labor for McGovern–Shriver" and "Jobs/Peace/McGovern" buttons with gear designs were among the headquarters items distributed nationally by the McGovern campaign, but conspicuously absent were endorsement buttons issued by labor organizations. Another telling void was the virtual absence of coattail buttons linking McGovern with local Democratic candidates, except for a few New York and Chicago varieties. A "Gay Citizens for McGovern" button may have been the first of its type in national presidential politics.

The Nixon re-election effort inspired roughly a hundred types of buttons and nearly that many bumper stickers, as well as tabs, flashers, jewelry items, posters, T-shirts, scarves, suspenders, tops, and bubblegum cigars, a

Figs. 225 and 226. These 1972 McGovern campaign items echoed the nominee's pleas for peace in Vietnam and a national renewal of spiritual values at home. (Edmund B. Sullivan)

rather lean material dimension in light of the unprecedented treasury raised by his heavyhanded Committee to Re-Elect the President (CREEP) operatives, but nevertheless more diverse and slightly more creative than his uncommonly sterile 1968 material culture. What Nixon's 1972 headquarters giveaway items may have lacked in variety and creative genius they surely made up in sheer abundance, for never in the history of American political campaigning have local party headquarters been so amply stocked with material. While visits to McGovern headquarters usually yielded a single button, bumper sticker, or piece of literature and a request for a contribution to cover its cost, it was not uncommon for smiling Nixon volunteers to fill boxes or bags with red, white, and blue buttons, bumper stickers, pencils, matchbooks, balloons, and other items bearing such slogans as "Re-elect the President," "Four More Years," and "Nixon Now More than Ever."

Undoubtedly the most pervasive theme projected by the objects issued by Nixon's national organization was the exceptional emphasis placed upon Nixon's identity as "The President," almost as if to suggest that the man had evolved into the very personification of the office. Headquarters buttons, bumper stickers, posters and the like occasionally referred to him as "President Nixon," but much more frequent (figs. 227, 228) were such legends as "Right On, Mr. President," "Re-elect the President," "Young Voters for the President," "Senior Power for the President," or simply "The President." Nowhere in evidence were echoes of 1960's Dick Nixon or even 1968's Richard Nixon, a semantic progression that might well be interpreted by some of Nixon's more imaginative detractors as a sign of his steadily burgeoning megalomania.

Nixon's withdrawal of most American military personnel from Vietnam by November 1972, and the other diplomatic triumphs of his first term inspired dove-design "Nixon for Peace" buttons, "Peace/Strength/Stability" license plates, "Work for Peace, Nixon Does Every Day" bumper stickers, and attractive posters featuring Nixon explaining to a little boy, "For the first time in 20 years we are spending more on human resources than on defense." A button sold at the Republican booth at the Illinois State Fair declared "America Anew in '72/NIXON–AGNEW for the Red, White and Blue." Buttons reading "Don't Be Taken for Granted" and "We're not in the Bag" were issued by a black Nixon support group, but the tangible results of this effort consisted primarily of a fawning endorsement by entertainer Sammy Davis, Jr. No official Republican items attacked McGovern, rather surprising in light of the seamy strain of character assassination prevalent in the television commercials sponsored by John Connally's "Democrats for Nixon." Buttons issued by independent conservative organizations or sold by vendors on the streets and at Republican campaign events bore such insults as "Acid/Amnesty/Appeasement—Vote McGovern," "Hanoi Needs McGovern and Fonda," "McGovern in 1984," and "Will Rogers Never Met

Figs. 227 and 228. Portraying Richard Nixon quite majestically as "The President" in 1972 were headquarters buttons (facing page) and this attractive poster, complete with Nixon negotiating with Chinese and Soviet leaders.

George McGovern," the latter most likely inspired by a "Will Rogers Never Met Howard Cosell" sheet banner made for a televised Monday night professional football game.

Few American political lives have been as rich in irony as Richard Nixon's, and one of the facets of politics over which he exerted an ironic influence was the realm of material culture. On five occasions Nixon represented the Republican party as a nominee for national office; on none of these occasions did his candidacy inspire a departure or innovation of any significance in the manner in which objects have been utilized to influence the outcome of a political campaign. Then, after the last of his political wars had been waged and won, "high crimes and misdemeanors" committed in the process began to come to light that would in campaigns to come exert a profound influence upon the role played by material culture in presidential campaigning.

NOTES

1. Despite its occasionally uncritical reliance upon the ideas and jargon of Marshall McLuhan, the best introduction to the role of television in recent presidential campaigns remains Joe McGinniss's *The Selling of the President, 1968* (New York, 1969).

2. Quoted in *Washington Post*, Oct. 8, 1976.

3. See Hake, *Political Buttons*, II, 95–119; Bristow, *Illustrated Political Button Book*, 187–208; Hake, *Encyclopedia of Political Buttons*, 179–92, 194–204; Collins, *Threads of History*, 486–98, 501–3; Fischer and Sullivan, *Political Ribbons and Ribbon Badges*, 371–74; Greenhouse, *Political Postcards*, 78–79, 83–88; Sullivan, *Collecting Political Americana*, 12, 101, 136–37, 161, 166, 168; and American Political Items Collectors, *Adlai E. Stevenson, 1952–1956–1960: An APIC Research Project* (1977).

4. Unable to come up with a vice-presidential candidate to put up against Nixon, a group of 1956 Republican convention delegates led by Nebraska gubernatorial candidate Terry Carpenter nominated and voted for the fictitious "Joe Smith," a gambit that produced a rare spark of excitement in a dull convention, attracted widespread public interest, and subsequently inspired many droll Democratic campaign items.

5. See Bristow, *Third Party and Hopeful Items*, 28, 31, 42–43, 45–47; Hake, *Encyclopedia of Political Buttons*, 250, 252–53, 255–56; and Fischer and Sullivan, *Political Ribbons and Ribbon Badges*, 387.

6. See Hake, *Encyclopedia of Political Buttons*, 206–16, 218–20, 251–56; Bristow, *Illustrated Political Button Book*, 209–19, 221, 224–26, 228–31, 236–37; Hake, *Political Buttons*, II, 120–37, 237; Collins, *Threads of History*, 506–13; Bristow, *Third Party and Hopeful Items*, 23–25, 30–32, 47–48; Greenhouse, *Political Postcards*, 89, 91–96; and Fischer and Sullivan, *Political Ribbons and Ribbon Badges*, 374–77. Especially valuable for Kennedy material is *The Campaign Items of John F. Kennedy*, comp. Bonnie C. Gardner and Harvey E. Goldberg (Clark, N.J., 1980).

7. Although Eisenhower's personal dislike for Nixon was obvious (during one 1960 interview he omitted Nixon's name from a list of possible successors, and in another he asked for more time to think of some Nixon virtues), he did endorse Nixon and spoke out in support of his election during the latter stages of the campaign. See Theodore H. White, *The Making of the President, 1960* (New York, 1964), 308–11.

8. White, *Making of the President*, 36.

9. See Hake, *Political Buttons*, II, 138–64, 231–33, 237; Bristow, *Illustrated Political Button Book*, 239–60; Hake, *Encyclopedia of Political Buttons*, 227–32, 234–38, 250–51, 253, 255–56; Sullivan, *Collecting Political Americana*, 12–13, 15, 166; Collins, *Threads of History*, 515–18; Bristow, *Third Party and Hopeful Items*, 23, 29, 31–32, 48–52; Fischer and Sullivan, *Political Ribbons and Ribbon Badges*, 378–79; and Greenhouse, *Political Postcards*, 90, 97–98.

10. All known items lampooning Jenkins were produced independently, primarily by commercial vendors, because Goldwater refused to make political capital of the incident and, much to the dismay of a few of his advisors, it never became a part of Republican campaign propaganda.

11. The most notorious manifestation of this propaganda ploy was a pair of monumentally tasteless television commercials, one juxtaposing a little girl eating an ice cream cone against a nuclear explosion and the other beginning with a child pulling petals from a daisy and fading into a nuclear count-down. For an excellent account of this issue, see Theodore H. White, *The Making of the President, 1964* (New York, 1965) 296–300.

12. An informative guide to 1968 presidential campaign buttons and tabs is *Project '68: The Presidential Election of 1968 as Seen Through Campaign Pins*, ed.

Marian A. Ford (American Political Items Collectors, 1969). For Robert F. Kennedy material produced before his assassination, a helpful source is *The Campaign Items of Robert F. Kennedy*, comp. Bonnie Gardner, Harvey Goldberg, and John Henigan (Clark, N.J., 1982). For other 1968 items, see Hake, *Political Buttons, II*, 165–80, 231–33, 235, 237; Bristow, *Illustrated Political Button Book*, 221–24, 225–28, 231–37, 261–70; Hake, *Encyclopedia of Political Buttons*, 221–22, 240–42, 249, 251–52, 255–56; Collins, *Threads of History*, 521–29; Bristow, *Third Party and Hopeful Items*, 17–22, 24–25, 29, 31–32, 48–57, 59–67; Fischer and Sullivan *Political Ribbons and Ribbon Badges*, 377, 379–80, 387; and Sullivan, *Collecting Political Americana*, 13, 112, 137.

13. The practice of creating campaign items primarily for collectors dates back to before the Civil War, when several medalets were struck en masse in base metals for general distribution and minted in limited quantities in different metals or in beautiful "proof" finishes for sale or trade to collectors of "exonumia." For the same purpose earlier campaign medalets were restruck and obverses of one variety "muled" with reverses of another to create rare collector oddities. Ever since the production of campaign items developed into a commercial endeavor, sales have been enhanced by the desire of partisans to retain items as souvenirs after the campaigns, individually or in large collections. It is clear, however, that the overwhelming majority of campaign items created from 1828 through 1964 were made to sell or give away to partisans for the purpose of political expression. Such was not the case in 1968, when hundreds of varieties of celluloid buttons were printed expressly for sale to collectors of political Americana. Other 1968 buttons were produced in small quantities for political purposes and subsequently run in huge numbers for the hobby market. Still others were created for potential sale to campaign organizations and commercial vendors but simultaneously sold directly to collectors through special catalogues. On the whole, nearly two-thirds of the presidential buttons produced in 1968 (including whole sets of state and ethnic language varieties) were never used for authentic political purposes.

14. See Hake, *Political Buttons, II*, 181–203, 231, 233, 237; Hake, *Encyclopedia of Political Buttons*, 223–25, 244–47, 251–53, 255–56; Collins, *Threads of History*, 535–36; Greenhouse, *Political Postcards*, 105–6; Sullivan, *Collecting Political Americana*, 98, 137; Fischer and Sullivan, *Political Ribbons and Ribbon Badges*, 380; Tom French, *The 1972 Presidential Campaign in Buttons* (Capitola, Calif., 1973); and Dick Bristow, *1972 Presidential Campaign Items* (Santa Cruz, Calif., 1973). Unfortunately, the vast majority of items pictured in the French and Bristow volumes are fantasy buttons produced exclusively for the collector market. It is probable that of every four varieties of campaign buttons ostensibly promoting 1972 candidates, three were collector buttons that never graced the lapel of a political partisan.

8

Watergate Legacy 1974–84

The Watergate crimes of Richard Nixon and his subordinates led not only to Nixon's August 9, 1974, resignation to avoid impeachment and to prison terms for many of his aides, but also to changes great and small in American government and politics. One facet of contemporary American politics altered dramatically by Watergate and its aftermath has been the use of material culture in the past three presidential contests, a result of sweeping campaign financing reforms enacted to avert future Watergates. Discovery of the venal manner in which Nixon's 1972 operatives had raised campaign funds and then used them to finance "dirty tricks" produced a groundswell for radical revision of the 1971 Federal Election Campaign Act to limit campaign contributions and expenditures during bids for federal office. Signed into law by Gerald Ford on October 15, 1974, amendments to FECA set ceilings on expenditures by presidential candidates of $10,000,000 for the primaries and twice that sum for the general election, limited contributions to a candidate to $1,000 per individual or $5,000 per political action committee and state party organization, sought to diminish the influence of contributors even further by providing partial public financing of primary campaigns and the option of full public funding for general election efforts, and created a bipartisan Federal Election Commission to monitor compliance.[1]

As a result, after proper allowances are made for fund-raising expenses, inflation, and other variables, presidential campaign organizations in 1976, 1980, and 1984 have been forced to fund their operations at levels substantially less than half of the financial resources enjoyed by Nixon's CREEP in 1972 and limit campaign activities accordingly. At the same time, however, subsequent congressional action and a Supreme Court ruling have paradoxically served to increase enormously the ability of independent political action committees (PACs) to spend money to influence elections. In 1976, Congress yielded to pressure from business and labor groups and amended FECA to allow corporations and unions to establish multiple PACs, an action soon rendered essentially meaningless by a Supreme Court decision in *Buckley* v. *Valeo* (1976) permitting independent PACs to spend unlimited funds promoting pet candidates or causes, so long as a maximum sum of $5,000 went directly to a candidate's campaign committee. Predictably, PACs quickly proliferated to fill the vacuum left by the emasculation of the committees, increasing in number from 608 in 1974 to 2,075 by 1980.[2]

If the Federal Election Commission was thus prohibited from exerting effective control over campaign spending by independent PACs, it operated under no such restraints in attempting to make sure that grass-roots party groups and campaigns did not develop into covert conduits for evading the intent of the 1974 reforms. Here the FEC encountered a fundamental conflict between law and political reality, for implicit in FECA was the premise that campaigns for federal office were distinct, self-contained entities, a naive notion hopelessly at odds with the organic nature of political party organization in the United States. Since the days of Jackson and Clay, the very hallmark of a smoothly functioning national party has been its ability to promote, harmoniously and simultaneously through the economy of shared effort and resources, the fortunes of its candidates at every level from the courthouse to the White House. Headquarters space, telephone banks, literature, promotional events, and material culture are traditionally pooled in such a manner as to make individual cost accounting impossible. In demanding such accountability, the Federal Election Commission created some truly ridiculous situations.

On August 25, 1976, the FEC issued a directive that city, county, state, and congressional district party committees would be allowed to spend up to $1,000 promoting presidential nominees and a warning that billboards bought by local groups at costs exceeding $1,000 would be classified as in-kind contributions, illegal for candidates accepting public funding. Two days later, New York congressman Ed Koch asked the treasurer of his campaign committee to request an FEC ruling on the legality of 3,000 buttons that read "Carter–Mondale–Koch" (fig. 229), purchased without consultation with Jimmy Carter's campaign committee for the sum of $409.28. After inspiring editorials denouncing such "regulatory ridiculousness" in the *Washington Post* and *New York Times*, the request elicited what Koch characterized as a "solomonic decision" when, on September 21, the FEC permitted the New Yorkers for Koch committee to distribute the buttons without the $409.28 being counted as an illicit in-kind contribution. The Republicans in Nassau County, New York, did not fare so fortunately, however; twenty-six billboards they commissioned to promote President Ford and several other candidates at a cost of $36,000 did not pass muster with the FEC, forcing local party officials to paint out Ford's name.[3] Along with small packets of Jimmy Carter peanuts ruled in Oregon to be in violation

Fig. 229. Promoting Jimmy Carter,
Walter Mondale, and New York Representative Ed Koch, three thousand
of these buttons were purchased for
$409.28 by New Yorkers for Koch and
distributed after a ruling by the Federal Election Commission that they
did not represent an illegal in-kind
contribution to the Carter–Mondale
campaign. (Kenneth J. Moran)

of a state law prohibiting candidates from giving out "items of value,"[4] the
Nassau County billboards symbolized the hazards of political material culture in the wake of Watergate.

Such legalistic nit-picking, however, did not represent Watergate's major
legacy to the material tradition in presidential politics. Much more significant has been the revolution in campaign budgeting wrought by the new
spending limits imposed upon campaign organizations and the concomitant
shifting of many campaign functions from central committees to allegedly
independent PACs. After meeting such inevitable expenses as staff salaries
and overhead, travel costs for candidates and campaign personnel, and
operational necessities, most remaining funds have been used for media
advertising, primarily television time and production expenses. In 1976, for
example, the Ford campaign committee could scrape together only
$3,000,000 (less than the 1972 Nixon effort had spent in California and
New York alone) for fifty state campaign organizations to spend on headquarters, travel, and political activities.[5] The once-familiar storefront presidential campaign headquarters has virtually disappeared from the American
landscape since 1976, with campaign workers forced to beg for desks and
storage space in offices leased for congressional and local campaigns not
burdened with spending limits. For the most part, headquarters campaign
items have suffered the fate of the storefronts that served as their
dispensaries.

This trend, in particular the sudden scarcity of the once-ubiquitous headquarters giveaway campaign button, attracted widespread commentary during the 1976 campaign. In December 1975, a Sargent Shriver supporter
told the *Washington Post*, "We can't buy buttons in unlimited supply these
days," and a Ford campaign official explained, "There is only so much we
can do, and one of the early widespread casualties is buttons." During the
spring Chicago and West Coast producers accustomed to orders of one

hundred thousand to a half million buttons reported that sales of five to ten thousand at a time were more typical in 1976. The situation did not improve after the conventions. For their general election effort the Ford forces purchased 1,500,000 buttons and the same quantity of bumper stickers with the proviso "when they run out, they run out," and the Carter campaign decided to distribute no buttons or bumper stickers at all, reluctantly reconsidering and ordering two hundred thousand of each in response to angry complaints from headquarters volunteers. By late October, veteran New York political item producer Al Cohen was fuming over the lack of Nixon professionals in Ford's operation and "Georgia hillbillies" in charge of Carter's, blaming poor button sales on "two stupid campaigns and a public that doesn't give a damn."[6]

Whether the fault lay with amateurs and Georgians or, more probably, with spending limits and television, orders for presidential campaign buttons did decline markedly from 1972 to 1976. Even the New York firm of N. G. Slater, which in 1976 established itself as the premier American producer of campaign buttons with a strong product line, aggressive marketing to vendors and local party organizations, and a bold Democratic convention coup,[7] experienced a sales slump of nearly 30 percent. Yet, like the rumors of Mark Twain's death, reports of the demise of the presidential campaign button in 1976 ("The Button Bottoms Out," "Outlay Limit Unbuttons Campaigners") were grossly exaggerated. Although neighborhood storefront headquarters with bins filled with buttons and shelves piled high with bumper stickers and other material became for the most part a thing of the past, American political partisans have not had to forego material culture "cold turkey" during recent elections. To a great extent, local party groups and PACs have filled this void, largely supplanting the national candidate organizations as suppliers of buttons, bumper stickers, and other paraphernalia. It has thus been less true that post–Watergate election reforms have stifled material culture than that they have served to decentralize it.

Among the political action committees, this was most true in 1976 of such pro–Carter labor groups as the PACs representing the United Auto Workers, the National Education Association, the Communication Workers of America, and the Brotherhood of Railway and Airline Clerks. Each of these PACs ordered massive quantities of Carter–Mondale buttons, bumper stickers, and other materials, ostensibly for distribution only to their own members to avoid a clear violation of *Buckley* v. *Valeo*, although in practice the distinction proved impossible to police. In one instance where an effort was made to do so, United Auto Workers officials chose to halt distribution of 150,000 Carter–Mondale bumper stickers purchased for $4,747 after UAW lawyers noted that voters on the streets would see the stickers; a few weeks later, the UAW bumper stickers were being distributed surreptitiously in Minnesota by Carter–Mondale campaign officials. In 1980, the UAW issued bumper stickers and buttons supporting Edward Kennedy and then Carter and a few other labor PACs distributed Carter materials, although only the National Education Association did so in a big way, its gratitude for creation of the Department of Education making NEA a last bastion of labor enthusiasm for the beleaguered Georgian. As might have been expected, conservative PACs cool to Ford in 1976 responded enthusiastically to Ronald Reagan's 1980 campaign, with such organizations as the Young Americans for Freedom, the Fund for a Conservative Majority, Americans for Change, and Farmers and Ranchers for Reagan distributing buttons and other items promoting their champion. In 1984, the PACs truly came of age as purveyors of political material culture, as right-wing organizations issued an abundant array of Reagan–George Bush re-election material and organized labor PACs responded with huge quantities of items, including more than one hundred different varieties of campaign buttons (see fig. 247).

Of equal importance in the decentralization of material culture in recent presidential elections—and even more a factor in endowing it with a degree of eclectic creativity not witnessed since the days of Bryan and McKinley—has been the 1976 amendment to FECA permitting local party groups to spend up to $1,000 each to promote their presidential nominees. Buttons, bumper stickers, posters, T-shirts, and political novelty items present an ideal way to do so, while simultaneously generating revenue for voter registration efforts, sample ballots, and other types of activity that provide additional benefits to presidential candidates without counting against their FEC spending limits. Although many local groups have found it expedient to order standard designs of buttons and other material marketed nationally by such firms as N. G. Slater, Millenium Group (Philadelphia), Adcraft (Chicago), and Creative Photo Crafts (Sylvania, Ohio), and others have used do-it-yourself button machine kits priced as low as $19.95 to produce rather drab but cost-effective handmade buttons, some local organizations have designed and sold truly distinctive varieties of buttons, posters, T-shirts, and other campaign items featuring state maps, mascots, and symbols and tributes to such local landmarks as the Empire State Building, Golden Gate Bridge, and Washington's Mount St. Helen. From wealthy Montgomery County, Maryland in 1976 came a "Horse People for Carter–Mondale" button, from Louisville in 1984 came a "Kentucky Thoroughbreds" Reagan–Bush variety, and Republican and Democratic organizations in Indianapolis have promoted recent nominees with distinctive buttons featuring checkered flag motifs.

The challenge of providing retail outlets and local party groups with campaign items sufficiently distinctive to capture the fancy of the buying public occasionally produced even more creative results. In 1976, North Carolina fund-raiser Howard Bloom brought with him to the Democratic national convention his solution to his party's fund-raising woes, a rectangular Carter buton with a small flashing red light powered by a hearing aid battery activated by coupling its safety-pin fastener.[8] Such devices enjoyed limited popularity in 1976 and 1980, but in 1984 the E. W. Novelty Company really made the blinker button a marvel of modern technology with its line of "Hot-Lites" (fig. 230), some of which both flashed and played the National Anthem when activated. Less spectacular but much more likely to establish a trend for future elections was another 1984 innovation, tasteful enameled lapel pins and tie tacs (fig. 231), enormously popular among political partisans relectant to sport large, garish buttons and successful fund-raising devices for the party and labor organizations selling them for $5 or $10 apiece. Examples of entrepreneurial genius during recent campaigns that do not seem destined to serve as trendsetters for future campaigns include a pornographic plastic Carter doll equipped with a large figural peanut penis that rose erect when the doll's head was depressed and a 1980 Reagan walking stick made from the petrified organ of a bull. Such bizarre items are excellent examples of the basic paradox of modern political material culture, that campaign items have enjoyed a renaissance in creativity while their functional role in the process of persuading the electorate has grown increasingly ephemeral.

Ephemeral or not, the 1976 presidential election inspired a rich and diverse material dimension, in part because of the excitement generated by spirited contests for both major party nominations and an extremely close general election race between Carter and Ford, and in part because of the decentralization of material culture resulting from the Watergate reform legislation. From early caucuses through victory night celebrations, nearly two thousand styles of buttons promoted the myriad candidates, as did many bumper stickers, posters, jewelry items, lapel stickers, and such diverse memorabilia as T-shirts, pocket knives, pencils, ballpoint pens, cigarette lighters, matchbooks, luggage tags, key chains, belt buckles, pocket watches, wristwatches, cloth patches, toy trucks, and plastic whistles and frisbees.[9]

Democratic primary and convention items included buttons and other pieces supporting Jimmy Carter's unsuccessful rivals Morris Udall, Fred Harris, George Wallace, Jerry Brown, Henry Jackson, Frank Church, Birch Bayh, Sargent Shriver, Terry Sanford, and Milton Shapp and non-candidates Edward Kennedy and Hubert Humphrey. Among the more imaginative of these were lunchpail "Jackson Means Jobs" buttons and stickers, a set of multicolor landscape buttons handpainted by Udall volunteers in Madison, Wisconsin, and several rather ideological Harris buttons with such legends as "Let's Take the Rich off Welfare," "Privilege Is the Issue," "Economic Democracy," "The New Populism," and "This Land Is Your Land." The battle for the Republican nomination between Ford and Ronald Reagan also begat a wealth of material objects. Promoting Reagan were perhaps a hundred different buttons, several bumper stickers and posters,

Figs. 230 and 231. Two major developments in political material culture during the 1984 campaign were these "Hot-Lites" Ronald Reagan buttons, some of which played the National Anthem as well as blinking, and the great popularity of enameled lapel pins and tie tacs like these Reagan and Walter Mondale varieties. (Kenneth J. Moran)

matchbooks, a belt buckle, and some campaign jewelry. In 1976 as in 1968, Reagan items with few exceptions (among them a Young Americans for Freedom button proclaiming him "The Choice of Young Conservatives" and a double entendre "Let's Start Our Third Century RIGHT!" button) were totally mute on the right-wing gospel of the candidate and his constituency. Ford primary and convention items almost invariably bore the legend "President Ford '76" to establish, as media expert Jack Frost explained, "that Gerald Ford was the President and, as such, entitled to the respect due the office."[10]

For the subsequent race against Carter, Ford commercials and headquarters buttons, bumper stickers, flyers, and posters switched to the slogan "He's making us proud again," an effort to credit Ford with restoring a measure of decency and dignity to the presidency, thus putting distance between him and predecessor Richard Nixon and hopefully blunting Watergate and the Nixon pardon as a campaign issues. It was without question a brilliant strategem, highlighting the essential humanity and integrity that was Ford's strongest selling point to a public still shaken by the sordid Nixon legacy, but with very few exceptions the theme was not echoed on the hundreds of different items produced for local Republican groups, a serious failing in a year when such organizations were ordering and distributing the lion's share of the objects.

A large number of these ignored Ford's virtues in an effort to lampoon Carter. The Democratic "Grits and Fritz" slogan inspired "Blitz Grits & Fritz" and "Gritz & Fritz Give Me the Shitz" buttons. Carter's ambivalence on the issues prompted a "Jimmy Carter's Favorite Color" button featuring plaid fabric. His toothy grin led to buttons insisting "Carter Hasn't Shown Me Anything but His Teeth!" The widespread belief that behind that grin was a rather unlovely personality led to "Will Rogers Never Met Jimmy Carter" buttons. Carter's singularly unfortunate admission during an interview for *Playboy* that he had lusted in his heart for many women inspired a heart-shaped "In His Heart, He Knows Your Wife" button that parodied Goldwater's epic 1964 slogan. Most of the satiric Ford items, however, lampooned the Carter campaign's emphasis upon the "politics of peanutry" (fig. 232). Many buttons depicted GOP elephants eating or stomping peanuts, and another rather indelicately urged, "Let's Crush Carter's Nuts!" Others read "Don't Settle for Peanuts," "Vote Ford or Eat Peanuts," "Carter's Brain Is the Size of a Peanut!," "Ford Hates Peanut Butter," and "Keep the Peanut Farmer on His Peanut Farm." A caricature button ordered by a California Republican group originally in the Reagan camp read "Your Chance to Put Another Nut in the White House," but it was replaced by one reading "Now We Can Put a *Real* Nut in the White House" after Ford supporters protested its ambiguity.

Although Carter was certainly a compelling target for satire and many of these items were genuinely witty, their cumulative effect was probably detrimental to Ford, for 1976 was simply a poor year for put-down politics, especially for a party whose 1968 and 1972 standard-bearer had been so recently driven from office for "high crimes and misdemeanors." Other 1976 Republican items were not much more helpful. After Ford's celebrated statement during the foreign policy debate with Carter that eastern Europeans did not feel dominated by the Soviet Union, he wore a "Ford" button featuring Russian cyrillic letting to a meeting with eastern European ethnics to explain his blunder.[11] Buttons (fig. 233) with such legends as "I'm Betting

Figs. 232 and 233. Many 1976 Gerald Ford buttons sold by vendors or local Republican groups either lampooned the peanut politics of opponent Jimmy Carter or
paid tribute to First Lady Betty Ford. More helpful to Ford's chances for re-election
were headquarters items accentuating his incumbency or the theme "He's Making
Us Proud Again." (Kenneth J. Moran)

on Betty's Husband," "Betty's Husband for President," "Keep Betty in the White House," "I'm Voting for Betty's Husband," and "Betty for First Lady" were distributed by Republican women's groups. Her citizen's band radio handle was saluted with "Citizens Band Together for First Mama" matchbooks and "First Mama" buttons. Although Betty Ford was a prime political asset in her own right, these items created an impression (in some cases no doubt deliberate) that President Ford was either a necessary evil or something of a nonentity. Other locally ordered Ford buttons, jewelry items, T-shirts, and other items played up the Ford name with Model-T slogans and symbolism. Only a few "proud again" and "Peace, Prosperity and Public Trust" buttons echoed the decency theme that Ford's national campaign committee labored to establish.

United and bouyed by prospects of their first victory in a dozen years behind a genuinely popular nominee whose muted style seemed tailor-made to the aftermath of Watergate, rank-and-file Democrats responded to the Carter candidacy with uncommon enthusiasm. One result was the creation of a material dimension that totally dwarfed Ford's, including as many as a thousand different buttons, perhaps one hundred varieties of jewelry items and bumper stickers, and such memorabilia as key chains, T-shirts, frisbees, pocketknives, pens, pencils, belt buckles, wristwatches, pocket watches, cloth patches, luggage tags, mirrors, plastic whistles, bandanna, scarves, and cigarette lighters. Carter media authority Gerald Rafshoon was able to impose on much of the 1976 Carter material culture a distinctive green color scheme (a legacy of the 1970 Georgia gubernatorial effort) and to project an image of an open and down-to-earth Carter with a "fence-post picture" of him wearing a faded denim work shirt, but Rafshoon's choice of the double-edged slogan "A leader, for a change" fared no better on items made for local Democratic groups and vendors than "He's making us proud again" did on Ford material. This was probably rather fortunate, for with the exception of a host of extremely dull buttons patterned after N. G. Slater's pilot design during the national convention, most Carter campaign items were endowed with a measure of creative exuberance conspicuously lacking in the headquarters material.

Like the log cabin in 1840, the split rail in 1860, and the red bandanna in 1888, the humble peanut evolved into the ubiquitous symbol of the 1976 Carter campaign. Metal peanut jewelry items included tie tacs, cuff links, necklaces, lapel pins, and earrings. Belt buckles, plastic whistles, mirrors, and embroidered cloth patches were shaped like peanuts. Peanut designs graced a multitude of buttons (fig. 234), as well as bumper stickers, plastic luggage tags, T-shirts, bandannas, scarves, tabs, and pocketknives. Buttons bore such mottos as "Peanut Power," "I Work for Peanuts," "I'm Nuts about Carter," and "I'm Your Peanut Pal." Many buttons (fig. 235), several utilizing the Planter's "Mr. Peanut" logo, went so far as to portray Carter as a peanut. A secondary Carter icon in 1976 was his celebrated grin, featured

Figs. 234 and 235. Like the log cabin in 1840 and the split rail in 1860, the lowly peanut evolved into an appealing political icon in 1976, featured on items like these buttons to exploit Jimmy Carter's background as a Georgia peanut farmer. (Kenneth J. Moran)

on many buttons (fig. 236) and other items. Many proclaimed "The Grin Will Win," a slogan pioneered on a handmade sign at the national convention. Buttons and jewelry featured grinning peanuts. An attractive caricature button worn by Nevada convention delegates urged, "Give the Smilin' Man a Chance," and a button used in Nashville, Tennessee, predicted "Carter by a Country Smile."

Carter's southern "good ol' boy" identity, so crucial to holding the regional base that assured his narrow victory in November, was developed on campaign items in a variety of ways. Many posters and buttons, one of them proclaiming him "A Man of the Soil," featured Carter dressed in a weather-beaten denim work shirt. His home town of Plains, Georgia, was highlighted on several objects. Buttons reading "Damn Yankees for Jimmy Carter" and (in a heart superimposed over a Confederate flag) "Scarlett O'Hara Loves Jimmy Carter" exploited his heritage as a southerner, as did many buttons (fig. 237) inspired by a handmade sign at the national convention referring to the Carter–Walter Mondale ticket as "Grits and Fritz."

Other themes were developed more sparingly. The only objects directly appealing to the crucial black vote were a few "For All of Us" button varieties featuring Carter and Martin Luther King, Sr. Although mother Lillian graced a senior citizen's button and wife Rosalynn a "Jimmy & His Best Friend" variety and miniature Amy Carter frisbees were given out at the Democratic convention, family members were exploited in moderation compared to their exposure ad nauseum in the media. The Carter campaign sought to woo evangelical Protestants as delicately as possible to avoid alienating Catholics, Jews, and infidels, but their efforts were undermined by some buttons, unwittingly inspired by a superb satiric variety portraying Carter as Christ sold through ads in such "fundamentalist" magazines as *Playboy* and *Penthouse*, exulting "J.C. Will Save America!"

A number of local and vendor buttons lampooned Ford and the Republicans, including many varieties (fig. 238) exploiting Watergate and the Nixon pardon. Nixon caricature buttons asked, "Would you buy a used Ford from this man?," and others proclaimed Ford "Nixon's Choice." Other buttons quipped "Vote for Carter/Ford Will Pardon You," "Pardon Me, Gerald," and "I Beg Your Pardon . . . " Ford's penchant for the veto inspired "Veto Ford" buttons, his lack of charisma invited "Bored with Ford" buttons and others depicting the Ford–Robert Dole slate as "The Sominex Team" and "Dull & Dole," and speculation that Lyndon Johnson had been correct in complaining, "The trouble with Ford, he played football too long without a helmet," led to "Carter Is Smarter" buttons and a caricature variety reiterating the LBJ remark. Ford's name inspired buttons featuring such legends as "A Ford Is No Lincoln," "There Is No FORD in My Future," and "Happiness Is Trading in an Old Ford." A National Education Association button characterized him as "A Pain in the Class." Secretary of Agriculture Earl Butz, who provoked a furor over his moronic observation that black

Figs. 236 and 237. Other excellent examples of creative 1976 Carter material culture include these buttons featuring the celebrated Carter grin and his southern identity. (Kenneth J. Moran)

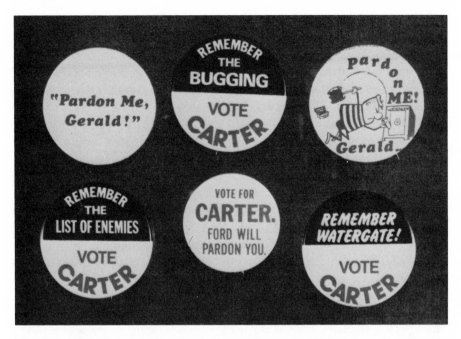

Fig. 238. These buttons represent a few of the many 1976 Democratic items designed to remind voters that Ford had pardoned Richard Nixon for his Watergate crimes, the decision that probably cost him the election. (Kenneth J. Moran)

voters cared about little but sex, loose shoes, and a warm place to defecate, provided inspiration for "No More Ifs, ands or Butz!" buttons and bumper stickers.

Many Carter items echoed the headquarters slogan "A leader, for a change" with such maxims as "New Generation of Leadership," "A New Vision for America," "Get America Moving Again," "For a Better Future," "The Best for America's Third Century," and "Why Not the Best?" With the exception of a button featuring Carter against a backdrop of disjointed policy statements from the 1976 Democratic platform, however, no known 1976 Carter items bore specific references to objectives in such areas as foreign policy, human rights, economic stability, labor relations, the environment, energy, education, or other salient national priorities. Rarely has the material culture of a nominee of a major party reflected such a vacuum of ideas on salient issues, a portent of things to come during Carter's troubled term in office.

Many expressive minor party items were produced in 1976. The Communist ticket of Gus Hall and Jarvis Tyner inspired "We the People Want . . . Jobs/Equality/Detente," "Freedom/Peace/Jobs," and "Beat Big Business" buttons. Among the nearly two dozen Libertarian buttons were ones urging "1776/1984/There Is No Middle Ground" and Break Free from Big Brother." Prohibition buttons included a "Vote Dry" variety featuring the camel symbol and a "One Is Already Mounted" caricature style depicting nominee Benjamin C. Bubar atop a camel. A Socialist button read "Socialism & Democracy," and a Socialist Labor variety demanded "Workers' Control of Industry." Some of the nearly two dozen Socialist Workers' buttons bore such legends as "Jobs for All!/Not One Cent for War," "Education Is a Right!/Stop the Cutbacks!," "ERA in '76," "By Any Means Necessary," "Human Needs Before Profits!," and "Capitalism Fouls Things Up." The American Independent candidacy of Lester Maddox inspired many buttons, including a "Maddox Is My Commander" variety and a series of crudely drawn button-machine pinbacks with such slogans as "Panama Canal?/It's Ours!," "When Guns Are Gone, So Is Freedom," "Pro-Life," and "Stop Inflation." Independent Eugene McCarthy was promoted by several buttons, none attempting to articulate either 1976 issues or the 1960's nostalgia that characterized his rather quixotic campaign.

In 1980, Ronald Reagan's victory over Carter, independent John Anderson, and several minor party entries produced a much smaller and generally much less imaginative material dimension than the 1976 election had done, primarily because the Reagan campaign established no real thematic focus, the Carter candidacy little popular enthusiasm, and the Anderson movement no money. A year in which a demented Iranian despot named Khomeini dominated the attention of press and public and the loudest cheers came not for statesmen but for twenty young Americans from the rinks of Minnesota and Massachusetts who skated to immortality at Lake Placid, 1980 was a year conspicuously lacking in that spirit of bouyant self-confidence that makes for creative, exuberant material culture. Despite spirited primary battles in both major parties and a general election contest that leading pollsters considered too close to call until a massive move to Reagan by undecideds during its final days, 1980 produced a rather meager harvest of presidential campaign items.[12]

Early Republican primaries yielded buttons and other items for such Reagan rivals as congressmen Anderson and Philip Crane, senators Howard Baker and Robert Dole, former Texas governor John Connally, and eventual running-mate George Bush, none of it running a risk of violating the party's "eleventh commandment" prohibiting slurs upon other Republicans. Edward Kennedy's bid to deny Carter the Democratic nomination inspired nearly as many items as were produced for Carter throughout the 1980 campaign, including buttons issued by such groups as the United Auto Workers, United Rubber Workers, International Union of Electrical, Radio and Machine Workers, William Wimpisinger's International Association of Machinists, Cesar Chavez's United Farm Workers, and Americans for Democratic Action. Few Kennedy items sought to reflect either the ideological dimensions of his challenge to Carter or nostalgia for Kennedys past, although a postconvention "And the Dream Shall Never Die" button, echoing the final words of his moving Madison Square Garden concession speech and issued as a token of thanks for campaign loyalists, surely evoked both nostalgia for a Kennedy present and hopes for Camelots yet to come. Buttons worn during the convention by Kennedy delegates bore such legends as "Keep It Open!," "Free the Carter 2000," and "We Want an Open Convention," engendered by the effort by Kennedy forces to overturn Rule F(3)(c) binding delegates to the candidate they were elected to represent unless they were released by that candidate.[13]

The 1980 Citizens' party ticket of Barry Commoner and LaDonna Harris inspired several buttons, none as creative or provocative as their use of the word "bullshit" in radio and television commercials. The Libertarian, Prohibition, Socialist, and Socialist Workers' tickets also engendered buttons and other material. "Put People Before Profits" buttons promoted Communist nominee Angela Davis, and Workers' World party candidate Dierdre Griswold was assisted by buttons bearing such demands as "Money for Jobs, not for War," "People's Needs, Yes! Profits, No!," and "Fight Racism/Stop the KKK and Nazis Now!" Among the items issued in support of American Independent nominee John Rarick were buttons urging "Gold & Silver Standard" and "Those Who Work Should Live Better than Those Who Don't." Truculent and unrestrained, such splinter-party memorabilia provided at least a small measure of thematic creativity. John Anderson's bid for the presidency left a rather small and disappointingly bland material legacy, perhaps because it was so preoccupied with struggles for ballot status, federal election funds, and access to a series of televised debates staged by the League of Women Voters. Perhaps the most unusual Anderson item was a button (fig. 239) featuring a panel from the cartoon series "Doonesbury," with Mike Doonesbury telling a man to whom he has handed a leaflet, "He's never heard of you, either. Just read it, okay?" Celebrating one of the signal highlights of Anderson's quixotic campaign, his endorsement by cartoonist Garry Trudeau, the button was worn by volunteers during the Republican primaries in New Hampshire and Massachusetts.[14]

The unsuccessful and rather listless campaign to re-elect Jimmy Carter inspired the smallest array of campaign items produced for an incumbent candidate since Franklin Roosevelt's effort in 1944, a year of critical wartime shortages in plastics and metals. Although a few Carter objects echoed the exuberant "goobers, grits, and grin" banality of 1976, most 1980 Carter material either avoided thematics altogether or sought to portray him (fig. 240) as a sober world statesman facing complex problems that defied simplistic solutions, a theme utilized in the most persuasive of Gerald Rafshoon's 1980 commercials. Rather surprising in light of other commercials characterizing Reagan as a war-monger and something of a half-wit, relatively few Democratic campaign items were overtly abusive. Student Democrats in Minnesota issued buttons calling Reagan "The Fascist Gun in the West," and a New York party button read "Carter Is Smarter," a slogan used much more effectively against Gerald Ford in 1976. Inde-

Fig. 239. Made from photocopies of a Garry Trudeau "Doonesbury" panel depicting the travails of young Michael Doonesbury advancing the cause of John Anderson in the snows of New Hampshire, these buttons were prized by many young Anderson volunteers during the republican primaries in New Hampshire and Massachusetts. (James R. Kotche; reprinted with Permission of Universal Press Syndicate)

pendent producers marketed buttons with such slogans as "Reagan for Shah," "Send Regan Back to Central Casting," and "Stop Pollution/Nuke the Trees," the latter making reference to one of Reagan's more celebrated campaign gaffes, his assertion that trees generate more pollution than industry.

If Carter's 1980 campaign items bore evidence of a spiritless campaign going through the motions primarily for lack of an alternative, Reagan's reflected in ample measure the enthusiasm among conservative Republicans for the first of their own to be nominated since Goldwater, and the first elected since the onset of the Great Depression. From the Iowa caucuses through election day, Reagan's candidacy inspired a large number of buttons and other regalia, like the campaign itself characterized primarily by zestful colors and designs and rather banal, upbeat messages. A favored slogan was "Let's make America great again"; others were "the time is now" and "a new beginning." Reagan was featured on distinctive posters and many buttons (fig. 241) wearing a Stetson, shrewd political imagery for a candidate dependent on the overwhelming support of western "sagebrush rebellion" country. Many of these items utilized a handsome multicolor campaign photograph that made Reagan appear much younger than sixty-nine. Although many buttons sold by vendors called attention to the shortcomings of opponent Jimmy Carter, few items issued by the Reagan campaign did so. Among the more interesting exceptions were two headquarters buttons that read "Ask Amy," inspired by Carter's inane and transparently self-serving reference to his daughter as an opponent of nuclear proliferation during a televised debate. Like Reagan material used in 1968 and 1976, 1980 Reagan items provided virtually no echoes of the ultraconservative tenor of his campaign, and among the few clues to the truly historic realignment in American politics it was producing were a hard-hat "Working

Figs. 240 and 241. While many 1980 Jimmy Carter buttons sought to project him as a strong and sensible national statesman, these 1980 Ronald Reagan varieties portrayed him as a virile westerner. (Kenneth J. Moran)

Man's Candidate" button (fig. 242) issued by the Fund for a Conservative Majority, a "Pro-Life for Reagan" button distributed by a midwestern anti-abortion group, and a "Christians for Reagan" variety issued by his national campaign.

Despite a first term during which he did more to reshape the basic scope and substance of national government in his own image than any American president in nearly half a century, Reagan's 1984 material culture was as blithely unencumbered by conservative slogans, symbols, and themes as his earlier campaign material had been. Festive colors, shapes, and designs again dominated, as did vague upbeat messages and multicolored photographs of Reagan wearing his Rancho del Cielo Stetson and denim shirt, visual denials that his western values had been corrupted by four years in Washington. Shabby vendor buttons urged "Victory over Communism" and denigrated both the Soviets and pro-ERA forces by using the letters of the ill-fated amendment to spell out "Eradicate Russians Atomically," and an especially venomous vendor button characterized the Democrats as the party of "Aids, Atheism & Appeasement," but material issued by Reagan's organization and supporting PACs unfailingly avoided such right-wing histrionics. Reagan's campaign issued special buttons for pro-life and Christian supporters, and various moral majority and anti-abortion groups did likewise for their constituencies, but such items provided the few clues to the fundamental realignment in American politics wrought by the "Reagan revolution." Whether a result of genius or accident, this surprising ideological vacuum on Reagan campaign items from 1968 through 1984 probably served well this man who was so adept at selling a rigidly conservative agenda to a philosophically diverse electorate by talking like a reactionary without sounding like one.

In only one respect did Reagan's 1984 items reflect a conscious effort by his campaign to project a clearly articulated message, that American women should vote for Reagan and were indeed going to do so in large numbers despite his opposition to affirmative-action quotas, ratification of ERA, and other feminist objectives. Alarmed by evidence of a sizeable gender gap in his 1980 support that grew even greater during his hawkish first term, Republican strategists feared that this could mushroom into an Achilles' heel in 1984, especially after opponent Walter Mondale made history by asking Geraldine Ferraro to join his ticket. One Republican response was an extraordinary variety of "Women for Reagan" campaign objects, including dozens of different buttons (fig. 243). These items were issued not by Phyllis Schlafly's Eagle Forum or other stridently antifeminist groups of right-wing women, but rather by the national Reagan campaign and by such mainstream Republican women's organizations as the National Federation of Republican Women and several of its affiliated state groups. Especially active in producing material culture to express support for Reagan by women was the Houston-based organization, American Women Supporting

Fig. 242. Distributed by the Fund for a Conservative Majority, one of the many independent political action committees working in 1980 on Reagan's behalf, this hard-hat button was one of the few examples of Reagan's material culture to reflect the fundamental political realignment his candidacy was creating. (Kenneth J. Moran)

the President. As a result, Reagan became the rather unlikely beneficiary of more women-oriented campaign items than any candidate in American history.

The extent to which 1984 was a referendum on Reagan pure and simple was reflected even more by Democratic items condemning him than by Republican items extolling him. During a long and often nasty series of Democratic primaries, buttons, bumper stickers, and other materials promoted such early casualties as John Glenn, George McGovern, Ernest Hollings, and Alan Cranston. Gary Hart's quest for the nomination was accompanied by a wealth of material as attractive and showy as the figure they promoted, and Jesse Jackson's spirited bid to become the first black major party nominee inspired many distinctive "rainbow coalition" items featuring many more colors than the coalition itself. Mondale's superbly organized campaign generated a large number of items, including several buttons asking "Who's Got the Beef?" or declaring "Mondale's Got the Beef," inspired by his clever parroting of a popular television hamburger commercial to belittle Hart's lack of substance. So many labor organizations flooded crucial primary states with their own Mondale buttons and bumper stickers as part of a strenuous effort to elect a pro-labor president and simultaneously restore their own political credibility that the cumulative result may well have harmed Mondale by reinforcing the popular perception of him as a pawn of the special interests.[15] Many Mondale items trumpeting the endorsement of the National Organization for Women may have had a similar effect, especially after NOW's shrill and painfully public arm-twisting on behalf of Geraldine Ferraro.

But items promoting their own candidates proved less popular among Democratic partisans than did the extraordinary array of buttons (fig. 244) and other objects attacking Reagan, who in 1984 inspired more hostile material culture than any candidate since Franklin Roosevelt running for

Fig. 243. Reflecting widespread fears that Reagan's chances for re-election in 1984 could be threatened by his gender gap problems with women voters, these buttons and many others were issued for Republican women to wear to demonstrate their support for the president. (Kenneth J. Moran)

Fig. 244. In 1984, Reagan inspired a larger array of hostile material culture than any incumbent running for re-election since Franklin Roosevelt in 1940. (Kenneth J. Moran)

a third term in 1940.[16] Many 1984 anti–Reagan items simply copied earlier items pioneered during protests over budget cuts or defense initiatives, featuring such slogans as "Dump Reagan," "Let Them Eat Jellybeans," and a rather cruel commentary on Reagan's unsuccessful first marriage, "Jane Wyman Was Right." More imaginative were buttons given to participants in a Lincoln Memorial potfest that read "Pot Is an Herb, Reagan's a Dope." Also impugning the president's intelligence were several styles of buttons pleading "No Mo'Ron for President." Several clever buttons patterned after the popular motion picture, *Ghostbusters*, probably inspired by "Fritzbuster" buttons sold during the Republican national convention that attracted nationwide attention, featured "Reaganbuster" and "Ronbuster" slogans and designs. A clever "Dump Reagan" caricature button sold during the Democratic convention featured Reagan upside-down in a trash can, surrounded by the verse "Impeach the Leech, Put the Button Out of His Reach." A button produced for the Oklahoma Democratic Women's Club featured a bulldog and the legend "Gr-r-r, Democratic Women Power." The "Gr-r-r" apparently stood for "Get Rid of Ronald Reagan." Teachers could wear "I Sent Ronald Reagan a Pink Slip" buttons that came with pink postcards dismissing him for his record on education. More graphic was a button worn by embittered unemployed workers in Wisconsin that read "Ron Reagan has done for America what panty hose did for finger fucking!"

The measure of excitement and novelty brought to the 1984 campaign by Geraldine Ferraro inspired many items saluting her candidacy and a few (fig. 245) lampooning it. Among the latter were buttons characterizing the Democratic ticket as "Fritz and Tits," a sexist update of the old "Grits and Fritz," and "Wally and the Beaver," a wordplay on both the television series "Leave It to Beaver" and a sexual vulgarism. Much more clever was a "Hurry Up Fritz!" caricature button featuring Mondale as a small dog being walked on a leash by Ferraro. Disclosure of irregularities in her congressional campaign contribution FECA reports and some truly venal transactions by husband John Zaccaro inspired a few "Come Clean Geraldine" buttons. Much more numerous were buttons (fig. 246) and other objects celebrating her nomination, although many of the more stridently feminist varieties served the ticket shabbily by belittling Mondale as they exalted Ferraro. One such button read "Ferraro and What's His Name," others were inscribed "Ferraro–Mondale," and other varieties made the same point by printing Ferraro's name much more prominently than Mondale's. One button utilizing this gimmick featured a large picture of Ferraro next to a dwarfish one of Mondale; to compound the insult, Ferraro was pictured at left, in the position traditionally reserved on jugate buttons for presidential nominees. Such items speak volumes on a doomed Mondale candidacy that was upstaged simultaneously by a charismatic running-mate and a charismatic adversary.

Fig. 245. The historic candidacy of Geraldine Ferraro in 1984 inspired many satiric buttons, some of them crude and sexually explicit. (Kenneth J. Moran)

Aside from the dimension provided by the first woman ever to grace a major party ticket, Mondale–Ferraro material culture was notable primarily for its ideological vacuity and the unprecedented proportion of items produced on behalf of the Democratic campaign by organized labor. Departing from a tradition of off-beat color schemes on Humphrey, McGovern, and Carter materials, Mondale-Ferraro headquarters items were most commonly red, white and blue with bland patriotic graphics to match, a pattern imitated on much vendor and PAC material. Almost nonexistent was rhetoric reflecting the imperatives of social justice and world peace, strange in light of the fact that Mondale's slim chance for victory was an ascendancy of the politics of conscience over the politics of personality. No such ambiguity was projected by the extraordinary number of buttons (fig. 247), lapel pins, bumper stickers, posters, and other items issued by such labor organizations as the United Auto Workers, National Education Association, AFL–CIO, and most major AFL–CIO affiliates to promote Mondale and Ferraro as labor's champions. Although their poor showing among rank-and-file union members illustrates the limitations of buttons and bumper stickers in winning the minds and hearts of modern voters, the fact that so

Fig. 246. Mondale running-mate Geraldine Ferraro also inspired many campaign buttons celebrating her candidacy, including several feminist varieties that mocked Mondale as they exalted Ferraro. (Kenneth J. Moran)

Fig. 247. Angered by Reagan's anti-labor record as president and alarmed by the decline of their own influence in national politics, labor leaders issued the buttons shown and many more as part of a concerted effort to elect the Mondale–Ferraro ticket. (Kenneth J. Moran)

many 1984 campaign objects were issued by PACs in an effort to do so indicates that material culture will continue to play a part in future presidential contests so long as political action committees are permitted to produce it.

NOTES

1. For an excellent summary of these developments, see *Congressional Quarterly Almanac*, 30, 1974 (Washington 1975): 611–35.

2. Nelson W. Polsby and Aaron Wildavsky, *Presidential Elections: Strategies of American Electoral Politics*, 6th ed. (New York, 1984), 32–33.

3. Vernon W. Thomson to Stanley Schlesinger, Sept. 21, 1976; *Washington Post*, Sept. 21, 1976; *New York Times*, Sept. 21, 30, 1976; Federal Election Commission, *News from Federal Election Commission*, Sept. 25, 1976, 30; *Congressional Record*, Feb. 22, 1977, E872.

4. *Washington Star*, Dec. 23, 1975. A law of long standing in Oregon and not a reaction to Watergate, this statute had been used in 1964 to prevent Lyndon Johnson's campaign from distributing matchbooks.

5. *Washington Post*, Oct. 8, 1976; *Newsweek*, Aug. 2, 1976, 77; *Time*, Oct. 11, 1976, 83.

6. *Washington Post*, Dec. 21, 1975, Oct. 8, 1976; *Time*, Apr. 26, 1976; San Francisco *Sunday Examiner and Chronicle*, May 16, 1976; *New York Times*, Oct. 25, 1976.

7. During the Democratic convention at nearby Madison Square Garden, Slater had plates prepared for button papers featuring Carter with each of the six vice-presidential possibilities he had listed. As soon as Carter announced his selection of Walter Mondale, Slater's presses began to turn out 15,000 buttons for distribution uptown three hours later, along with the company's sales brochure. See *New York Times*, Oct. 25, 1976.

8. Ibid., July 14, 1976.

9. Especially valuable for 1976 campaign material is The American Political Items Collectors, *Project '76*. See also Hake, *Political Buttons*, II, 204–30, 232–33, 235–36; Greenhouse, *Political Postcards*, 101, 107–8; Fischer and Sullivan, *Political Ribbons and Ribbons Badges*, 381–83; Collins, *Threads of History*, 542–43; 553; and Sullivan, *Collecting Political Americana*, 13, 98–99.

10. *Washington Post*, Sept. 30, 1976.

11. *Washington Star*, Oct. 13, 1976.

12. Extremely informative on 1980 campaign material is Joe Wasserman, "APIC Project 1980," *APIC Keynoter*, issues 80 (Spring 1980) through 82 (Spring 1982). James R. Kotche, *John B. Anderson: Congressman and Candidate* (Rockford, Ill., 1981) provides an excellent catalogue of the material culture inspired by Anderson's independent candidacy. See also Fischer and Sullivan, *Political Ribbons and Ribbon Badges*, 381, 383; and Greenhouse, *Political Postcards*, 102, 109.

13. See Calvin Anderson, "'Free the Carter 2000': The Fight for an Open Convention," *APIC Keynoter* 85 (Summer 1985): 20–21.

14. *Washington Post*, March 6, 1980. For the cartoon series from which this item originated, see G. B. Trudeau, *He's Never Heard of You, Either* (New York, 1981).

15. Labor's role in Mondale material culture was so pervasive that even many Mondale buttons and bumper stickers that did not exhibit union logos or disclaimers were supplied surreptitiously by labor sources. An excellent example was a little "Virginia Is for Mondale" button with a disclaimer indicating its source as an "Arlington Delegate Committee." In this instance, the Arlington delegate in question was also president of the Virginia AFL-CIO.

16. See Roger A. Fischer, "Anti-Reagan Buttons," *The Political Collector* 14 (May 1985):1, 6–7, 14; and 14 (June 1985): 1, 7, 11, 13.

9

Coda

"Buttons, stickers, and songs have little substantive impact on a voter's ultimate decision at the polls," Ed Koch observed in 1977, "but they are the sparkle and glitter of which our campaigns are made."[1] It would be difficult to quarrel with the peripheral role assigned by Koch to political material culture today, but it would constitute the worst sort of presentist myopia for scholars to assume that such has always been the case. Before television and other marvels of modern civilization pushed material culture into the shadows of our political process, banners, badges, posters, prints, trinkets, and an eclectic array of other objects served to familiarize millions of Americans with the themes and issues of presidential campaigns and the faces and popular images of the men who did battle for the White House. Almost a century and half ago, tokens and shinplasters lampooning his party's monetary policies sent Thomas Hart Benton into a towering rage over "derisory manufactures intended to act on the thoughtless and ignorant through appeals to their eyes and passions," and what Jackson described as "Logg cabin hard cider and coon humbugery" in the 1840 Harrison–Tyler campaign caused many Democrats and a few Whigs to question the sanity of staging popular elections.[2] However overblown, such emotions were not evoked by "sparkle and glitter," but by a central component of the new politics of popular entertainment.

Scholars seeking to determine whether specific presidential elections have been won or lost through the use of material culture face a difficult, probably impossible task. Why Americans have voted for this candidate or that one is a question that has generated an enormous body of research but few hard and fast answers. Geographic determinism, class divisions, denominational and socioethnic heritage, and many other theories of voter behavior have not suffered from lack of persuasive proponents. In *Rendez-vous with Destiny*, Eric F. Goldman cited a workingman foursquare for Franklin Roosevelt because FDR would understand that the man's boss was a son of a bitch, a good example of what Lee Benson characterized as "negative orientation to reference individuals or groups" in his excellent study of Jacksonian politics in New York.[3] I know a woman whose presidential vote goes invariably to the man whose wife she loathes the least, and the ability of such publications as the National Enquirer to sway votes is probably as considerable as it is unfortunate. In short, voter behavior remains too much a mystery for pat postmortems. Even when presidential contests have been determined by a few votes in one or a few key states, assumptions are dangerous. We are told, for example, that Clay's rakish reputation and waffling on Texas prompted enough New Yorkers to vote the Liberty party slate in 1844 to tip the state and the presidency to Polk, that an 1884 slur by a Presbyterian minister angered enough Irish voters to send Cleveland to the White House by virtue of a 1,119-vote plurality in New York, and that crossing a picket line in 1916 cost Hughes California and the presidency. These claims are valid, of course, only if more votes were lost than won in these states for these reasons while no comparable or greater shifts in voter sentiment were occurring there or in other marginal states because of any other factor.

Likewise, it cannot be stated with any degree of certainty that the outcome of any American presidential election has been determined by its material culture. It could be argued, I think, that such was most likely the case in 1840, when theatrical spectacles featuring log cabins, cider barrels, slogan balls, floats, banners, and badges constituted virtually the sum total of Harrison's campaign. Given the extraordinary attention paid to material culture by the Whig high command and by editors of both persuasions, the enthusiastic participatory dimension it engendered, and the modest majorities for Harrison in a few key states where barrels and balls theatrics had been most prevalent, there is strong circumstantial evidence to suggest that material culture might have made the difference. It is possible, however, that a strong voter reaction against such revolutionary and unrefined displays may well have had the opposite effect, transforming a potential Harrison landslide into a reasonably close race. We simply cannot be sure. What is apparent from the perpetuation of the practice in subsequent elections is that most of the men who managed the great nineteenth-century campaigns, especially Whigs and then Republicans, shared the belief that creative utilization of material culture enhanced their chances for a popular mandate. Given the extraordinarily thin margins between victory and defeat in the contests between 1876 and 1888 and the pervasive localism and festive exhibitionism that characterized the campaigns of the period, the assumption that material culture may have on occasion meant the difference would not be altogether capricious, especially if one considers the vital importance of "Boys in Blue" patriotic appeals to the 1876, 1880, and 1888 Republican victories.

While the number of votes cast on the basis of themes and images con-

veyed wholly or in large part on banners or floats or more recently on
buttons or bumper stickers will almost certainly remain forever a mystery,
material culture can at least provide students of our past political campaigns
with a wealth of specific evidence on how those themes and images were
projected to the American electorate. At its best, political material culture
has served to portray to the public the ultimate economy of a campaign,
condensing onto a single banner or button or badge the barest essence of
the central themes and appeals expressed in infinitely greater detail in
platforms, position papers, and stump speeches. For millions of voters without access to or patience for the latter, a candidate's likeness and "Jackson
and No Bank" or "Lincoln and Union" or "Sound Money and Protection"
provided a bare-bones substitute. In this respect, material culture served
much the same function as the economic advisors to the apocryphal sultan
who finally compressed their collective wisdom down from many thick
volumes into the terse edict "there is no such thing as a free lunch."
Reducing a complex political appeal to slogans or symbols that fit a banner
or bumper sticker may demean both the campaign and our cherished illu-
sions about democracy in action, but scholars who seek to understand the
behavior of voters limited in literacy, attention span, and political curiosity
would do well not to dismiss altogether the relevance of such artifacts to
their endeavors.

The claim of campaign objects to legitimacy as scholarly resources would
be a stronger one, no doubt, if such items had been designed personally by
the masterminds in charge of presidential campaigns, representing a clear
consensus of the candidate's high command on the bottom-line appeal it
chose to pitch to the political grass roots. In many instances, of course,
campaign managers and media specialists have performed precisely such a
function. When material culture was in its infancy, local party leaders had
no alternative, for mass-produced material was not available. In 1840, the
first log-cabin Harrison visual was a transparency designed by Harrisburg,
Pennsylvania, party chieftains Thomas Elder and Richard S. Elliott, and
the enthusiastic response it elicited prompted Whig campaign officials elsewhere to emulate their example.[4] In 1860, much of the material culture
that served the interests of Abraham Lincoln so splendidly did little more
than exploit the brainstorm of friend and party activist Richard Oglesby,
creator of the "Railsplitter of 1830" identity for Lincoln.[5] Through much
of the nineteenth century, the floats, the majority of parade banners and
transparencies, most posters, and most of the badges made for local clubs
and celebrations were designed by local party officials and produced by local
printers, party activists, or their wives. Such custom-made material constituted an ever-diminishing minority of the total number of items created,
to be sure, but for the most part the designers of mass-produced commercial
material tended to imitate such themes, slogans, and symbolism or they
resorted to the expedient of issuing safe, generic designs in matched sets

for all combatants. So long as presidential politics remained an essentially localized phenomenon in the United States, much of the creative impulse exhibited on its material culture emanated directly or indirectly from political activists.

Since the genesis of the centralized national presidential campaign, the direct role of senior political operatives in the creation of material culture had decreased markedly, although a few exceptions must be noted. In 1896, Mark Hanna personally decided to order huge quantities of American flag stickpins to distribute at McKinley rallies and appearances to equate his candidacy with patriotism.[6] In 1960, Hubert Humphrey and his "Minnesota mafia" made the prudent command decision to order buttons proclaiming "It's Humphrey in '60" so that they could be given out in his bid for a third term in the Senate if his quest for the Democratic presidential nomination was unsuccessful.[7] In 1976, Gerald Rafshoon enjoyed remarkable success imposing upon much of the vast array of independently produced material promoting Jimmy Carter his green and white color scheme, the slogan "A Leader, for a Change," and a favorite photo of Carter accentuating an image of rustic integrity.[8] On rare occasion even the candidates themselves have become involved, not just in budget decisions on how much of which material to order, but in the actual process of creation. In 1972, George McGovern personally approved many of the designs, including several distinctive varieties featuring multicolored rainbows, used on buttons, stickers, and other material promoting his candidacy. During his earlier House and Senate campaigns, McGovern had taken an even more active role in designing his campaign items. According to longtime friend and supporter George Cunningham, "McGovern used to sit in a booth at the Lawler Hotel in Mitchell drawing out different designs for buttons on placemats. A lot of them never got made, but he was always interested in playing around with different ideas."[9]

The vast majority of campaign items, however, have been designed and produced not by candidates or key campaign officials to carry the day, but rather by commercial producers to generate profits. On some occasions such firms have won the approval of national campaign committees, who have in turn served as middlemen in promoting products for purchase by local party organizations. Such was the case in 1964, when the Democratic National Committee prepared a "'64 Democratic Campaign Materials Catalog" featuring buttons, ribbons, and tabs by the Philadelphia Badge Company, jewelry items by the Green Duck Company of Chicago, antenna flags by Jet Stream, bumper stickers by the Avery Label Company, matchbooks by the American Match Company, and an eclectic assortment of other approved items that included balloons, pens, car-top signs, cowboy and skimmer hats, potholders, litter bags, and little "LBJ for the USA" stuffed toy donkeys.[10] More typically, however, such producers have marketed their wares directly to party groups, street vendors, and other retail outlets by distributing directly their own brochures. From the 1807 "True Madisonian" Sheffield razors through "Adams Forever" and "Jackson and Reform" French thread boxes, Zachary Taylor parlor stoves, and Lincoln–Hamlin cut crystal punch bowls down to 1984 Mondale and Reagan designer sunglasses, items too expensive for ordinary political utilization have been marketed directly to well-heeled partisans, bypassing the campaign processes altogether. A very different genre of campaign material, scurrilous put-down items, has been marketed in a similar manner, with such buttons as "No Crown for Franklin," "Goldwasser for Fuhrer," "All the Way with LBJ, but Don't Go Near the YMCA," and "Reagan in '80, the Angel of Death in '81" clearly unsuited to distribution by campaign organizations but providing brisk business for street vendors.

If a majority of campaign items have been seen first by candidates, their managers, and party leaders on the lapels or car bumpers of their supporters, the authenticity of such material as legitimate campaign relics faithfully reflecting the candidacies they promoted is less than absolute. Indeed, this laissez-faire approach to political material culture has on occasion produced bizarre results. Many Republican medalets and other items manufactured early in the 1860 campaign promoted presidential candidate "Abram" Lincoln, often with fiery free-soil rhetoric totally alien to the cautious, muted approach to the sectional crisis that Lincoln's campaign would adopt. Singularly unfortunate was an 1888 bandanna promoting the grossly obese Grover Cleveland as "Our Sturdy Nominee." In 1968, a Millenium Group "My Man Humphrey" caricature button featuring HHH's high forehead and receding hairline with a set of stuffed-animal "goggle eyes" (see fig. 202) was deemed so offensive by Humphrey that it was withdrawn from sale at his Washington boutique. Such grotesqueries might have been averted by campaign committee screening, but official material issued by the campaigns themselves has not always been free from humorous or unfortunate connotations. An excellent example is a 1972 "Cubans for President Nixon" button issued by Nixon's national committee just after several men of Cuban extraction were arrested for the Watergate break-in.

Although commercial producers have more often than not created their items without any direct guidance from campaign officials, their record over more than a century and a half of producing material reflecting faithfully the thematics and spirit of a long succession of campaigns has been on the whole remarkably successful. In a business characterized by fierce competition for a limited market of brief duration, the firms that have anticipated accurately public tastes and party dictates have survived and prospered, while those that have not have foundered or abandoned politics for more predictable markets. Producers of such "elite" memorabilia as multicolored woven ribbons, ceramic and glass bric-a-brac, Currier and Ives and Kellogg multicolored prints, and the more elaborate celluloid buttons have generally relied upon superior aesthetics and downplayed or avoided political relevance, producing ornate standardized designs prized for their beauty. In many instances, virtually identical designs appeared election after election, distinguishable only by the passing parade of party nominees. For companies marketing enormous quantities of inexpensive headquarters giveaway items like Green Duck lithographed buttons, the formula has been cost-effectiveness and simplicity, with thematic expression beyond name or facial identification rarely attempted. Firms specializing in material rich in ideological or symbolic content, however, have always had to remain alert to every nuance emanating from campaign headquarters, for thematic relevance and timeliness have spelled the difference between brisk profits and hard times. This has been true especially of the producers of such vendor merchandise as the 1940 buttons denigrating Roosevelt or Willkie, for many of them played upon transitory events (an egging, a reference to "my" ambassador, or FDR supporters a "paupers") destined to be forgotten in a week or two.

Although presidential material culture has frequently been extremely innovative in the forms it has taken, from the log-cabin bitters bottles and breastpins of 1840 through the musical blinker "Hot-Lites" buttons of 1984, it has rarely exhibited such experimentation in exploitation of campaign themes. On rare occasion such as the Elliott-Elder log-cabin transparencies in 1840, the Oglesby split rails in 1860, and buttons by Emmanuel Ress and A. G. Trimble pioneering the slogan "I Like Ike," material culture has made possible the debut of new campaign symbolism and sayings. For the most part, however, it has been not innovative but reactive in its exploitation of political themes. For this among other reasons, scholars looking to 1828, 1860, 1896, 1932, and 1980 campaign items as harbingers of the so-called "critical elections" producing epic political realignments are likely to be disappointed. Another reason, of course, is that to candidates, partisans, and many voters every election is considered critical at the time, every campaign strategy projects inroads into opposition strength, realignments become apparent only after the votes have been counted, and that such follow-up races as 1832, 1900, 1936, and 1984 have provided more meaningful indications of enduring shifts in voter sentiment. Scholars mining material from these campaigns for appeals intended to reinforce or counteract these swings in allegiance will usually be more successful.

Elections attain significance for many different reasons, of course, and many of the contests most critical to the development and utilization of material culture have not been those resulting in epic realignments or the coming to power of an exceptional national leader. Only the 1828 Jackson triumph that pioneered the use of objects as campaign devices, the 1860 election of Lincoln as the split-rail candidate, and the 1896 McKinley–Bryan "battle of the standards" represented elections as critical for students of material culture as for students of party alignments or American political history in general. Most of the other presidential contests that inspired truly exceptional material dimensions—1840, 1844, 1884, 1888, 1940, and

1976 in particular—are not commonly cited by scholars as epic milestones in the political odyssey of the Republic, and some of them traditionally merit no more than cursory paragraphs in standard survey textbooks. The ascendancy of Franklin Roosevelt in 1932 inspired a mediocre material response and the Reagan counterrevolution of 1980 a less than substantial one, probably because in both cases more voters were quietly resolved to write the epitaphs of the ruined presidencies of their opponents than were ebullient over the prospect of ideological departures. Great changes in American government have not always been welcomed with great fanfare.

Indeed, no correlation whatever can be made between a presidential nominee's ability to engender exceptional material culture during a campaign and performance in the Oval Office afterward. Perhaps the only generalization about material culture in presidential campaigns that has been true without exception is that it has never flourished unless a candidate, party apparatus, or ideological imperative has succeeded in creating genuine enthusiasm in a substantial segment of the grass-roots electorate. Such support need not constitute a popular majority or anything even approximating one, for such landslide losers as John C. Frémont, William Jennings Bryan, Barry Goldwater, and George McGovern all managed to inspire unusually creative and colorful material dimensions, whereas such landslide winners as Warren Harding, Calvin Coolidge, and Herbert Hoover have not. Frémont, Bryan, Goldwater, and McGovern did so, of course, by waging intensely evangelical, narrowly ideological campaigns that enraptured minorities of likeminded partisans while alienating much larger numbers of voters. In such instances "Free Soil and Free Men," "16 to 1, No Compromise," "In Your Heart, You Know He's Right," and "Come Home and Stop Killing Little Babies" made for more memorable banners or buttons than vote counts.

Another group of candidates who have inspired even more exceptional material culture while enjoying much greater political success have been a succession of dark-horse nominees so obscure that their campaigns have been afforded the luxury of substituting for distinguished public careers or ambitious blueprints for national progress such thoroughly frivolous symbolism as Lincoln split rails in 1860, Harrison log cabins and hard cider in 1840 and nostalgia for them in 1888, and Carter peanuts and grins in 1976. Wendell Willkie, surely one of the most obscure nominees ever annointed by a major party, also inspired an extraordinary array of material culture in 1940, although most of it reflected not escapist symbolism but alarmist hostility to a third term in office for FDR. It is significant that no incumbent president seeking re-election has successfully utilized material culture that could be characterized as capricious, frivolous, or irrelevant, although the "bandanna mania" on behalf of Grover Cleveland and octogenarian Allen Thurman came close. The candidacies of extremely well-known men have not typically enjoyed notable material dimensions, although the 1844 Clay campaign and the reelection efforts of Cleveland in 1888, McKinley in

1900, FDR in 1940, and Lyndon Johnson in 1964 provide graphic exceptions to the rule.

Just as the ambitions of many presidential contenders have been assisted by creative exploitation of material culture, many other candidates have been served poorly by the campaign objects produced to promote them. It is unlikely that more than a relative handful of voters in 1828 even saw a John Quincy Adams bandanna, medalet, or thread box bearing such inscriptions as "His Excellency John Quincy Adams" or "Adams Forever," which may have constituted a kindness for a man so widely regarded as an effete aristocrat with royalist tendencies. Because their campaign objects reflected so faithfully the tenor of their stridently ideological candidacies, material culture promoting such nominees as Frémont, Bryan, Goldwater, and McGovern surely added to their problems with crucial constituencies. It is difficult to regard as political assets slogans such as "No More Rule of Nigger Drivers" among Lower North moderates in 1856, "No Crown of Thorns, No Cross of Gold" among immigrant midwesterners in 1896, and "I'm *Extremely* Fond of Barry" or "Come Home and Stop Killing Little Babies" among independent voters genuinely alarmed by the fanaticism of the John Birch Society in 1964 or the New Left in 1972. Much of Thomas E. Dewey's material culture in 1948 evinced the annoying smugness that proved to be his Achilles' heel, just as the campaign items of Walter Mondale in 1984 did much to reinforce a widespread perception of the Minnesotan as a captive candidate of such special interests as organized labor, radical feminists, and gays.

Material culture has bestowed its blessings capriciously upon occasion. It was instrumental in facilitating the improbable metamorphosis of a refined country gentleman into a rustic backwoodsman in 1840 and in making his grandson, a man so remote and aloof he had been nicknamed "the human iceberg," into an object of compelling nostalgia. In 1860, it helped make possible the unlikely transformation of a corporation attorney and behind-the-scenes party professional into a prairie rail-splitter. In 1888, it helped create an even more improbable celebrity, a doddering octogenarian vice-presidential nominee whose fondness for snuff decreed the use of a red bandanna. As difficult to explain as these unlikely inspirations for such creativity have been a few much more promising political figures whose exciting personalities and backgrounds have failed to inspire material culture reflecting their charisma. Perhaps the most notable example of a failure of this sort occurred in 1960, when the material culture promoting John Kennedy was so uncommonly boring and bland, echoing his naval heroics with a few PT–109 lapel pins and his Irish heritage and image of youthful "vigah" not at all. A facet of presidential campaigning capable of transforming JFK into a dullard and Allen Thurman and Benjamin Harrison into creatures of charisma merits further study by the men and women who plan and execute our campaigns and the scholars who study them.

NOTES

1. *Congressional Record* Feb. 22, 1977, E872.

2. Benton, *Thirty Years' View*, II, 26; Ward, *Andrew Jackson*, 97; Heale, *The Presidential Quest*, 107.

3. Eric F. Goldman, *Rendezvous with Destiny*, rev. ed. (New York, 1956), 268; Lee Benson, *The Concept of Jacksonian Democracy: New York as a Test Case* (Princeton, N. J., 1961), 281.

4. Gunderson, *Log-Cabin Campaign*, 75–76.

5. Fischer, "Republican Presidential Campaigns of 1856 and 1860," 132–33; Baringer, *Lincoln's Rise to Power*, 181–85; Nevins, *The Emergence of Lincoln*, 2, 244–46.

6. Jones, *Presidential Election of 1896*, 291–93.

7. White, *The Making of the President, 1960*, 36.

8. *Newsweek*, Aug. 2, 1976; *Washington Post*, Sept. 30, 1976.

9. Quoted in David Kranz, "The House and Senate Buttons of George McGovern," *APIC Keynoter* 82 (Winter 1982): 19.

10. Democratic National Committee, "'64 Democratic Campaign Materials Catalog" (Washington, 1964).

Sources

The body of interpretive scholarly literature relating to the material culture of American presidential campaigns is unfortunately skimpy. Among the few general volumes on American political history to pay heed to campaign objects as more than pictorial window-dressing are Robert Gray Gunderson's *The Log-Cabin Campaign* (Lexington, Ky., 1957), a fine study of the campaign so critical to the evolution of material culture in presidential politics; John William Ward's pioneering *Andrew Jackson: Symbol for an Age* (New York, 1955); M. J. Heale's study of antebellum political campaign styles and images *The Presidential Quest: Candidates and Images in American Political Culture, 1789–1852* (London, 1982); and H. Wayne Morgan's thoughtful and splendidly written *From Hayes to McKinley: National Party Politics, 1877–1896* (Syracuse, 1969).

My own efforts to direct scholarly attention to campaign objects as research resources have included "The Republican Presidential Campaigns of 1856 and 1860: Analysis through Artifacts," *Civil War History* 27 (June 1981); "Pinback Put-Downs: The Campaign Button as Political Satire," *Journal of Popular Culture* 13 (Spring 1980); and "1896 Campaign Artifacts: A Study in Inferential Reconstruction," *Journal of American Culture* 3 (Winter 1980). The same issue of the *Journal of American Culture*, recently reissued as *American Material Culture: The Shape of Things Around Us*, ed. Edith Mayo (Bowling Green, Ohio, 1984), also contains Mayo's essay "Campaign Appeals to Women," an excellent and thought-provoking comparison of women's campaign items produced before suffrage to those created afterward, and Otto Charles Thieme's "Wave High the Red Bandanna," an informative and entertaining essay on 1888 campaign handkerchiefs. A cogent contribution to the argument for artifact study in general is Thomas J. Schlereth's *Artifacts and the American Past* (Nashville, 1981), although the most eloquent plea for this approach remains Ivor Noel-

Hume's compelling essay "Material Culture with the Dirt on It: A Virginia Perspective," in Ian M. G. Quimby's uneven volume, *Material Culture and the Study of American Life* (New York, 1978).

Scholars willing to broaden the dimensions of their research endeavors to include the material legacy will find useful a rapidly growing number of publications providing thorough surveys of presidential campaign objects. Edmund B. Sullivan's *American Political Badges and Medalets, 1789–1892* (Lawrence, Mass., 1981), a substantially revised edition of J. Doyle De-Witt's 1959 classic *A Century of Campaign Buttons*, is a meticulous and well-documented survey of nineteenth-century political tokens and lapel badges. Herbert R. Collins's *Threads of History: Americana Recorded on Cloth, 1775 to the Present* (Washington, 1979) provides a thorough survey of the larger political textiles with generally accurate attributions and an excellent introductory essay, and Roger A. Fischer and Edmund B. Sullivan, *American Political Ribbons and Ribbon Badges, 1825–1981* (Lincoln, Mass., 1985) surveys the smaller political textiles worn as badges. Helpful on early political clothing buttons is Alphaeus H. Albert's *Record of American Uniform and Historical Buttons, with Supplement* (Hightstown, N. J., 1973). Two model studies containing a few examples of campaign glass are Ruth Webb Lee and James H. Rose's *American Glass Cup Plates* (Northborough, Mass., 1948), and the massive and meticulously researched Helen McKearin and Kenneth M. Wilson's *American Bottles and Flasks and Their Ancestry* (New York, 1978). Combining useful illustrations with singularly inane commentary is Bessie M. Lindsey's *American Historical Glass*, rev. ed. (Rutland, Vt., 1967).

Theodore L. Hake's trilogy *The Encyclopedia of Political Buttons* (1974), *Political Buttons: Book II, 1920–1976* (1977), and *Political Buttons: Book III, 1789–1916* (1978), all available from Hake at Box 1444, York, Pa., 17405, catalogue thousands of varieties of buttons and an eclectic assortment of other types of campaign material. Much less useful is Richard P. Bristow's fuzzily illustrated and error-filled *Illustrated Political Button Book*, 4th ed. (Box 1741, Santa Cruz, Calif., 1973). Edmund B. Sullivan's *Collecting Political Americana* (New York, 1980), a very useful volume for scholars as well as for the collectors for whom it was written, provides a cogent overview of the various types of campaign items and many sound insights into their political utilization. A much less successful attempt to fulfill the same mission, Stan Gores's *Presidential and Campaign Memorabilia* (Des Moines, 1982), is useful primarily for its many photographs of unusual political ceramic, glass, and novelty items. No adequate survey of campaign ceramics has been written. Marian Klamkin's *American Patriotic and Political China* (New York, 1973) features some superb color plates, but the volume is rendered practically useless by its incompleteness and an unfortunately banal and error-laden narrative.

An even more serious handicap for researchers has been the lack of volumes surveying such significant varieties of political paper as posters, electoral tickets, prints, and postcards. Bernard L. Greenhouse, *Political Postcards, 1900–1980* (by Greenhouse, Box 6736, Syracuse, N. Y., 13217) provides something of an introduction to these entertaining and significant vehicles for political expression, but suffers from superficiality and a failure to create a historical context. A scholarly contribution of genuine significance to students of Abraham Lincoln and political material culture alike is Harold Holzer, Gabor S. Boritt, and Mark E. Neely, Jr., *The Lincoln Image: Abraham Lincoln and the Popular Print* (New York, 1984). Also informative on Lincoln political paper is James W. Milgram, *Abraham Lincoln Illustrated Envelopes and Letter Paper, 1860–1865* (Northbrook, Ill., 1984), a volume distinguished less by its historical scholarship than by its superb illustrations. Despite the enormous impact of the automobile on American presidential campaigning, no survey volumes devoted to bumper stickers (scorned by collectors and most curators, but probably the most important of all contemporary items for future political historians) or other automobile-related artifacts have been published.

Several privately published catalogues of the campaign material promoting individual candidates are worthy of note, including Edwin M. Stahl, *We Want Willkie: A Pictorial Guide to the Campaign Memorabilia of Wendell L. Willkie* (909 East Drive, Bordentown, N. J. 08505, 1972); Nixon Political Button Collectors, *Catalogue of the Campaign Buttons of Richard M. Nixon* (Box 2354, Mission Viejo, Calif. 92690, 1979); Bonnie C. Gardner and Harvey E. Goldberg, *The Campaign Items of John F. Kennedy* (Box 922, Clark, N. J. 07066, 1980); Gardner, Goldberg, and John Henigan, *The Campaign Items of Robert F. Kennedy* (Box 922, Clark, NJ, 07066, 1982); and James R. Kotche, *John B. Anderson: Congressman and Candidate* (3410 High Crest Road, Rockford, Ill. 61107, 1981).

Two quarterly journals published by collector organizations have been instrumental in broadening our knowledge of campaign items and their use in presidential politics. Especially informative in the *APPA Standard* (back issues available from the now-defunct Association for the Preservation of Political Americana, Box 211, Forest Hills, N. Y. 11375) was a series of articles by Donald L. Ackerman in 1977–79 issues that surveyed such early political objects as thread boxes, snuff boxes, and glass cup plates. Oriented even more toward serious artifact analysis and interpretation has been the *APIC Keynoter*, issued by the American Political Items Collectors (Box 340339, San Antonio, Texas 78234). Also published by the APIC have been comprehensive survey projects on the campaign items of Alton Parker, John W. Davis, Adlai Stevenson, and election years 1968 and 1976. Available as well through the APIC is Tom French, *The 1972 Presidential Campaign in Buttons* (Capitola, Calif., 1973), a volume marred by its failure to distinguish the buttons used for legitimate political purposes from the fantasy pieces produced for sale to collectors.

For scholars willing to carry their inquiries beyond the literature, the outstanding public collections of presidential campaign memorabilia are the J. Doyle DeWitt Collection of Political Americana of the University of Hartford and the political history collection of the Smithsonian Institution's National Museum of American History. Access to the Smithsonian collection is very difficult to obtain, but the equally impressive and much better organized DeWitt collection has recently been given a permanent home in a new University of Hartford library annex providing access to scholars and other interested parties. Many of the better state and local historical societies and presidential libraries and museums house excellent specialized collections of campaign objects. The Lincoln National Life Insurance Company's Louis A. Warren Lincoln Library and Museum in Fort Wayne, Indiana, boasts an outstanding collection of Lincoln campaign material. A superb collection of Franklin Roosevelt political paper assembled by Joseph M. Jacobs is located in the archives of the University of Illinois-Chicago.

Because most unusual campaign objects are acquired through mail order dealers or auction sales, the ultimate research resource in presidential material culture would be the display advertisements in such collector publications as *The Political Collector* (444 Lincoln Street, York, Pa. 17404), the sales catalogs of such dealers as Charles McSorley and Kenton Broyles, and the hundreds of auction catalogs issued by such specialists in political Americana as Leon Weisel, Allan Anderson, Ted Hake, George LaBarre, Tom Slater, Robert Coup, George Rinsland, and Rex Stark. Especially valuable for its large number of uncommon and historically significant campaign items, crisp photography, and outstanding explanatory notes is the catalog of the Don Warner collection printed in 1981 by New England Rare Coin Auctions. Over the past century or more, a large number of flyers and catalogs have been printed for the manufacturers and distributors of campaign materials and for national campaign organizations to send to local headquarters. It is unfortunate for scholars that much of this material is virtually impossible to obtain, although the University of Hartford's DeWitt Collection has made an impressive start toward rectifying this situation.

Index

ROGER A. FISCHER received his doctorate in history in 1967 from Tulane University and since 1972 has taught at the University of Minnesota-Duluth, where he is currently professor and chairman of the Department of History and director of American Studies. Author of *The Segregation Struggle in Louisiana, 1862–1877*, and co-author of *American Political Ribbons and Ribbon Badges, 1825–1981*, his major scholarly interest is American political culture in general and American political cartoon art in particular.